Defense Industries in
Latin American Countries

Defense Industries in Latin American Countries

Argentina, Brazil, and Chile

José O. Maldifassi and
Pier A. Abetti

Westport, Connecticut
London

Library of Congress Cataloging-in-Publication Data

Maldifassi, José O.
Defense industries in Latin American countries : Argentina, Brazil,
and Chile / José O. Maldifassi and Pier A. Abetti.
p. cm.
Includes bibliographical references and index.
ISBN 0–275–94729–7 (alk. paper)
1. Defense industries—Brazil. 2. Brazil—Defenses. 3. Defense
industries—Argentina. 4. Argentina—Defenses. 5. Defense
industries—Chile. 6. Chile—Defenses. I. Abetti, Pier A.
II. Title.
HD9743.B682M35   1994
338.4′76233′0981—dc20   93–43070

British Library Cataloguing in Publication Data is available.

Library of Congress Catalog Card Number: 93–43070
ISBN: 0–275–94729–7

First published in 1994

Praeger Publishers, 88 Post Road West, Westport, CT 06881
An imprint of Greenwood Publishing Group, Inc.

Printed in the United States of America

The paper used in this book complies with the
Permanent Paper Standard issued by the National
Information Standards Organization (Z39.48–1984).

10 9 8 7 6 5 4 3 2 1

The views and opinions expressed in this book are the sole responsibility of the
authors and in no manner do they commit, reflect, or represent the positions,
opinions, or policies of any other person, group, private or public organization,
or institution in the United States or in any other country.

To our wives Carmen Gloria and Betty Burr

Contents

Illustrations

TABLES

FIGURES

Defense Industries in
Latin American Countries

1

Introduction

Historical experience, gained from the major wars of this century, has taught the world that military technological superiority is one of the decisive factors in the final outcome of any armed conflict. This military technological superiority is also a very powerful element of any deterrent strategy. Thus, all nations, industrialized or not, have attempted to acquire the most advanced military equipment for their armed forces within their industrial, technological, and economic capabilities and constraints. This equipment is obtained either through domestic manufacturing or by purchasing abroad.

Unlike industrialized countries that produce the great majority of the weapons needed by their armed forces, semi-industrialized countries are faced with two basic alternatives in order to develop and maintain their defense capabilities:

1. purchase the defense systems they need from the international market, or
2. develop their domestic defense industries to satisfy their defense needs.

Obviously, a combination of the two alternatives is possible and often adopted in practice. However, a semi-industrialized nation that depends almost entirely on external suppliers to equip its armed forces with sophisticated weapons is extremely vulnerable to international political pressures. This vulnerability through dependency occurs first in the acquisition of equipment and arms systems and then later when imported spare parts and other products are required for the operation, maintenance, repair, and upgrade of the equipment purchased abroad (Maldifassi, 1989).

The defense industries[1] of all countries possess some unique characteristics that render them more complex than other industrial sectors of the economy. In particular, these characteristics include the total government involvement in such matters as national security, defense policies, defense spending, and defense decision making; the reliance on ever increasing levels of technological sophistication; the confidentiality required by national security; and the international nature of the weapons market. Moreover, as will be explained later, in the economic sense there is no such thing as a "defense industry"—like the garment, housing, construction, or similar industries—that could be easily isolated and targeted in order to apply specific "industrial" policies.

In the case of industrialized nations, technology developed originally to satisfy defense needs was a driving force for several industrial innovations during the post–World War II period (Freeman, 1986, pp. 109, 191). In some of these countries, increased government spending in defense was even considered as a Keynesian tool to improve the overall economic conditions (Mosley, 1985; Kolodziej, 1987b). In developing countries, however, because of the high prices of sophisticated foreign military equipment, the impact of government policies and spending on the purchase of defense-related equipment and weapons has shown, and continues to have, significant economic impact and ramifications.

In developing countries, given their weak industrial infrastructure and inferior technological capabilities, arms and equipment for the armed forces historically came from abroad. However, as national industrial capabilities improved, so did the domestic capacity to manufacture arms of greater sophistication. Provided with an enhanced capability to produce more advanced weapons, the defense industries of semi-industrialized countries were established to cope with the strategic need to reduce the dependency—technological, political, and economic—associated with the international supply of arms and equipment for defense, particularly in case of conflict, when

---

1. In broad terms the defense industry can be defined as a set of private and state-owned firms that provide goods and services needed by the armed forces to perform their normal peace-and wartime activities. A more detailed definition will be presented in Chapter 2.

they are most needed.[2] Besides helping to reduce foreign dependency, the existence of a local defense industry also allows semi-industrialized countries to withstand a longer-lasting conflict without the need of building up major inventories of foreign equipment.

For semi-industrialized countries, more sophisticated, domestically produced defense equipment can also help to reduce the expenditures in hard currency needed to purchase advanced military supplies from international sources. In the case of Latin America, where the debt burden is extremely heavy (Frankman, 1992), this procurement practice can be considered as a tool for import substitution as well as a mechanism for generating hard currency through increased exports. However, as some countries that adopted an import substitution policy can testify, it has been found that import substitution may not save foreign exchange in its initial phases because of the need to import manufacturing equipment (Frank, 1969, pp. 234–235, cited in Vayrynen, 1992, p. 96). Thus, what changes is the structure of the imports and not the total amount imported (Herrick and Kindleberger, 1983, p. 426).

It can also be argued here that in semi-industrialized countries an increased internal demand for sophisticated defense products could act as a catalyst for technological innovation of the manufacturing sector. More advanced requirements in research, development, design, and manufacture of advanced goods, as well as on-the-job training of the labor force and its managers, could be the final outcome of this relatively more sophisticated demand.

1.1   THE DEFENSE INDUSTRY OF LATIN AMERICA

Like Southeast Asia, Latin America is a region that has experienced a steady increase in the level of industrialization and also where some degree of international tension still persists (Varas, 1985). These regional dynamics gave rise to the simultaneous emergence of domestic industrial capabilities and enhanced defense needs, resulting in the establishment of defense industries intended originally to satisfy national defense requirements through import substitution. As will be shown, the enhanced industrial capabilities created in the defense sector were later used to boost exports in order to obtain hard

---

2. This proposition is supported by Vayrynen (1992, p. 26), and Ross (1984, pp. 9–13).

currency for the highly indebted economies of the Latin American region.

Latin America, more specifically the group of semi-industrialized countries of the region composed of Argentina, Brazil, and Chile, represents a fruitful field of research because a major industrialization process occurred during the last 20 years (1970 to 1990) and also because during this same period these three countries converted from being net importers of defense equipment to worldwide net exporters of military supplies (ACDA, 1990). It is evident that this transformation has already had, and will continue to have, a major impact on the industrial, economic, and technological structure of these semi-industrialized countries.

Most studies analyzing the defense industries of Latin American countries have either been descriptive of the national defense capabilities of such countries as Argentina (Porth, 1984; Millán, 1986; Waisman, 1986), Brazil (Barros, 1984; Brigagao, 1986; Lock, 1986; Perry and Weiss, 1986), and Chile (Sohr, 1990) or inserted into a wider sociopolitical analysis of regional defense spending, dependence, and militarization on a world scale (Varas, 1986, 1989; Ross, 1984; Brzoska and Ohlson, 1987).

A recent publication by Vayrynen (1992) analyzes the process of military industrialization on a historical and worldwide basis. Vayrynen explores the importance of the military industrialization process in Japan, Brazil, Britain, and the United States and how it relates to economic development, depending on the country's condition as a rising or declining power. As such, Vayrynen's study covers to some extent the Brazilian military industrialization process, tangentially addressing some of the topics to be discussed here.

It has not been possible to find any in-depth analyses that attempt to measure empirically the economic effects of the substitution of imports for defense purposes, the overall employment generated by the defense firms, the hard currency generated by defense exports, or the efficiency of the defense industries. This vacuum of economic analysis in the literature arises because the scholars mentioned above have concentrated principally on the sociopolitical conditions and dynamics of the militarization process and not on the characteristics and industrial structure of the defense industry and its economic and technological impact. Therefore, it is the goal of this book to help fill this analytical gap by performing a systematic analysis of the defense industries of Argentina, Brazil, and Chile and an empirical analysis of their overall economic and technological impact on the economies of the three countries.

1.2   BOOK OBJECTIVES

The objectives of this book are to analyze the conditions that gave rise to the emergence and subsequent development of the defense industries of Argentina, Brazil, and Chile and to determine empirically their impact on the respective national economies. The main aspects to be examined here are the ones related to the emergence of domestic defense industries and technological capabilities, the factors that shaped the process, and the relationship between defense production and certain economic and technological indicators at the national and manufacturing levels.

As will be shown, during the last two decades Argentina, Brazil, and Chile turned from being net importers of defense equipment to net exporters. Thus, they underwent important industrial and technological changes in their economies and institutional conditions, which are worthy of being studied and explained.

In regard to the assumed—and sometimes highly controversial—impact of the defense industry on the economic, technological, and social development of semi-industrialized countries, we will advance the hypothesis that in such countries the military industrialization process can strengthen the country's scientific, technological, and industrial infrastructure. In order to prove the validity of this hypothesis, we will analyze the emergence and evolution of defense industries in Argentina, Brazil, and Chile and show how this military industrialization process relates to scientific, technological, and economic development.

The defense budget or military spending of a country is generally set by high-level government decisions and policies. Therefore, the analysis performed in this book will not address the issue of whether the defense budget should be modified. Rather, considering this budget as an exogenous variable in the assessment, we will focus only on the nonpolitical aspects of industrial production of defense equipment and arms. We will analyze to what extent the present domestic defense industry affects the overall economy, given the historical spending levels and the existing defense industrial structure.

The underlying premise of this study is that the defense industries of semi-industrialized countries are part of the front end of the national technological innovation process, much like they are in the industrialized countries. Thus, the defense industries are an important tool in the national development and industrialization strategies of semi-industrialized countries, such as those of Latin America. This military industrialization process could be considered an example for designing industrial policies for other areas of the economy.

The emergence of an indigenous defense industry in developing countries is normally the outcome of an explicit industrial policy carried out by the government and the armed forces. Therefore, the study of such policies, the associated governmental actions, and their outcomes can be used as examples—good or bad—of ways and means to implement effectively other industrial policies in such countries. Some of these policies can be targeted specifically toward technological self-reliance and industrialization of the much broader civilian economy.

1.3 METHODOLOGY AND BOOK OUTLINE

The sensitivity of the topic and the sometimes scarce and inexact data make this a difficult topic to pursue in an unbiased and exact manner. The lack of precise data and information—and of reliable sources with respect to the defense industries in general and the Latin American countries in particular—is due to confidentiality. Data regarding defense acquisitions, and research and development amounts devoted to defense systems, are often suppressed or distorted. As will be explained in Chapter 2, several of the defense firms in the semi-industrialized countries studied are owned by the government and operated by the respective Ministries of Defense, and no financial information is publicly available to assess their economic performance. When equipment is exported or imported for the defense sector, sometimes only the number of pieces of equipment is revealed but not the amount of the sales. In some cases, trade magazines are the sole source of information. However, there are also some more serious studies performed by international institutes devoted to peace and disarmament initiatives or by government agencies (e.g., Vayrynen, 1992; Brzoska and Ohlson, 1986; OTA, 1991c) that provided useful basic data.

Before embarking on the process of analyzing the defense industry, we needed an operational definition of *defense industry*. This definition had to be broad enough to include all its components and relationships and applicable to all countries in the same developmental condition. The work done in studying and defining the defense industry in industrialized countries was used as the basis for this definition. As the defense industry is part of the larger national economy, it was necessary to place the defense industry in the national context. Thus, a systemic model was derived in order to help identify all the interrelations of the defense industry with the rest of the national economic, political, and industrial settings. All these topics are covered in Chapter 2.

Chapters 3 to 5 look in great detail at the defense industries of Brazil, Argentina, and Chile, recognized as the most important within Latin America. The description of the defense industries of these countries is included in order to facilitate the assessment and cross comparison of their emergence, performance, and characteristics. The data base on which to ground the analysis and perform the cross comparisons was obtained from secondary sources.

The examination of the historical and contemporary issues described in each of the country's chapters, and the cross comparison between their defense industries, is used to explain the reasons for the growth of industrial defense output and exports and the differences in industry performance. An overall comparison between the defense industries of Argentina, Brazil, and Chile is carried out in Chapter 6 in order to determine the most viable reasons that could help explain their relative success, characteristics, and industrial performance.

In Chapter 7 the relationship between defense production, degree of sophistication of the arms produced, and national technological indicators is empirically studied. This analysis is performed to derive conclusions about the implications of countrywide science and technology policies and how they affect the emergence of domestic defense industries. The science and technology policies adopted by Argentina, Brazil, and Chile are described and cross-compared. To assess the interdependence of the science and technology policies and military production, qualitative and—depending on the availability of reliable data—also quantitative methods were used. As total defense production figures have been derived using approximate methods, and given the imprecise and sometimes unreliable data of science and technology indicators for Latin America, the conclusions to be derived by comparing both factors (i.e., defense production and science and technology indicators) have a preliminary rather than a conclusive nature.

Chapter 8 covers the analysis of the economic impact of the defense industries of Argentina, Brazil, and Chile by focusing on such indicators as defense employment, defense exports, substitution of imports, and relative industry efficiency. The overall empirical analysis of the defense industries was done at the national industrial level, given that there are no data available at the firm level. The approximate efficiency of the defense industries of industrialized countries is also derived and used to assess the main differences between the defense industries of semi- and fully industrialized countries.

To analyze the economic impact of the defense industry, there was a need to determine first the levels of defense production in each of the countries. As precise production volumes were not available, an approximate method was used. Consequently, it must be recognized that the conclusions to be derived are also imprecise. Thus, there was a need to validate the results obtained by means of cross comparisons and by making reference to conclusions derived by previous researchers. Whenever possible, the robustness of the results has been assessed by means of statistical procedures and sensitivity analysis.

Finally, the analysis of the findings and conclusions concerning the overall economic impact of the defense industries of Argentina, Brazil, and Chile is presented in Chapter 9. Recommendations are also made in this last chapter concerning the identification of future research needed in order to better understand the economic and industrial implications of the emergence and institutionalization of defense industries in semi-industrialized nations.

2

A Model of the Defense Industry in Semi-Industrialized Countries

In this chapter the "defense industry" is defined, and a model is developed for the placement of the defense industry in the economy of semi-industrialized countries. This model will highlight the key elements in the emergence and subsequent growth of domestic defense industries in semi-industrialized countries and, later, help explain the dynamics of the military industrialization process of Argentina, Brazil, and Chile.

2.1 DEFINITION OF THE DEFENSE INDUSTRY

As mentioned in Chapter 1, the defense industry can be broadly defined as the set of private and state-owned firms that provide goods and services needed by the armed forces to perform their normal peace- and wartime activities.

According to Hax and Majluf (1991, p. 36), "An industry can be defined as a group of firms offering products or services which are close substitutes of each other." However, the set of firms that support the armed forces provides them with a very large variety of products and services that are not substitutes of each other. What unifies all these firms is the final customer. Thus, the name *defense industry* is generic and in no way represents an industry in the absolute economic sense.

There needs to be an agreement on an operational definition of *defense industry* in order to study it more properly. One possible way of doing so is by defining it by extension, that is, by identifying each firm that provides the goods and services to the armed forces. It is possible to identify which firms belong to the defense industry by focusing on the origin of the products and services purchased by the armed forces. According to Mosley (1985), Table 2.1 shows the distribution of industry shipments to the Department of Defense (DoD) of the United States for 1980, ordered by industrial sectors.

As can be seen from Table 2.1, the defense industry is a blend of many industrial sectors with quite different characteristics. However, as can be clearly seen from the table, most of the firms in the defense industry belong to the manufacturing sector of the economy (SIC[1] code 3). Therefore, the economic impact of the defense industry can be expected to be easier to detect and measure by assessing its importance at the manufacturing level. Thus, it can be argued here that a semi-industrialized country needs to have a strong manufacturing base to develop an important defense industry. As weapons are technologically sophisticated products that require the integration of many different kinds of parts and components, the more advanced and consolidated the manufacturing sector, the easier it will be for a semi-industrialized country to develop an efficient defense industry.

The Office of Technology Assessment (OTA) of the U.S. Congress (OTA, 1991a) provides a comprehensive definition of the defense industry in somewhat more specific terms:

> The defense technology and industrial base can be broadly defined as the combination of people, institutions, technological know-how, and production capacity used to develop and manufacture the weapons and supporting defense equipment needed to achieve our [U.S.] national security objectives. It contains three functional elements:
>
> 1. a "technology base" that includes private industry laboratories and research facilities, university laboratories conducting defense research, government laboratories (e.g., those run by the National Aeronautics and Space Administration and the Departments of Energy, Commerce, and Defense), test centers, and the trained scientific and technical personnel to staff these facilities;

---

1. SIC = Standardized Industrial Classification code.

Table 2.1

Military Production by Industrial Sector, United States, 1980

SIC Code	Industry	Shipments DoD (%)	Empl't. DoD (%)
28	Chem. & allied products	1.4	4.9
29	Petroleum & coal products	1.2	1.4
30	Rubber & misc. plastic products	2.1	2.5
33	Primary metals industries	1.5	2.5
34	Fabricated metal products	5.6	7.1
3463	Nonferrous forging	21.4	19.4
3482	Ordinance	39.2	39.2
3483			
3484			
3489			
35	Machinery, except elec.	2.6	2.8
36	Electrical and electronic equip.	13.1	14.0
3662	Radio & TV comm. equip.	43.6	43.6
37	Transportation equip.	34.5	39.6
3721	Aircraft	29.8	35.1
3724			
3728			
3731	Shipbuilding & repairing	36.2	38.7
3761	Guided missiles, space vehicles	64.2	78.3
38	Instruments & related products	3.9	4.2
3811	Eng. & Sci. instruments	10.0	

Source: Mosley, 1985, p. 51.
Shipments: Value of Military products' shipments as percentage of total value of shipments in each industrial sector.
Employment: Defense-related employment as percentage of total employment in each industrial sector.

2.   a "production base" composed of private industry as well as
      government enterprises (both government-owned and
      government-operated [GOGO] and government-owned and
      contractor-operated [GOCO]); and

3.   a "maintenance base" consisting of government facilities
      (arsenals, depots, etc.) and private companies that maintain
      and repair equipment either at their own facilities or in the
      field (p. 2).

This definition clearly indicates that an important share of the
national research and development capacity of the country is also part
of the defense industry.   Thus, this technology-generating
infrastructure needs to be included when assessing and analyzing the
impact of the defense industry on the economy.

Vayrynen (1992, p. 2) points out that "civilian and military
technologies have a common basis in the scientific establishment of
the country." To illustrate this point, Figure 2.1 shows the relationship
between defense and civilian technologies.   As can be seen, the
technological infrastructure, supported by the fundamental scientific
and technological disciplines, provides for the industrial base of the
economy. Civilian and military industrial sectors derive from this
common industrial base.

Figure 2.1 highlights how military technology requires the pre-
existence of technological expertise in a very broad range of
disciplines and cannot be isolated from technological innovation
oriented to civilian applications.   Due to stringent operational
requirements, the production of sophisticated military hardware
requires further specialization beyond similar civilian applications.
Thus, research and development activities with pure military
orientation need to be carried out to achieve this higher degree of
sophistication. However, in the case of developing countries that do
not have the capacity to develop their own technology, the only way
to acquire more sophisticated weapons is by means of embodied
technology transferred in the form of imported arms and military
equipment.   The semi-industrialized countries that do have some
capacity to generate domestic technology will attempt to develop
defense equipment by their own means, with or without the assistance
of more developed countries, and in doing so, they will need to resort
to the civilian industrial infrastructure.

On the other hand, it can be argued that if a semi-industrialized
country attempts to create an important domestic defense industry in
isolation from the rest of the national industrial and technological

Figure 2.1

Relationships Among Defense Sectors
And The Industrial Base

INDUSTRIAL SECTORS

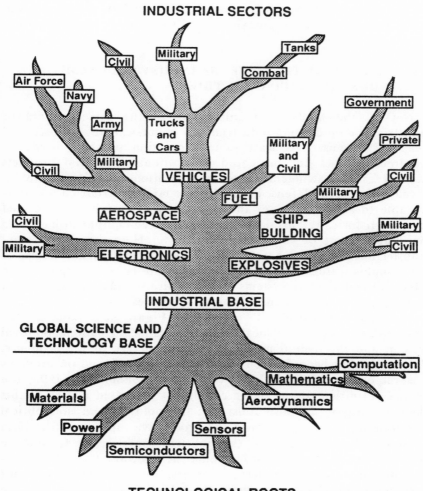

TECHNOLOGICAL ROOTS

Source: OTA, *Redesigning Defense*, 1991, p. 40.

infrastructure, discouraging results might result from such a forced process, and production costs of the few weapons produced would be extremely high.   Under these conditions of forced military industrialization by means of a closed defense industry, higher production costs will most probably occur because of scope inefficiencies in the overall production process, in addition to scale inefficiencies resulting from low production volumes.   Scope inefficiencies will result from extensive vertical and horizontal integration to replace the nonexistent civilian industrial infrastructure.

2.2   A MODEL OF THE DEFENSE INDUSTRY IN SEMI-INDUSTRIALIZED COUNTRIES

Not all the hardware requirements of the armed forces of industrialized and semi-industrialized countries are sophisticated weapons systems.   At least some proportion of these hardware requirements can be considered conventional industrial products adapted for more stringent operational conditions (Maldifassi, 1988b). Because of this, the defense industries of semi-industrialized countries are able to supply some of the equipment needed by their armed forces. Historically, this domestically produced equipment has had a low embodiment of advanced technology.   However, some semi-industrialized countries have been able to develop weapons systems of some sophistication for their local use and later to export these relatively sophisticated systems to other Third World countries and, on some occasions, even to industrialized countries.

For semi-industrialized countries, Figure 2.2 models the relationships between the local defense industry, the national political system, and the overall productive infrastructure of the economy. This model has been derived by the first author based on previous research on the defense industry (Maldifassi, 1988b, 1989, 1990) and on the definition of the defense industry presented earlier in this chapter.   Figure 2.2 also illustrates the political and nonpolitical conditioning factors that affect the productive capacity of the local defense industry.   Some of the political conditioning factors are international constraints that influence the trade and transfer of arms and defense technology across borders, the availability of hard currency to purchase weapons in the international market, and the geostrategic situation of the country that mandates the level of defense expenditures.   Some of the nonpolitical constraints and influencing elements that affect the defense industry are the lack of skilled

Figure 2.2
The Defense Industry in Semi-Industrialized Countries

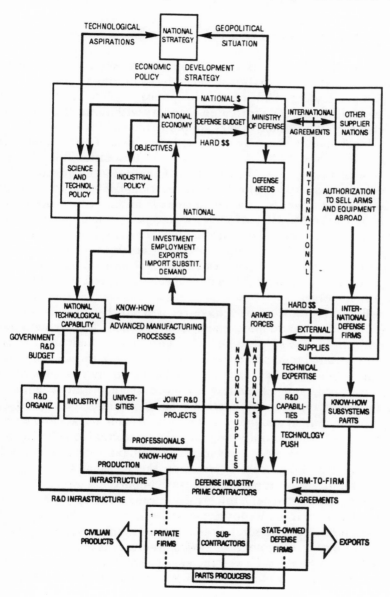

human resources, outdated productive capacity, and inadequate technological capabilities. The general explanation of the model proposed here will proceed starting from the *top left* of Figure 2.2 and working to the *bottom right*.

2.2.1   National Influencing Factors

The overall national strategy adopted by semi-industrialized countries affects the national economy through the chosen development strategy and economic policy. Thus, while some countries decided on a state-oriented economy with centralized control and decision making, some others adopted free market economies.

The development strategy followed by most Latin American countries up to the 1970s was based on a substantial state-owned productive infrastructure. In the case of the defense industry, this state-owned production policy led to the establishment of military factories and shipyards that historically have been under the supervision of the Ministry of Defense and managed by members of the armed forces. These factories tended to be large in overall size, employed conventional equipment and machinery to produce unsophisticated items, and performed mainly the general repair and maintenance of the equipment—that had been purchased abroad—in use by the armed forces.

Several developing countries have recognized that technology is a driving force that would allow them to attain their development and industrialization goals. Some of these technologically aware developing countries have adopted important and forward-looking industrial policies. They also have formulated and implemented explicit, focused, and adequately financed science and technology policies to aid in the industrialization process. The degree of political support and technical adequacy of these industrial and technological policies varied substantially among these technologically aware developing countries. As a result, they achieved correspondingly different degrees of success in creating the national technological capability required to support a modern economy.

The more successful technologically aware developing countries advanced from their underdeveloped condition to a state of semi-industrialization. In these semi-industrialized countries the enhanced productive and technological infrastructure created by the industrialization process allowed the emergence of an earlier capacity to assimilate foreign defense technology and to produce domestic defense equipment.

Taking now into consideration the geostrategic situation of a nation, there will be a higher or reduced need for more advanced defense systems, depending upon the kind and characteristics of the perceived external threats. The higher the external threat (either perceived or real) and the weaker the local industrial capacity, the larger the quantity of foreign weapons that will be required.

In order to cope with the geostrategic situation, and depending on the capacity of the national economy, a defense budget is allocated to satisfy the personnel, operational, and material requirements of the armed forces. This defense budget is normally divided into a national currency portion (shown as "$" in Figure 2.2) and a hard currency portion (shown as "$$" in the same figure), clearly signaling the purpose and orientation of the procurement effort. Developing countries with high availability of hard currency and low industrial capacity will tend to favor imports of defense goods over domestic production.[2]

2.2.2   International Influencing Factors

Because of existing international agreements and restrictions in the international transfer of arms, prospective weapons buyers can gain access to the international defense market exclusively through bilateral government contracts. Only with the official authorization of the local government can a firm transfer defense systems, arms, equipment, or military-related technology to another country. Occasionally, the political constraints imposed on this defense-related technology transfer process have been so severe that locked-out countries have been forced to develop their domestic defense industries to satisfy their particular needs, for example, South Africa, Israel, and Taiwan. On the other hand, easy access to foreign weapons relatively more sophisticated than the ones the local industry is able to produce will destroy the incipient capabilities of the domestic defense industry and will also discourage the emergence of national defense firms (Molero, 1988). This easy access to defense equipment can be a function of the availability of large amounts of hard currency (e.g., oil-exporting

---

2. According to the figures provided by the Arms Control and Disarmament Agency (ACDA, 1990), in the 1980s Venezuela imported arms equivalent to an average of 30 percent of its defense budget. Also, the oil-rich countries of the Middle East have been the most significant importers of arms during the past decade (p. 7).

countries) or the strong political support provided by an industrialized nation (Israel and the U.S. support for aircraft). Thus, a hypothesis can be offered here: The more difficult the access to advanced weapons, the more advanced the local defense industry would tend to be.

2.2.3   Economic Impact of the Defense Industry

Like any other industry, the direct impact that the defense industry has on the overall economy can be measured by:

- the employment (direct and indirect) that it generates,
- the investment in infrastructure and equipment carried out by the defense firms,
- the hard currency generated by exports,
- the substitution of imports that reduce the need for hard currency expenditures, and
- the increased internal production of defense goods.

From a purely economic perspective, it can be argued that the effects of import substitution and exports of the defense industry can be considered to be the main issues. This economic effect of the defense industry on the economy is illustrated by the long feedback loop in Figure 2.2.

Since the defense industry is mostly a subset of the manufacturing sector of the economy, its economic impact (either positive or negative) will be felt directly at this level. The larger the share of the defense industry output with respect to the overall manufacturing sector, the more profound will be this impact. For this reason, in Chapter 8 we will quantify this economic impact by analyzing the defense industry and its relationship with the manufacturing sector.

2.2.4   National Technological Capability

The technological sophistication of the manufacturing sector, the technical qualifications of the technicians and professionals that work in manufacturing, and the research and development capacity of universities and other local laboratories are the industrial, social, and technological pillars on which the defense industry is supported.

The degree to which any industry incorporates technology as a value-added component of its final output is determined by its national technological capability. Also, the demand for more skilled workers and technically qualified professionals is determined by the complexity of the products and manufacturing processes of industry. To ensure that the professional requirements of industry are met, a strong linkage between industry and universities is needed. Unfortunately, this university-industry link has been weak in most developing and semi-industrialized countries (Herbert-Copley, 1990, p. 1459).

The conceptual and detailed design of defense systems requires the expertise of professionals in several technical areas, including all engineering disciplines. This expertise needs to be based on experience and technical training, as well as on the previous generations of defense systems historically available at the national level.

A static economic model of the relationship between the defense industry and the manufacturing sector would suggest that the defense industry, with its need for sophisticated manufacturing equipment, highly skilled human resources, and large capital investments, presents a very high opportunity cost for the overall economy (Sivard, 1987). On the other hand, a dynamic model suggests that the defense industry, with higher technological requirements and more advanced products and services, enhances the national technological capability through know-how, trained personnel, and more sophisticated manufacturing equipment. This dynamic process will exist only if there is a strong and continuous interaction between defense and civilian production units. When the defense industry is not properly linked with and supported by the rest of the manufacturing sector—for example, through state ownership of "closed" military factories or inorganic defense industrial growth—larger inefficiencies in the production processes can be expected. The opportunity cost issue is resolved either (1) by government overfinancing of inefficient state-owned factories and by subsidies for local production or (2) through the market mechanisms in countries with market-oriented economies, for instance, by raising the prices paid by the armed forces.

As the armed forces of developing countries resorted to foreign equipment because of lack of local industrial and technological capacity, it can be argued that historically the armed forces had a more sophisticated technological base than the civilian industry. Thus, with the emergence of an indigenous defense industry capable of supplying the local armed forces with more advanced equipment, it can be said that a qualitative improvement in the industrial base of the country took place. Considering again a dynamic model, some of the technical advancements and developments in the defense industries may be transferred to the civilian industries by several mechanisms, which include personnel migration or the participation of civilian industries in the production of defense systems that increase their technological know-how. This dynamic process leads to increased technological self-sufficiency and higher industrial capacity at the national level. The short feedback loop shown in Figure 2.2 illustrates this dynamic positive effect.

2.2.5   The Armed Forces

For unsophisticated equipment, as well as goods and services in general, the local industry of semi-industrialized countries is able to satisfy most of the requirements presented by the armed forces, with purchases made in national currency. These products and services are either the same ones traded in the civilian market or slightly adapted items to be used under more stringent operating conditions by the armed forces. Besides the international market, the armed forces of semi-industrialized countries can rely to some extent on the local defense industry to supply some of their weapons and purely military equipment. However, these products normally have been of low-technology content when compared with the ones available in the international market.

In order to productively utilize the scarce human and capital resources available in semi-industrialized countries, only a small number of weapons and defense systems can be developed and produced simultaneously. This means that major defense projects should be prioritized according to overall needs, through coordination and centralized decision making, particularly at the armed forces or Ministry of Defense level.

The operations and maintenance infrastructure of the armed forces, the technical expertise and skills of their members, and the research and development organizations they operate provide the innovational "technology push" for the local defense industry. This technology push is enhanced by the diffusion of the know-how and defense equipment acquired from abroad, as well as by the technical and commercial literature about foreign defense systems.

Arms and defense equipment available in the international market that could benefit the local armed forces and be reproduced with domestic technology, but not readily procurable because of prices or political constraints, generate the "market pull" in the defense industry at the national level.[3]   According to this demonstration effect, the local armed forces would like to incorporate these advanced weapons into their arsenals to provide a technological edge against their potential adversaries.   Thus, restricted in their purchases in the international arms market, the armed forces increase the technological demand by placing orders for the production of the desired items by the local defense industry.

In this way, according to the model of technological innovation developed by Marquis (1969), the two elements that drive the technological innovation process—market pull   and   technology push—occur simultaneously, increasing the pressure for further expansion of the domestic defense capability. Given such growth forces, some semi-industrialized countries made the mistake of establishing inorganic defense industries in spite of inadequate industrial infrastructure and capabilities.   These industries were protected by strong import substitution policies, based on state-owned factories and capable of producing relatively more advanced military equipment but at very high costs.[4]   Other semi-industrialized countries, using a more cautious approach, created a domestic defense industry based on the existing and emerging civilian manufacturing capabilities, while at the same time they continued their reliance on imported weapons of higher sophistication.[5]

In semi-industrialized countries, the product and process technology needed by the defense industry can be provided either by:

1.   transfer of know-how and manufacturing equipment by the set of foreign defense firms authorized to do so by their respective governments, or

2.1. internal research and development of proprietary technology by both private and state-owned firms, and

2.2. research and development activities carried out by the armed forces alone or in conjunction with universities and other national research and development organizations.

---

3. This phenomenon of consumers being attracted to superior goods existing in other markets has been called the "demonstration effect" (Kindleberger and Herrick, 1977, p. 136).

4. As will be shown in Chapter 8, an example of this inorganic growth is Argentina.

5. The example in this case is Brazil, whose defense industry is described in Chapter 3.

The joint research and development projects undertaken by the armed forces with the cooperation of local universities, private firms, and other research and development organizations provide another means to increase the "technology push" and to enhance the technological capabilities of the defense industry, in particular, and of the manufacturing industry, in general.

In semi-industrialized countries, the undertaking of research projects financed by the defense sector helps domestic research and development establishments to (1) utilize some of their unexploited capabilities and expertise, (2) train young researchers in more advanced technologies, and (3) finance research equipment and infrastructure that will also be used for other nondefense projects. Thus, where there are not many work positions available for highly skilled professionals and scientists, the defense industry, with its heavy reliance on research and development as well as advanced manufacturing technology, becomes an attractive and challenging working environment.

The development and production of defense systems also require a high degree of expertise at the managerial level in the firms that develop and produce the systems, as well as among the officers of the armed forces that are in charge of the projects. These enhanced managerial capabilities will be useful later in other activities carried out by these managers, increasing the overall managerial capacity of the local industry through managerial spin-offs. This beneficial effect has been found in a study of 67 laboratories performing government-financed research and development in the United States, where improved managerial practices and technologies have been voluntarily adopted as a result of experience with government contracts. These contracts and the administrative standards they impose thus become a vehicle for technological innovation (Black, 1969). Because of the high reliance of the defense industry on advanced technology, we hypothesize that the emergence of modern defense industries in semi-industrialized countries strengthens the interrelationships of the technological infrastructure of the economy: universities, research establishments, and industry.

2.2.6   The Defense Industry

The central element of the model is the defense industry itself. As was already indicated, in semi-industrialized countries the defense industry is composed of private firms and state-owned firms and factories, all of which act as prime contractors, taking full responsibility for the final systems delivered to the armed forces. In the process, both private and state-owned firms sometimes act as subcontractors for each other when the need arises. It has been found that private ownership increases the efficiency performance of firms and that factor inefficiencies tend to increase with the size of the company (Frantz, 1985). Thus, with such significant government involvement in the defense industry and given the large sizes of the state-owned factories, lower efficiencies in the utilization of factors of production could be expected. Accordingly, it is possible to hypothesize that the more significant the state ownership of the defense industry, the lower the efficiency it will have.

Since the late 1970s and early 1980s in the developing world in general, and in Latin America in particular, there has been a shift from state-oriented development strategies and economies to free market economies with lesser government intervention. This policy shift gave rise to the emergence of small, privately owned defense firms that employed relatively more advanced production equipment and were driven by a broader economic vision. These private firms have been able to fill the technological gap created by the traditional state-owned defense firms. At the same time, the new market-oriented economy imposed on the traditional state-owned defense factories the need of self-financing. In order to reach this self-financing goal, these factories and shipyards had to evolve or perish. This change resulted in higher efficiencies, the production of civilian-oriented products, and a wave of technological innovations in terms of advanced manufacturing equipment, new machinery, the production of more sophisticated products, and the provision of more advanced services.

In the case of private firms, their involvement in the defense industry can range from total to minimal. Given the historical pattern of large state ownership of defense firms and factories, it appears that private firm involvement has increased over time. We do not expect to find private firms totally dedicated to defense production because of the inherent commercial risk that this entails.

The state-owned defense firms, thanks to their installed capacity and technological expertise, sometimes may become involved in the manufacture of products and the provision of services for the civilian market in order to increase capital and labor utilization.[6] These firms also contribute to exports of defense goods and services to foreign companies and armed forces.

Another group of firms that are as important as the prime contractors are the parts suppliers. According to Gansler (1980, p. 6), even in the case of the United States with its enormous production capacity, these parts producers may become the bottleneck in the case of a sharp increase in demand for arms and equipment, such as a mobilization surge. As will be shown in the following chapters, given their limited technological capacity, semi-industrialized countries are more dependent on parts and components for their domestic products than on complete systems. This means that there has been a change in the structure of the technological dependence from systems to parts, and from parts to critical components. Thus, even though semi-industrialized countries have the capability to produce somewhat advanced weapons systems, they possess a reduced logistical depth. With the extreme complexity of highly sophisticated weapons systems, this parts-and-components technological dependency has also spread to industrialized countries, where even the United States is considering the security implications of this dependency, and actions are being carried out to search for alternatives either to reduce it or to cope with it (Kellman et al., 1992; Saadawi et al., 1992).

In semi-industrialized countries, the defense sector possesses three advantages over the civilian sector vis-à-vis the development and application of technology (Simon, 1986):

- higher quality and quantity of technical personnel,
- better and more sophisticated testing equipment and instrumentation, and
- greater access to funding.

Besides these general advantages, it is possible to add a fourth one:

- ability to focus on the specific technology needed to reduce the technological risk.

These four advantages can help explain in part the disparity

---

6. During the mid-1980s, for example, the Peruvian naval shipyards began producing steel towers for power transmission lines. In Chile, the army's FAMAE (Army's Factories and Workshops) produces hand tools as well as weapons (see Chapter 5).

existing between the development of civilian technological capabilities and the development of military technological capabilities in semi-industrialized countries. While market mechanisms in the civilian sector operate with low demand and low purchasing power to promote technological change, the technological innovation process in the defense sector is driven by the ever increasing operational requirements of the armed forces, accelerating the development and adoption of new technologies.

The final performance of the indigenous defense industry of semi-industrialized countries can thus be measured along several parameters:

- total number of different types of equipment produced (diversity),
- technology incorporated into the products and services (sophistication on an absolute basis),
- degree of incorporation in the local armed forces (local acceptance),
- number of recipient countries (diffusion and international acceptance),
- technological level of the recipient countries (sophistication on a relative basis), and
- amount of sales.

In semi-industrialized countries one of the main objectives of the domestic defense industry has been the substitution of imported equipment to reduce political and technological dependency. Thus, acceptance of the equipment and arms produced at the national level is almost guaranteed, provided technical and quality requirements are satisfied. The most important parameters to be analyzed are diversity, sophistication in absolute and relative terms, diffusion, and sales volume. From a technological perspective the most important of these parameters is considered to be sophistication in absolute terms, which reflects the degree of technical expertise attained in the arms development and manufacturing process. Unfortunately, diffusion and international acceptance are often a function of international political considerations that may obscure some of the other factors.

In the following chapters, some of these indicators will be used to assess the performance of the defense industries of Argentina, Brazil, and Chile.

2.3   CHAPTER SUMMARY

In this chapter an overall model of the defense industry at the national economy level of a semi-industrialized country has been presented.   This model suggests that the establishment of an indigenous defense industry requires the integration of the overall industrial and technological capabilities of the nation.   As the integration achieved between the defense industry and the rest of the economy increases, higher benefits can be expected in terms of manufacturing and managerial skills and also in technological innovations of manufacturing processes for the production of civilian goods.

As can be seen from the model shown in Figure 2.2, in a semi-industrialized country the relationship of the local defense industry with the productive infrastructure and the overall political and economic state of affairs creates many elements in the industrial environment that affect the production volume as well as the degree of sophistication of the products.   The model suggests that the higher the integration of the local defense industry with the overall manufacturing sector of the economy, the higher the efficiency and the better the utilization of resources.   On the other hand, if there is lack of interaction between the two industrial sectors, the defense industry may become a burden to the rest of the economy.   The classic example of industrial defense burden is provided by the defense industry of the former Soviet Union that was highly criticized and repudiated because of its isolation, excessive use of capital and prime resources, and inability to transfer technology to the civilian sector.

3

The Defense Industry of Brazil

In this and the following two chapters, detailed descriptions of the defense industries of Argentina, Brazil, and Chile are presented. The information contained in these chapters will be used later to determine the impact that the defense industry of those countries has had on the national economies. We will start with Brazil because of its proven capability and high level of defense exports.

3.1 THE EMERGENCE OF THE BRAZILIAN DEFENSE INDUSTRY

Since the beginning of this century, Brazil relied upon defense imports coming from Europe and the United States to equip its armed forces (Lock, 1986; Vayrynen, 1992, p. 83; Ross, 1984, p. 175). Because of a shortage of international currency during the crisis of the 1930s, a small defense production capability emerged. When the Brazilian Army joined the Allies during World War II, large quantities of U.S. weapons were made available to Brazil, with this supply continuing to the late 1950s. No local production of major weapons systems was recorded during this period; only small arms and small naval units for the fluvial branch of the navy were manufactured in Brazil at that time. Brigagao (1986) argues that the availability of U.S. weapons during the 1950s and 1960s created political and economic dependency in Brazil, also helping to increase the burden of the national debt.

With respect to the origins of the Brazilian defense industry, there are different opinions. Perry and Weiss (1986) indicate that the Brazilian defense industry began as a modest attempt to supplement Brazil's limited and outdated military capabilities and enhance the nation's autonomy in defense matters. Sohr (1990, p. 23) points out that Brazil placed commercial considerations first in the development of its defense industry, with a large number of its products expressly designed for export, without even considering the possibility of incorporating them in the national arsenals. On the other hand, Brigagao (1986) maintains that the emergence of a strong defense industry in Brazil resulted from the need to project national power and protect national interests on a global scale. This political need led to the creation of a policy of expansion and consolidation of the defense economy, with the goal of providing for Brazil's security while simultaneously achieving the military production capacity to enter the international arms market. Vayrynen (1992, p. 87) indicates that in Brazil the creation of a modern defense industry had as the ultimate goal greater military industrial autonomy, regarded as the key to greater national power and national security. Ross (1984, p. 165) argues that

> The principal objectives underlying Brazil's investment in a large-scale arms manufacturing program include—in addition to reducing dependence upon foreign suppliers—force modernization, solidifying a hegemonic position in Latin America, and lending credence to the ongoing campaign for major power status.

Rather than being contradictory, all these hypotheses about the reasons for the emergence of a strong defense industry in Brazil can be considered to be complementary. The varied opinions of these researchers help to infer that the origins of the defense industry in Brazil have a combination of geopolitical, military, and commercial roots, strongly supported by the Brazilian government and its armed forces in the best interest of the country.

Lock (1986) mentions that international events helped in the inception of the Brazilian arms industry. He indicates that in the mid-1960s U.S. decisions to limit transfers of military technology to Brazil served to strengthen its defense capabilities, additionally helping it to move away from U.S. sources of weaponry. This was further reinforced when in 1977, because of international political reasons, the Brazilian government renounced the 1952 agreement with the United States for military assistance. Also, the heavy involvement of the United States in Vietnam during the 1960s reduced Brazilian access to

U.S. weapons, creating a perception among the Brazilian military leaders of vulnerability, which led to the search for alternative sources of arms in Europe. This resulted in large purchases of European arms from 1967 to 1972 (Brigagao, 1986).

Brigagao points out that the Brazilian defense industry, being the most robust sector of the economy, took up the excess capacity in other technological and industrial sectors resulting from Brazil's economic recession during the 1960s. Although figures for the whole industry are not available, it appears that during the 1970s and 1980s Brazil's arms export industry was profitable, making a contribution to the balance of payments. In fact, Brazilian arms exports represented an average of 1.4 percent of total exports between 1978 and 1988, with a total amount exported during that 10-year period of $4.1 billion (ACDA, 1990). However, the termination of hostilities between Iran and Iraq in 1988 has had a debilitating effect on two of the most important Brazilian defense firms: Avibrás and Engesa. Both are currently in financial trouble, despite the settlement in 1988 of a major arms deal with Libya (OTA, 1991b, p. 143).

From the beginning of the Brazilian military industrialization process in the mid-1960s, the armed forces and private industry combined their interests and efforts to create a modern defense industry (Brigagao, 1986). During the period 1964 through 1967 the emerging defense industry took advantage of the growth and modernization in the automobile and steel industries. Because of an economic recession and with funds provided by government soft credits, firms that previously manufactured civilian goods were transformed into factories producing military equipment, including firms in the automobile, heavy equipment, medical supply, textile, aeronautic, and electronic industries (Lock, 1986). This indicates that the Brazilian defense industry was not developed apart from the rest of the economy but grew in an organic and coordinated manner at the same time as other related industries modernized and expanded. The presence of private industry in such an early stage is noteworthy because, as will be shown later, the emergence of the defense industry in Argentina and Chile was mostly the result of a centralized government effort carried out by the armed forces alone.

The fact that private firms were employed as the basis for the emerging Brazilian defense industry in its early stages provided well-defined commercial, market, and cost-efficiency considerations, giving to the Brazilian defense industry structure a close proximity to perfect market characteristics. As will be shown in Chapter 8, this important and early private participation in the Brazilian defense industry carried with it the corresponding benefits of improved and efficient use and allocation of resources, both human and capital. This defense industrialization process based on private investment and civilian-oriented firms contrasts with the policies followed by other developing countries where strong involvement of the state is the norm and also where defense firms are managed as separate and independent entities from the rest of the economy.

The new defense industrial policy of Brazil adopted around 1965 led to the creation of military research institutes closely linked with private industry (Lock, 1986; Vayrynen, 1992, p. 99). Between 1964 and 1967, foreign defense technology in the form of licenses was purchased from industrialized countries (Brigagao, 1986), with the goal to enlarge the military industrial base by concentrating resources on national defense. As will be shown, these research institutes were later instrumental in improving the technology transfer and assimilation process that followed and, in the long run, in developing indigenous technology.

In the mid-1960s government subsidies were applied to indigenously produced equipment to make them more competitive in the international market (Lock, 1986). Defense exports without political affiliation and with favorable commercial terms transformed Brazil into a viable international commercial partner (Barros, 1984). Perry and Weiss (1986) indicate that the Brazilian defense industry could not have developed adequately if it had relied only on supplying the domestic defense market. Thus, from the beginnings of the Brazilian military industrialization the market was visualized as being global in nature, not restricting the industry with autarkic import substitution schemes alone. The export subsidies helped to further reinforce this perception and to accelerate the institutionalization of the technology acquisition and development process. So, based on free market economic principles and strong government support, the Brazilian defense industry grew fast during the 1960s with a long-term vision of a global defense market.

With the technical experience gained in the previous years, larger and more sophisticated weapons were developed during the period 1967 through 1978. In addition, these weapons were priced to compete in the international market. Horizontal coordinating mechanisms emerged among different local firms for the development of complex weapons systems (Lock, 1986). Extraordinary resources were devoted to research and development in the weapons industry, indicating the trust of policymakers in the technological innovation process under way. This trust was probably based on the successful results attained by the research and development institutes founded in the early 1960s.

During the late 1960s, the shift to domestic production of military equipment was encouraged by reducing imports and subsidizing products intended for export. A new legislative policy promoting the production and commercialization of the Brazilian weapons industry also emerged, with a National Program of Military Material Exports established by the Brazilian National Security Council, with goals to make the defense industry self-sufficient and to penetrate foreign markets. Legislation was written to encourage military exports by reducing taxes, providing access to preferential bank financing and subsidies to military goods destined for foreign markets. All exporters received subsidies, for instance, through tax exemptions for value added in exported goods, as well as tax exemption for all of their imports (Lock, 1986).

During the 1970s, cheap, rugged Brazilian weapons became an alternative to supplies from industrialized countries for a large number of Third World recipients (Brzoska and Ohlson, 1987, p. 115). Joint ventures with foreign firms were developed, further aiding the integration of Brazil's defense industry into the world arms market. More than 100 joint ventures with European firms were established, and Brazilian-made defense equipment combined many foreign-made sophisticated parts and components (Ross, 1984, pp. 260–261). However, according to Brigagao (1986), this technology transfer process was inefficient, not achieving the complete transfer of defense technology. Thus, it can be argued that the incorporation of large quantities of sophisticated imported parts and components to Brazilian-made defense goods precluded the technology transfer of know-how and manufacturing technology to develop and produce the same components in Brazil.

It is also possible to assert that low-priced Brazilian-manufactured defense products were used by U.S. and European defense companies to further penetrate the international—as well as the Brazilian—defense market with cheaper weapons systems not produced in their own countries. Using Brazilian-made defense platforms that incorporated their advanced components, this process of increased market penetration by the firms of industrialized countries would have also increased the subsequent demand for spare parts and repair and maintenance services, known to be very profitable in other industries such as automotive and electronics.

One reason for the upsurge of arms production in Brazil was the specialization in the use of civilian-use components—produced commercially by multinational companies in Brazil—employed for the manufacture of weapons systems. During the 1970s, products manufactured for the civilian market by private firms were incorporated into defense systems by means of a technology adaptation process, increasing even further the interrelation of the civilian and defense industries (Lock, 1986; Vayrynen, 1992, p. 96).[1] In Brazil, then, this process of adapting civilian technology for the production of defense goods can be considered an important factor for the simple designs and low prices at which Brazilian weapons sell in the international market, perhaps the key elements for their wide acceptance in the Third World (Sohr, 1990, p. 23).

In order to avoid U.S. embargoes on components or technology, the use of U.S. defense technology was limited to components that were not under military export control by the United States government (Ross, 1984, p. 308; Lock, 1986, p. 97), further reinforcing the technology adaptation and learning process. Lock (1986) adds that the arms control approach of the Carter administration in the United States enhanced Brazil's position as a weapons supplier of Latin American countries. In this way, the restrictive practices of the United States for the export of defense equipment helped to transform the Brazilian defense industry into a world player.

As can be seen, during the 1970s the Brazilian government became strongly involved in the formulation of an explicit industrial policy to render the emerging defense industry stronger and more fruitful. At this point in time, it can be said that the institutionalization process of integrating the Brazilian defense industry into the rest of the economy and into the world arms market was successfully completed.

Coproduction agreements were signed in the 1980s with the United States, Italy, France, the United Kingdom, and the Federal Republic of Germany (Brigagao, 1986). This means that in less than two decades Brazil moved from being fully dependent in defense technology to the position of technological partner of the same countries that supplied Brazil before the establishment of the indigenous defense industry. Also, transfer of military production capabilities to other Third World countries started during these years, with an agreement to build an entire arms factory in Saudi Arabia (Lock, 1986).

---

1. In the case of the United States, the lack of interrelation of the civilian and defense industries has been recognized as one of the critical issues in the problems experienced in the production of military items (Gansler, 1989, p. 273).

Brigagao (1986) argues that the decision to expand and develop the military economy and defense industries, with a corresponding expansion in research and development (R&D), would renew the Brazilian industrial base, upgrade managerial methods, and alter the profile of the industrial labor force. The latter change can be considered a social impact not envisioned even by the most audacious.[2]

Just as in Europe after World War II, the indigenous development of defense technology also helped in the modernization of the Brazilian industry. The principal mechanism to achieve this modernization process through defense technological innovation can be considered to be the early and extensive involvement of private firms and civilian manufacturing factories in the production of military equipment. Currently, state ownership of defense firms in Brazil is almost negligible, with the exception of Embraer, a mixed company with 51 percent owned by the air force and 49 percent by private investor shareholders (OTA, 1991b, p. 143). Many defense firms are located in the private transportation and capital goods sectors.

Arms production in Brazil is highly concentrated in the fields of aircraft and armored vehicles, with an output in these two categories that far exceeds domestic demand. Of the total production, about two thirds comes from indigenous designs and the other third from designs licensed by firms outside of Brazil (Brzoska and Ohlson, 1986, pp. 11, 13). Even though it is estimated that in Brazil there are over 500 manufacturers of defense-related equipment (OTA, 1991c, p. 143), Sohr (1990, p. 23) indicates that the three major firms—Engesa, manufacturer of wheel-mounted armored vehicles; Avibrás, specialist in artillery rockets; and Embraer, manufacturer of civilian and military aircraft—have been responsible for roughly 90 percent of military exports.

Brazil has built up a domestic defense production capability at a high pace, with a marked increase after the second half of the 1970s (Brzoska and Ohlson, 1986, p. 28). Kolodziej (1987b, p. 313) reports that between 1970 and 1980 Brazil produced domestically, either under license agreements or as nationally developed systems, a total of 22 different weapons systems, including various types of aircraft, ground equipment, missiles, and naval vessels. With that number of

---

2. Brazilian defense industry workers are now, on average, 72 percent more productive than civilian manufacturing workers. Chapter 8 provides verification for this surprising phenomenon.

weapons systems produced locally during that decade, Brazil was the second-most diversified Third World arms producing country, with China being ranked first by producing all kinds of weapons systems.

For the years between 1985 and 1989, the Stockholm International Peace Research Institute (SIPRI) (1990) ranked Brazil ninth among the world's arms exporters to the Third World, with a cumulative total of $1.3 billion. For the same period, SIPRI ranked Brazil as number eleven when considering military exports to all countries. As can be inferred by the figures of defense imports and exports reported by ACDA (1990), Brazil has had a positive trade balance in military equipment since 1982, achieved by a combined effort of reducing imports and boosting exports. Currently Brazil stands as the sixth largest arms exporting country in the world (OTA, 1991b, p. 143).

The Brazilian arms market consists of more than 70 countries, mostly in the developing world of Latin America, Africa, the Middle East, and Asia. The large number of weapons exported to the Middle East is for counter-trade in the form of oil (OTA, 1991c, p. 150). This process has helped alleviate Brazil's heavy dependency upon imported oil. It also reduces the uncertainty of supplies. Egypt, Iraq, and Libya have been Brazil's major arms customers, as well as its major oil suppliers (Perry and Weiss, 1986). According to OTA (1991c), Iraq has been Brazil's most important customer, purchasing armored personnel carriers, missiles, and aircraft, often in exchange for oil. The arms embargo against Iraq has weakened the ability of Brazil to maintain its industrial base at 1980s production levels. Furthermore, negotiations for the proposed sale to Saudi Arabia of Engesa's Osorio main battle tank (an estimated $7 billion deal) remain suspended (OTA, 1991b, p. 143).

The military goods exported by Brazil range from military uniforms to fighter planes, armored vehicles, rockets, and missiles. OTA (1991b, pp. 144–145) lists 35 countries as recipients of Brazilian weapons and specifies the kinds of arms purchased. It is noteworthy that OTA's list includes the industrialized countries of Belgium, Canada, France, and the United Kingdom as importers of Brazilian weapons. All exports to these industrialized countries are aircraft, indicating that in relative terms these Brazilian military goods are the ones with the most sophisticated technology. The one sector lagging behind has been shipbuilding, which has never been part of the general arms export drive (Brzoska and Ohlson, 1987, p. 115).

Lock (1986) has indicated that Brazil contributed, by its example, to the initiation or expansion of military production in several developing countries. It is possible to argue that Chile is one of them.

In the introduction to his article, Brigagao (1986) expressed: "It is no overstatement to suggest that in many respects the new Brazilian industrialization—the Brazilian "economic miracle"—has been led by military production and technology" (p. 101). The Brazilian defense industry has established itself as one of the most reliable pillars in the export sphere, an area critical to Brazilian economic prospects, given its high indebtedness (Perry and Weiss, 1986).

3.2 STRUCTURE OF WEAPONS PRODUCTION IN BRAZIL

As was already explained, the defense industry of Brazil is a combined effort shared between private and state-owned companies, with heavy emphasis on the private industry. Lock (1986) indicates that even though Brazilian arms production is marked by commercial interests, state participation through ownership—in particular, of the shipbuilding and aircraft industries—special fiscal incentives and government-financed R&D are also essential ingredients.   State ownership is dominant in the field of naval construction and small arms production. The vehicle sector is private, while the aerospace sector is both privately and publicly owned.

The former state arsenals (except for the naval yard) and other state enterprises producing small arms and ammunition were combined in 1975 under IMBEL (Industria Brasileira de Material Bélico). The objective was to streamline, commercialize, and coordinate their production. The state arsenals had previously been organized under the individual armed services. In 1980, Luis Whittacker, an arms industrialist and the chairman of Engesa (Engenheiros Especializados, a private defense company), also took over the chairmanship of IMBEL, replacing a four-star general. This action marked the commercialization of the enterprise and transformed it into a state-owned firm run like a private company (Brigagao, 1986; Lock, 1986; Barros, 1984).

With respect to government policies, Vayrynen (1980; 1992, pp. 87–88) contends that the procurement policy of the Brazilian government visibly favors private companies at the expense of the government-owned military factories. The coalition of a foreign company and a private domestic firm appears to be in many cases the most favored solution. The close interrelation of the civilian and defense industries is noteworthy, with private companies certainly giving great importance to the commercial success of the overall effort, with due significance to the marketability of its products and services on a national and international basis. OTA (1991b, p. 143) adds that owing to budgetary constraints deriving from massive foreign debt, the government has provided little support for these firms through increased domestic defense procurement.

According to Brigagao (1986), the number of firms participating in the Brazilian defense industry is on the order of 350 medium-to-large public and private, national and international enterprises, with 50 of these solely producing weapons.   Using the employment figures provided by Lock (1986) for the major arms producing firms in Brazil, reproduced in Table 3.1, an employment figure of roughly 36,400 people is obtained. Using a direct-employment multiplier of two (the largest suggested by Mosley [1985] to obtain total military-related employment in the United States)—because of the large number of firms not included in Table 3.1 and to take into account smaller firms and second-tier suppliers—this results in an overall figure of 72,800 employees for the Brazilian defense industry.   This overall figure is lower than what other researchers have estimated (200,000 workers according to Brigagao [1986]; 100,000 workers in the arms producing industry according to Brzoska and Ohlson [1987]) and closer to the figure of 75,000 employees reported by Renner (1989) for the early 1980s.

The most important defense firms and defense-related research institutes of Brazil are all located in the area of São José de Campos, where a technology park similar to those existing in the industrialized world has been created by the government (Lock, 1986). There are several multinational corporations that operate in the Brazilian defense industry, including Beretta and FN (Fabrique Nationale, a Belgian firm) in small arms and ammunition; Northrop, Piper, Aernautica Macchi, Aerospatiale, and Fokker in the aeronautical sector; Thomson-CSF in the electronics and air defense systems; Ferranti, Philips, AEG-Telefunken, L. M. Erickson, General Electric, and Texas Instruments in military electronics; and Mercedes-Benz in military vehicles (Lock, 1986; Vayrynen, 1980).   No employment figures for these firms are available, but they have been accounted for by the indirect employment multiplier introduced above.

Table 3.1

Major Brazilian Arms Producers, 1982

Company	Location	Ownership	Sales $ M	Employees
Arsenal da Marinha	Rio de Janeiro	State	N/A	(7,000)
Embraer	São José dos Campos	Private/State	205	6,732
Engesa	São José dos Campos	Private	220	(5,000)
Cobra	Rio de Janeiro	Private	(80)	(1,900)
Mecánica Pesada	Rio de Janerio	Man (FRG)/Creusot Loire (France)	(60)	(2,700)
Avibrás	São José dos Campos	Private	38	(1,500)
CBC	Santo Andre	State	(35)	(1,800)
CBV	Rio de Janerio	Private	N/A	(1,500)
Taurus	São Paulo	Private	12	840

Table 3.1 continued

Major Brazilian Arms Producers, 1982

Company	Location	Ownership	Sales $ M	Employees
Moto Pecas	São Paulo	Private	8	(1,500)[a]
Bernardini	São Paulo	Private	7	365
Helibras	Itajuba	State/Aerospatiale (France)	5	(200)
Neiva	São Paulo	Embraer	4	345
Imbel		State	N/A	(4,000)[b]
Gurgel		Private	N/A	(500)
Sago		Private	N/A	(500)
				Total 36,382

Source: Lock, 1986, p. 83.
Note: Figures in parentheses indicate estimated values.
[a] Original table says 496; Lock (1986) reports 1,500 for 1986.
[b] Estimated by the authors considering the scope of operations and number of employees of FAMAE, Chile, with estimates of 3,000 employees in Chapter 5.

3.3   DEFENSE RESEARCH AND DEVELOPMENT IN BRAZIL

It can be said that the research expertise developed since the early 1960s to support the defense industry is highly capable in several different fields, including advanced fighter aircraft, main battletanks, nuclear-powered submarines, and missiles (OTA, 1991b, p. 143). This indicates that the long-term investment and vision of policymakers have paid off.

Military research and development are carried out at several institutions of the armed forces: CTA (Centro Técnico Aereonáutico, the Aerospace Technical Center) for the air force and for aircraft and missiles; Departamento de Ensino e Pesquisa (Department of Teaching and Research) and others for the army and for armored vehicles; and Instituto de Pesquisas da Marinha (Naval Research Institute) and others for the navy, as well as by the private defense companies. These organizations are concerned with both basic research and engineering. The armed forces themselves also have some research and design capabilities (Lock, 1986). According to Varas (1989), the Brazilian aeronautical industry is supported by the Aerospace Technical Center (CTA), around which the institutes of Space Technology, Research and Development, and Aerospace Research are grouped. The center provides wind-tunnel capabilities and physics laboratories.

OTA (1991b, p. 143) adds that in Brazil the most direct form of government support to the development of defense systems is the encouragement of linkages between these research institutes and the respective industries. In spite of the capacity of major Brazilian companies for developing weapons systems, joint operation with the armed forces is the rule (Lock, 1986). Today, scientists and engineers from the military sector work in private enterprises and factories, and research institutes closely cooperate with private enterprises to upgrade or develop new defense products (Lock, 1986). Thus, not only was production of defense equipment done in close interrelation with civilian factories, but in this later stage, technology for defense equipment was developed jointly by private firms and civilian industry professionals. This process undoubtedly has helped to reduce the technological dependence from industrialized countries and to further increase the technological self-reliance of the overall economy. As can be seen, the Brazilian government also fosters the development of new defense equipment at the front end of the product development cycle, besides providing subsidies at the back end to boost exports.

With respect to the financing of research and development activities for the defense industry in Brazil, an official publication of the Brazilian government (*A Política Brasileira de Ciencia y Tecnología: 1990-95*, 1990) indicates that the development of military technology, besides having its own budgetary resources, found significant support in the traditional system of incentives for science and technology. According to the same official publication, within the first program for the development of science and technology established during the early 1970s, it was contemplated that roughly 20 percent of the resources considered for the industrial sector should be assigned to the military ministries. This figure illustrates the high importance assigned by the federally funded science and technology development system to support the development of technology for the defense industry.

Between 1970 and 1980, the National Fund for the Development of Science and Technology (FNDCT) disbursed $113 million in direct support of research programs and projects under the immediate responsibility of the armed forces, which is a significant amount of the total devoted by the Brazilian government to science and technology during the period. During the years 1981 to 1990, the FNDCT maintained its contributions to the defense sector, but now on a lesser scale with a total of $58 million, because the fund itself experienced a drastic reduction during the decade (see Figure 3.1). However, to gain a better understanding of the relative effort made by the Brazilian public sector in the development of science and technology for military applications during the later years, the overall budgetary assignments of the Brazilian government to science and technology need to be considered. As can be seen from Figures 3.2 and 3.3, the share of government R&D resources devoted to the military sector were on average 12.7 percent of the total amounts spent in science and technology between 1987 and 1989, and 13.5 percent when the budgeted years 1990 and 1991 are included. The fact that the R&D funds assigned to the Brazilian Air Force (almost 69 percent) have been the highest can be justified in terms of technological complexity and, as will be shown below, because aircraft have been among the most important export items of the Brazilian defense industry.

The amounts shown in Figure 3.2, corresponding to funds assigned to the military ministries for research and development between 1987 and 1991, add up to the totals shown in Table 3.2. This is an extremely large amount for a country that, in terms of its gross national product (GNP) per capita, belongs within the lower-middle-

Figure 3.1

Brazilian Science and Technology Funding of R&D Projects Controlled by the Armed Forces

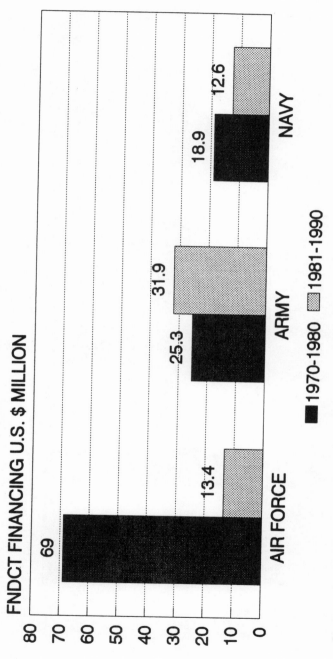

FNDCT FINANCING U.S. $ MILLION

■ 1970-1980 ▨ 1981-1990

Source: "A Política Brasileira de Ciência e Tecnología," 1990, p. 29.

Figure 3.2

Brazilian Federal Funding of R&D for Military Ministries

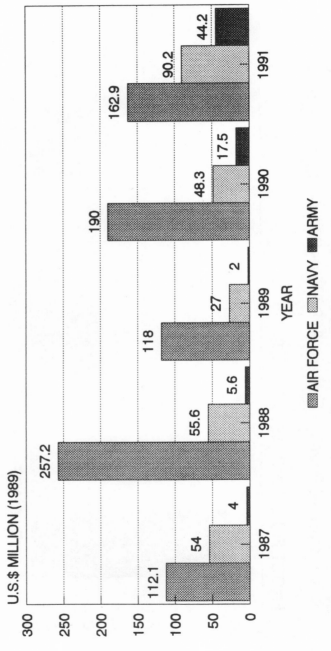

Source: "A Politica Brasileira de Ciência e Tecnologia," 1990, p. 30.

Figure 3.3

Military Ministries Percent Share of Brazilian Federal Funding for Science and Technology

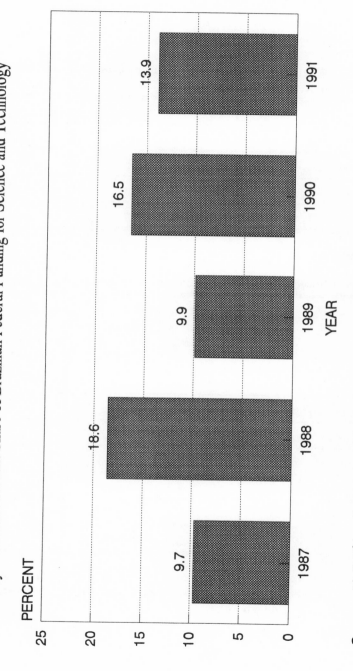

Source: "A Política Brasileira de Ciência e Tecnología," 1990, p. 31.

43

Table 3.2

Funds Assigned to the Brazilian Military Ministries for Research and Development, 1987–1991

Service	Millions of Dollars	
Air Force	849.2	(70.9%)
Navy	275.1	(23.0%)
Army	73.3	(6.1%)
Total	$1,197.6	

Table 3.3

Research and Development Expenditures of Selected Countries

Country	Defense R&D as Percent of Federal R&D, 1987	Estimated Federal 1987 Defense R&D Expenditures (1982 $Million)
France	34.1	2,380
West Germany	12.5	873
Japan	4.5	352
United Kingdom	50.3	2,707
United States	68.6	31,808
Brazil	13.7	325
	Average 1987–1991	(1988 approx.)

Sources: National Science Board, 1989; National Science Foundation, 1991; *Política Brasileira de Ciencia y Tecnología: 1990–95 A*, 1990, p. 30.

income economies of the world. If half the resources provided by the national program for science and technology devoted to defense technology during the decade ending in 1990 are also considered ($28 million), the total allocated amount devoted to research and development for military purposes during the late 1980s and early 1990s adds up to $1,226 million, or roughly $245 million a year. For comparison purposes, the percentage ratios devoted to defense research and development in 1987 for some industrialized countries, as presented by the National Science Board (1989, p. 289), are shown in Table 3.3.

From this table it is possible to observe that the percent allocation of resources for defense R&D in Brazil compares with the resources allocated by industrialized nations for the same purposes, even though it is much less than in the United States. In terms of amount of resources, the approximately $324 million invested by the Brazilian government in 1988 for defense research and development compares not only in relative terms to the funds devoted in the industrialized countries but also in absolute terms to that of Japan a few years before. In 1979 alone, Embraer spent $23.3 million in research and development, representing 13.6 percent of sales (Ross, 1984, p. 220). This figure is noteworthy because it is comparable with R&D expenditures of high-tech companies of industrialized countries, both in terms of dollar amounts and percent of sales.

From these amounts, it is clear that the development of weapons systems and military technology has had a significant importance within Brazilian science and technology policy. This effort was financed not only by the funds allotted to the armed forces but also by the federal budget assigned to the development of science and technology.

Perry and Weiss (1986) indicate that because of the continuing technological dependence for the manufacture of technology intensive weapons such as fighter aircraft and guided missiles, Brazil's National Security Council has established a government funded advance electronic research and production center near São Paulo. Barros (1984) points out that the R&D program of the Brazilian Navy has made remarkable progress in electronics and microelectronics, allowing for the development of a specialized manpower and technological base.

3.4   THE AIRCRAFT INDUSTRY IN BRAZIL

After several failures to persuade experienced aircraft manufacturers to establish a Brazilian subsidiary that would produce light and medium aircraft, the Brazilian government decided to set up a factory of its own in the 1960s. With a majority of shares controlled by the government, Embraer was founded in the second half of 1969 (Lock, 1986). Private capital was invited to subscribe under extremely favorable conditions, and, as of 1981, the private ownership of Embraer totaled almost 93 percent (Lock, 1986). At present, private ownership of Embraer amounts to only 49 percent (OTA, 1991b, p. 143), indicating that during the 1980s the Brazilian government increased its ownership of the company, probably through direct investment. Since its creation, Embraer has coordinated approximately 250 firms in a unified national aviation effort and has expanded production of a broad line of civilian and military aircraft (Perry and Weiss, 1986).

In only five years, Embraer's output increased from only five aircraft produced in 1971 to 469 units in 1976, at the same time that the number of employees increased only fourfold, from 1,128 to 4,225. In less than 10 years the export sales of Embraer increased from $5 million in 1975 to an estimated $450 million in 1983 (Lock, 1986). This growth of export sales can be attributed to an increase in the number of units sold abroad together with an increasing level of sophistication of the aircraft being exported that allowed for higher prices.

OTA (1991b, p. 143) expressed that the evolution of Brazil's aircraft industry has been driven largely by Embraer's concern for profitability and technological learning, rising from a fledgling company composed only of 595 employees in 1970 to the world's fifth largest aircraft manufacturer in the late 1980s. According to OTA, the development approaches used by the Brazilian aircraft industry were:

- commitment to domestic design and manufacture,
- joint ventures with foreign aircraft producers to acquire and upgrade technological capabilities,
- phased introduction of domestic components, and
- product development balanced between military and civilian aircraft for domestic and export markets.

The first project undertaken by the emerging Brazilian aircraft industry was the replacement of the old Beech C-45 flown by the Brazilian Air Force. This was accomplished with the development of the twin turbo-prop IPD-6504, which later became the EMB-100. Development of this plane began in June 1965, and the first prototype was built in 1966. Outfitted with Pratt & Whitney PT-6 engines, its first flight occurred on October 1968. The Brazilian Air Force ordered 80 of the EMB-110 Bandeirante version. Lock (1986) indicates that the EMB-110 Bandeirante won international recognition for its reliability, cost-effectiveness, and serviceability, with 450 units produced up to 1984. Of these, 200 units were sold abroad. By 1990, 500 units of the Bandeirante had been produced and were operating in 24 countries, primarily in the United States (over 147 units) and in Brazil itself (OTA, 1991b). The modified version of the Bandeirante alone—the EMB-110P—was extremely popular with local airlines and air forces in and outside the region. In 1976 Embraer developed three versions of the Bandeirante: the K1, for military use; P1, a modified version of the K1; and the P2, strictly for passengers. In order to increase the possibility of exporting these aircraft, Embraer strived to obtain U.S. certifications for its products (Lock, 1986).

One of the drawbacks that the Bandeirante design had to overcome was the inability of Brazilian industry to provide parts and components. Thus, the aircraft included mainly components that were used in other aircraft and available on the world market. On the positive side, OTA (1991b) highlights the enormous flexibility in the design of the Bandeirante. Using the same airframe, it can be manufactured for air drop, search and rescue, maritime surveillance, and ambulance missions. Thus, this technological capability of Brazilian engineers deserves to be recognized.

This achievement of the military aeronautical industry made it possible for Embraer to develop civilian aircraft such as the EMB-200 Ipanema for agricultural use. It made its first flight in July 1970, and five versions were built, amounting to a total of 400 units. The model following the Bandeirante was the EMB-120 Brasilia, targeted for commuter airlines and currently being flown in the United States by three airlines. The principal attractions of the Brasilia are its cruise speed of 300 km/h—making it the fastest in its class—and its price and financing package.

Embraer is currently developing another commercial airplane in association with the Argentinean firm Fábrica Argentina de Materiales Aeroespaciales (FAMA). The aircraft will use the fuselage and the cockpit of the Brasilia and an innovative "twinprop pusher" engine—

mounted on the rear of the airplane—developed by Garret. In this latter venture, the production and financing have been split: 67 percent by Embraer and 33 percent by FAMA (OTA, 1991b, p. 147).

With respect to the fabrication of military aircraft, Lock (1986) adds that Embraer signed a contract with the Italian manufacturer Aeronautica Macchi for licensed production of the MB-326 Xavante jet-trainer. Lock also indicates that technologically the Xavante was a safe aircraft with which to start fighter aircraft production, probably because of its simpler design and ease of manufacturing. Almost 200 Xavante aircraft were manufactured in Brazil, most of them for the Brazilian Air Force, with only two dozen for export (Perry and Weiss, 1986).

The next model developed jointly by Embraer and Aeronautica Macchi was the AMX trainer/light strike aircraft, with an estimated price of $10 million and development costs of at least $720 million. One third of the development costs ($240 million) were to be borne by Brazil and the rest by Italy, with Embraer owning a 29.7 percent share; Aeritalia, 46.5 percent; and Aeronautica Macchi, 23.8 percent (OTA, 1991b). By 1986 the AMX had reached the prototype stage, with 500 units originally considered for manufacturing: 200 for Italy, roughly 100 for Brazil, and 200 for export (Lock, 1986). OTA (1991b) indicates that the AMX project is the one that has contributed the most to Embraer's technological development and the least in terms of profitability, with the Brazilian Air Force receiving only 79 AMX units and Italy's air force the remaining 187 units of the total of 266 AMX units manufactured.

Continuing with the description of the production of military aircraft, Lock (1986) indicates that in response to a tender by the Brazilian Ministry of Aeronautics in 1987 for a turbo-prop trainer, Embraer won over other domestic competitors with the EMB-312 Tucano. Interesting to note here is the procedure chosen to select the producer of the aircraft: an open tender. Taking into consideration the world stature of Embraer at that time, this procedure reflects the pragmatism of the Brazilian government with respect to defense contracts.

With a low price of only $1.9 million and over 600 units sold worldwide, the Tucano has become the world's sales leader in the military turbo-prop trainer field. The Tucano was the first military sale by Brazil to a North Atlantic Treaty Organization (NATO) country. In 1985 the British Royal Air Force selected the Tucano over established domestic and European competitors, such as the Swiss's

Pilatus PC-9 and the British Aerospace's Hawk (Lock, 1986; OTA, 1991b). As indicated by OTA (1991b, pp. 144–145), the Tucano has also been sold to several other countries in North and South America, the Middle East, Africa, and Europe.

The military government took every chance to enhance the technological capabilities of Embraer. When 42 F-5 fighter aircraft were purchased from Northrop of the United States, the Brazilian government insisted that parts of the production program shift to Brazil, resulting in elements of the wing being produced by Embraer. Embraer has stressed the use of offset agreements when selling to industrialized countries. In the case of the sale to Great Britain, currently 30 percent of the Tucano aircraft (the wings, the landing gear, and canopy) is made in Brazil, and 60 percent is fabricated under license from Embraer by a British firm in northern Ireland. The Tucano is also license produced in Egypt, with full parts manufactured in Brazil and shipped for assembly (OTA, 1991b, p. 147).

With respect to the overall strategy adopted by Brazil in its aircraft industry, OTA (1991b, p. 147) indicates that Brazil's economy, with its $120 billion debt and its need for exports, is the compelling reason why Embraer has so heavily focused on its export customers when engaging in product development. Embraer has also avoided the mistake that some countries starting aircraft industries (such as India and Argentina) have made of relying almost exclusively on domestic military procurement. The company has maintained a balance between military and civilian aircraft production from the start. In 1987, for example, Embraer exported aircraft worth $320 million, which represented 68.1 percent of total production. For 1987, out of the 31.9 percent that constituted domestic sales, the civilian market accounted for 25.7 percent. International sales are divided 33.4 percent for military and 67.6 percent for civilian (OTA, 1991b, p. 147).

As can be seen, the Brazilian aircraft industry can be considered of world stature not only for the various kinds of aircraft offered but also because of the advanced technology it has been able to master in only two decades. However, it is still not capable of domestically producing supersonic fighters and heavy transport aircraft, nor turbines. Another weakness of the Brazilian aircraft industry is the lack of capability in the manufacture of some components (Lock, 1986; Sohr, 1990, p. 28), in particular, electronics and avionics (Vayrynen, 1980), requiring the import of large amounts of equipment to be incorporated in the manufactured aircraft for export. In fact, Sohr (1990, p. 28) indicates that 62 percent of Embraer's export sales between 1983 and 1986 corresponded to imported equipment. On top of this, Lock (1986) adds that, according to French sources, 41 percent of the value of the Xingu aircraft that has been purchased by the French Air Force originated from the United States and 28 percent from France. This leaves at most 31 percent production value added in Brazil.

This would indicate that a large share of the sales price of the manufactured aircraft corresponds to the value added to these imported components in the systems integration part of the domestic designs. In this case, Embraer performs not much more than the assembly of foreign sophisticated parts with its less expensive labor force.

According to Fialka (1991), one of the latest innovations in the aircraft industries of several countries is the upgrading of aging fighter planes from the 1960s. These aircraft—after being stripped of the outdated electronics and avionics—are re-equipped with the latest computerized technology, becoming serious contenders to the latest generations of fighter planes and at only a fraction of the cost of new ones. Among the various countries that actually perform such upgrades, Fialka includes Brazil, reflecting the high engineering capability of its aircraft industry.

3.5   ARMORED VEHICLES MANUFACTURED IN BRAZIL

Engesa, a São Paulo-based company, was the first firm to present prototypes of military trucks and armored vehicles that were particularly adapted to the conditions prevailing in Brazil. The designs embodied many standard components already produced in Brazil by subsidiaries of foreign manufacturers. Reliability, operability, and serviceability ranked high and made the military vehicles particularly suitable for the bad roads in the outback of the vast territory. The first export of armored vehicles made by a Brazilian firm occurred in the late 1970s, to fulfill a large order placed by Libya (Lock, 1986). The vehicles exported were 200 Cascavel armored cars (OTA, 1991b, p. 143)[3] manufactured by Engesa. When these vehicles were successfully utilized by Libya against Egypt, the reputation of the Brazilian firm rose worldwide.

Lock (1986) indicates that while the design of Engesa's armored vehicles is indigenous, the most sophisticated components are

---

3. Half the 400 units reported by Sohr (1990, p. 25).

produced under license or imported. Sohr (1990, p. 28) reports that only 25 percent of Engesa's exports correspond to imported equipment and components, reflecting a much higher degree of domestic integration and technological capability when compared with the aircraft industry.

Army research facilities and certain laboratories of the University of São Paulo were involved from the very beginning in the development of military hardware for Engesa (Lock, 1986). Thus, the early involvement of local universities, with their external research capabilities, should be added to the high level of participation of private companies in the Brazilian defense industries.

In 1970 Engesa had only 240 employees, 28 of whom were classified as engineers, which suggests that at least during that time few technological achievements could have been generated in-house. OTA (1991b) expressed that the meteoric rise of Engesa from a small equipment and transport producer to a major armored vehicle manufacturer attests to strong private entrepreneurship and product development through linkage to the Brazilian and transnational transport industries and to government-university research centers, as well as to international marketing abilities. To this list Lock (1986) adds strong financial support provided by the government in the form of tax exemptions and soft credit lines.

With respect to the export and marketing policies of Engesa, Lock (1986) indicates that they have been one of the most important ingredients in the economic success of the firm. Engesa offers weapons specifically suitable for Third World environments, concentrating its efforts on rugged wheeled vehicles—as compared with industrialized countries' tracked armored vehicles. Sohr (1990, p. 23) lists the following elements of the marketing strategy followed by Brazil in the export of weapons in general:

- inexpensive weapons that could easily be maintained, not requiring frequent revisions or complex installations;
- weapons of simple operation that a semiliterate soldier could use; and
- weapons designed for the harsh climatic and geographic conditions that prevail in most parts of the Third World.

OTA (1991b, p. 143) adds that the main characteristics of the armored vehicles fabricated by Engesa are simple and flexible design concepts, low cost, good performance and reliability, ease of use, and simple maintenance. All these corroborate the strategic marketing

elements delineated by Sohr. Another important element stressed by
OTA in the sales strategy of Engesa is the highly knowledgeable sales
force, as well as the after-sale support in terms of guaranteed spare
parts, training, and maintenance. In fact, Engesa has a dedicated
subsidiary firm for international marketing, fully responsible for the
commercialization of military and civilian products (Vayrynen, 1992,
p. 90).

The marketing strategy followed by the Brazilian defense industry
in general, and of Engesa in particular, can be considered highly
professional and well structured, providing further evidence that the
participation of private firms with marked economic interests aided
the overall performance of the industry and its export orientation.

Perhaps the most ambitious, but least successful, commercial
project that Engesa has undertaken is the development of the track-
mounted main battle tank (MBT) EE-TI Osorio that started trials in
1984 (Lock, 1986). Sohr (1990) describes the tank as a 41-ton vehicle
that can move at a speed of 70 km/h, with an autonomy of 550 km,
and a price tag between $2 and $2.5 million, designed exclusively for
export. However, Vayrynen (1992, p. 91) indicates that the Osorio is
also considered to be used by the Brazilian armed forces.

OTA (1991b, p. 149) reports that the development of the Osorio
MBT responded to a requirement of Saudi Arabia for a light main
battle tank, after which Engesa conducted a market feasibility study
of other developing countries, where bridges and roads could not
support 60-ton MBTs such as the U.S. M-1A1 or the French AMX.
Second, OTA adds, Engesa searched worldwide for the best available
armor, engine, suspension system, electronics, and gears. In keeping
with its strategy of finding suppliers who would share the
development costs, Engesa succeeded in attracting many international
defense equipment suppliers because the Osorio program represented
the only new tank development project in the 1980s and 1990s.

Sohr (1990) indicates that the engine and the gearbox of the Osorio
are of German design, being provided within Brazil by the
transnational German automotive industry (OTA, 1991b, p. 149). The
hydropneumatic suspension system was designed by the same division
of Dunlop that manufactures the British Challenger I MBT. The
optional equipment can include either a 105-mm cannon fabricated by
the Royal Ordnance Factory of the United Kingdom or a 120-mm
cannon fabricated by the French firm Group Industriel Armements
Terrestres (GIAT), or even its German counterpart. For night vision
the Osorio can use either French SEGEM equipment or equipment
produced by Philips of Holland. For tracking and detection systems

the British firm Racal has offered its systems (Lock, 1986; Sohr, 1990; OTA, 1991b). According to Sohr (1990, p. 30), the Osorio is "a real example of European integration in Brazil." As with other Brazilian defense products, the foreign firms were looking after the parts market created by the Brazilian tanks, leaving to Engesa the role of assembler and manufacturer of the supporting frame.

With respect to the profitability of Engesa, Sohr (1990, p. 30) indicates that in 1988 this firm required the financial assistance of a Brazilian bank to overcome a severe crisis. Engesa requested $65 million, which was rejected because the firm was not able to provide acceptable warranties[4] and was already highly indebted at around $126 million.

It appears that one of the main reasons for the poor financial situation of Engesa is the Osorio contract signed with Saudi Arabia. Since Saudi Arabia gave the go-ahead for prototype production of the Osorio in 1985, Engesa proceeded to spend $60 million in R&D and prototype development. It had been widely rumored that Saudi Arabia provided financial assistance for the initial R&D costs. However, when Engesa officials were asked whether such reports were accurate, they said that they had not been able to "recover" the money previously offered by Saudi Arabia. Despite an announcement in August 1989 by the Saudi government to buy 318 Osorios, the contract worth $7.2 billion has yet to be finalized. In April 1990, after laying off 3,000 workers, Engesa filed for bankruptcy protection (OTA, 1991b, p. 149).

It is interesting to note that the Brazilian government did not interfere (as far as the literature indicates) in the bankruptcy of one of the major arms manufacturing and exporting firms of the country, indicating its pragmatism with respect to this kind of an event in an industry that can be considered highly strategic in military and geopolitical terms. It appears that the overall defense industrialization process of Brazil has given more weight to commercial than strategic or geopolitical objectives—otherwise, the Brazilian government would have rescued Engesa from bankruptcy.

Besides Engesa, there are two other Brazilian firms engaged in the manufacture of armored vehicles. One of these firms is Bernardini, which previously manufactured safes and office furniture and has a work force of 365 employees. This firm's entry into the defense

---

4. "Not a single bank is willing to accept tanks as a warranty for a loan," stated the vice-president of Engesa (Sohr, 1990, p. 31).

industry came about with the refurbishing of World War II tanks still serving in the Brazilian Army. After being modernized by Bernardini and with new Daimler-Benz diesel engines, they were offered for export (Lock, 1986; Ross, 1984, p. 287; Vayrynen, 1992, p. 92).

After this initial success, two more modernization projects were undertaken by Bernardini for other aging armored vehicles: the M-41 tank and the M-113 armored personnel carrier, with the same auspicious results. The final step of the involvement of Bernardini in the defense industry was the development—in close cooperation with the corps of engineers of the Brazilian Army—of a medium-tracked tank designated the MB-3 Tamoyo. Even though Engesa would have been able to design and manufacture such a new vehicle, the Brazilian Army seemed to be eager to increase the number of domestic defense firms competing in the defense market.

Perry and Weiss (1986) indicate that Bernardini has had less commercial success than Engesa in specializing in the fabrication of tracked vehicles, several designed specifically for the requirements of Brazil's military, who have become its principal customers. Thus, it may seem that the entry of Bernardini into the Brazilian defense industry was due to the Brazilian Army's intention of increasing the number of local manufacturers of armored vehicles and to foster competition in the internal market. It reduced Engesa's bargaining power and increased the efficiency of the market. It can be argued that the apparent lack of an export policy on the part of Bernardini is one of the main reasons for the lower performance it has shown when compared with Engesa.

The third firm in the armored vehicles segment is Moto Pecas, an established producer of transmissions and gearboxes with 1,500 employees. The firm has offered to completely refurbish the aging U.S.-built M-113 armored personnel carrier, serving in many countries of the world. The M-113 modernization kit offered by Moto Pecas includes a Mercedes-Benz diesel engine, new electronic equipment, a new transmission, and amphibious equipment (Lock, 1986).

3.6   MISSILES IN THE BRAZILIAN DEFENSE INDUSTRY[5]

Vayrynen (1980) reports that as early as 1976 Brazil had the capability to produce indigenously designed missiles, and, according to Klare (1990), the Brazilian capability has increased to the point of being able to develop ballistic missiles.

As in industrialized countries, the emergence of a missile industry in Brazil has a strong link with space research activities, first funded as early as the 1950s. These activities have been carried out by the IAE (Institute for Space Activity) of the CTA (Technical Center for Aerospace) and the INPE (National Space Research Institute). In the 1970s, CTA began to design small missiles, the MAS-1 Carcará air-to-surface missile and the MAA-1 Piranha air-to-air missile, aided by a license agreement between the Brazilian Army and West Germany for the local manufacture of the Cobra antitank missile.

In 1962, a graduate from the CTA founded Avibrás, a privately owned aerospace firm, currently with a reputation for professionalism, a low-profile image, and great autonomy from government agencies as well as from the armed forces. Avibrás started on a very small scale, producing propellants and parts used in space research and closely associated with the space research activities of CTA. This company assisted CTA in the Sonda I, II, III, and IV experimental rockets and satellite launch vehicle research programs, contributing with its expertise in design, guidance electronics, and solid-fuel propellants. It has been suggested that the Brazilian Sonda series of rockets, supposedly designed to launch weather satellites and supported by the West German Corporation for Aerospace Research, has provided Brazil with the technology to produce its own medium-range missiles. In the late 1970s Avibrás started offering rockets, bombs, and integrated weapons systems of considerable complexity.

Since the early 1980s, Avibrás has been one of Brazil's leading export companies, concentrating in defense-related areas such as space research and satellite communications, rocket and missile development, and electronics and chemistry (propellants and explosives). In addition to these aerospace-related areas, Avibrás has developed meteorological radars and satellite communication antennas, as well as the terrestrial stations for Brazilian satellites being launched

---

5. This section has been summarized from the work of Lock (1986), Ross (1984, pp. 297-302), and OTA (1991b, pp. 149-150), except where other sources are explicitly indicated.

by the European Space Agency. Lock (1986) indicates that Avibrás accepted orders to mass-produce spare parts for Soviet weapons systems—needed by Egypt, for example—that require high standards of machine tooling and are labor-intensive. Sohr (1990, p. 28) maintains that 41 percent of the products exported by Avibrás correspond to imported parts and components, much less than the imported parts of the aircraft produced by Embraer, again reflecting a relatively higher technological expertise in this area.

Currently Avibrás is at the forefront of tactical rockets and missile production among the developing countries. Its most important product is the Astros II, an artillery saturation rocket bombardment system, which can be employed against targets located from 9 to 70 km away, with rockets of 127 mm, 180 mm, and 300 mm. The latter rocket system uses an armored launch vehicle, an ammunition supply, and a fire control vehicle, all manufactured by Avibrás' Tectran division. The development of this weapon system was partially funded by Iraq, which during the 1980s was Avibrás' largest customer. The other two countries that have purchased the Astros rocket system are Libya and Saudi Arabia.

Avibrás also markets air-to-ground missiles and a full line of bombs. In addition, Avibrás has assisted in the prototype development of the SM-70 Barracuda coastal defense missile, with the intention of installing these missiles in the Brazilian Navy's Inahuma corvettes, originally designed to be equipped with the French Exocet missile. Avibrás also has developed the SS-300 long-range missile, with a range of 170 miles, with Libya providing some of the required financing.

The export performance of Avibrás can be considered extraordinary, starting with $4 million in 1980, $35 million in 1981, and passing $90 million in 1982. In 1987 it had the largest export earnings of any private Brazilian company, with over $340 million as compared with Engesa's $300 million for the same year. As can be seen, the export performance of these two defense firms can be considered among the best of all the Brazilian private industry, undoubtedly helping to obtain the hard currency needed by the highly indebted Brazilian economy.

According to Lock (1986), in 1986 Avibrás had a work force of 1,500 employees, 300 of whom were engineers. This high proportion of engineers shows that the activities of Avibrás are geared toward the development and manufacture of sophisticated products at a low-volume rate.

Even though between the years 1986 and 1991 Avibrás exported approximately $700 million, the company has had increasing difficulty obtaining the necessary financing for the development of new weapons systems. In fact, SIPRI (1990, p. 328) ranked Avibrás as number 92 among the largest weapons-producing firms in the world, with 95 percent of sales corresponding to arms, amounting to a total of $370 million in 1988, and with an overall profitability of only 1 percent. This low profitability can be presumed to be a consequence of the difficult access to capital that this firm is facing, thus requiring internal financing to develop sophisticated new products at a very high cost.

3.7   NAVAL SHIPBUILDING IN BRAZIL

Naval shipbuilding is perhaps the area of the Brazilian defense industry where the least had been done up to the early 1980s. Beginning in the 1930s, Brazilian shipyards irregularly received orders to build small vessels for the Brazilian Navy. These ships were designed to serve as river patrol craft or were simple support ships. Neither in design nor in production did any continuity emerge because supplies from the United States were always at hand. For years the navy was fully occupied with operating its fleet—made almost exclusively from U.S. World War II vintage units—rather than seeking new vessels to be built in Brazil. More than a dozen large patrol craft, river patrol ships, and similar naval crafts were built between 1971 and 1976 at three local shipyards, but all these projects were marginal in terms of modern naval construction (Lock, 1986).

A large contract to procure six modern antisubmarine frigates—the Niteroi Class—was announced in 1970. The British partner in the deal, Vosper, was contracted to secure the transfer of the technology involved in the construction of modern warships. Four frigates were built in Scotland, where Brazilian engineers and technicians participated in the construction work as part of the scheme to transfer technology. As many Brazilian components as possible were to be used in the construction of all six frigates. The fifth and sixth frigates were laid down in June 1972 in the Arsenal of the Navy in Rio de Janeiro. Whereas the four frigates built in Britain went into service in the mid-1970s, it took the Brazilian yard the whole decade to finish construction of its two frigates (Lock, 1986; Sohr, 1990). Barros (1984) and Vayrynen (1992, p. 95) argue that the cost for the construction of the six Niteroi frigates, built under the contract with the British company, was more expensive than the purchase of similar new units in another Western country.

According to *Jane's* (*Jane's Fighting Ships, 1990-1991*) the first Brazilian-made frigates of this class were commissioned in 1979 and 1980, respectively. Another unit of this class, the training ship *Brasil*, was laid down in 1981 at the navy shipyard in Rio de Janeiro and commissioned in 1986. This latter unit was built with the same overall frigate specifications but without the sophisticated electronic and weapons systems. It is also equipped with a helicopter platform.

Though severe budgetary constraints may have contributed to the delays in the production of the Niteroi frigates, and may have worked against a continuation of the production series, there is agreement that the delays and the discontinuation reflected the deficient technological base of the Brazilian shipyards (Lock, 1986). This is something to be expected because no major warships had ever been built in Brazil before.

In the early 1980s a major expansion of naval production was announced. One project was the production of a new class of corvettes, the V-28 type. Initiated by the Ministry of the Navy in 1977, the design was carried out with the support of Marinetechnik Planungsgesellschaft GmbH, a West German consulting firm (Lock, 1986). These corvettes have been designated as "Inahuma," and the program calls for a total of 12 ships.

The first Inahuma unit was laid down at the end of 1983, launched in 1985, and commissioned in 1989—two years behind schedule—with the second unit expected to be commissioned in 1991. The second pair of units is actually being built not in the navy shipyard of Rio de Janeiro but at the privately owned Velorme shipyard. Vayrynen (1992, p. 93) indicates that the Inahuma construction program has proved an economic disaster for the Velorme shipyard, prompting the diversification of the company away from the military business.

According to *Jane's* (1990), as was already indicated above, the plan was that later ships of the Inahuma class might carry Brazilian-made Barracuda surface-to-surface missiles, instead of the French Exocet; eight Avibrás SSAI-N antisubmarine rocket launchers; and an Avibrás FILA 20-mm antiaircraft gun system, instead of the Bofors 40 mm with which the first units were equipped. All of these plans have been canceled. Clearly, the intention was to incorporate several Brazilian-made weapons systems in the following corvettes. Not so clear were the reasons for not implementing this plan. Perhaps the development of naval weapons systems in Brazil has not been mastered to the point of being able to fully replace highly sophisticated, reliable, and readily available imported equipment, without losing operational effectiveness. In this case, quantity might not be able to replace quality.

According to Lock (1986), two other shipbuilders with military production are Maclaren and Ishikawajima do Brasil. Maclaren won the first export order for naval units. In 1980 the Chilean Coast Guard placed an order for 10 fiberglass coastal patrol craft of 40 tons. This was followed by an order from Paraguay for a large river patrol boat.

With respect to the construction of submarines in Brazil, *Jane's* (*Jane's Fighting Ships, 1990-1991*, 1990) indicates that a contract was signed with Howaldtswerke-Deutsche Werft of West Germany in 1984 for the construction of a total of four conventional submarines U-209 type 1400. Of these, the first unit was laid down in Kiel, West Germany, in 1985 and commissioned in 1988. Two more units are being built at the Brazilian Navy shipyard in Rio de Janeiro, expected to be commissioned in 1992 and 1993, respectively. Another submarine of the same class has been planned without indication of the construction date. *Jane's* (*Jane's Fighting Ships, 1990-1991*, 1990) reports that because of program delays there are doubts as to how many submarines of this class will finally be built.

Besides the four submarines mentioned, under the German contract two additional units were considered. These two submarines— consisting of a stretched version of the U-209 submarine—would be designed and built in Brazil. According to *Jane's* (*Jane's Fighting Ships, 1990-1991*, 1990, p. 51), "These submarines will be called S-NAC 1." The same publication (*Jane's Fighting Ships, 1991*, p. 53) reports that plans for the construction of nuclear-powered submarines are advancing, with a prototype nuclear reactor being built at São Paulo.

The intent of the current submarine program is to complete up to six U-209 class units and then embark on three nuclear submarines (SSN) to replace the British Oberon class, of which there are three actually in service in the Brazilian Navy. The prototype SSN is to be about 2,700 tons and have a power plant developing 12 MW (megawatts) for a speed of 28 knots. In spite of delays in the diesel U-209 submarine program, *Jane's* (*Jane's Fighting Ships, 1991-1992*, 1991, p. 53) reports that the SSN program has very high priority.

If Brazil builds its nuclear-powered submarine, it will be among the few countries in the world to achieve such an ambitious goal. Only five countries have this kind of unit: the United States, the former Soviet Union (Russia), the United Kingdom, France, and China. India has also operated a nuclear submarine through lease of a used unit from the Soviet Union in 1988, which was returned in 1991 because of operational and technical difficulties. It appears that the technical support provided by FR (Federal Republic of) Germany to Brazil has been essential in order to reach such a high level of technological development.

Even though the shipbuilding activity in Brazil is somewhat new, in only two decades (between the 1970s and the 1990s) Brazil has been able to master the construction of large naval vessels through an effective program to acquire and transfer the technology first from the United Kingdom for surface units and later from West Germany for small corvettes and submarines.

The apparent inability to provide naval weapons systems for the corvettes reflects a common shortcoming found in other segments of the defense industry (aircraft, armored vehicles, and missiles). Brazil is still not able to produce the sophisticated parts and components needed to reach a level of self-sufficiency in the naval shipbuilding industry and depends on foreign technology to achieve operational levels comparable with weapons systems manufactured in industrialized countries. Under these circumstances it is highly probable that several imported components will be needed to make the Brazilian nuclear submarine fully operational.

3.8   OTHER WEAPONS

It is interesting to analyze how other smaller firms have entered the Brazilian defense industry. The visible success of manufacturers like Engesa, Avibrás, Embraer, and Bernardini has spurred other companies in the metalworking sector to pursue similar strategies. This is partly facilitated by the experience they gained as suppliers of components to established arms manufacturers and is especially true for companies in the automotive industry.

An automotive company based in Rio de Janeiro has launched a series of small military vehicles marketed under the name SAFO. The different configurations have been developed in cooperation with the Army's Engineering Institute (IME). Its history resembles that of Engesa: It uses components and engines that are produced domestically. Another small manufacturer has taken up the production of light military vehicles, which rely heavily on mass-fabricated components of Volkswagen do Brasil. Gurgel S.A. (São Paulo) is already an established supplier of light jeeps with a fiberglass body.

Both companies are small, even in terms of the Brazilian industry, employing fewer than 500 people each (Lock, 1986).

The steady expansion of domestic manufacture of guns and cannons is technologically more demanding. Engesa and others have acquired licenses for cannons and automatic guns of large calibers that contribute considerably to the autonomy of Brazilian export strategies. A similar expansion has been reported in the other branches producing military hardware. Some of these companies have been in the field for 50 years or more, but it was the recent export drive that allowed them to expand so rapidly. There is also extensive production of electronic components for a large range of weapons systems. This is integrated with civilian production in the electronic sector.

One of the main elements in the emergence of the Brazilian defense industry can be seen again in this description: the high degree of integration at the small firm level of military and civilian-use products. This allows for an increased and effective use of capital and human resources in the design and manufacture of defense and civilian equipment, reducing financial and technological risk. In this manner risk is localized at the private company level, where it is more easily handled, and also diluted in a series of different companies. The other element in the industrial development strategy is the high market orientation of the products offered, as discussed above.

3.9   CHAPTER SUMMARY

In the long run, the creation of a strong Brazilian defense industry has been possible because of the continuous support provided by the government, by the armed forces, and especially by private industry. However, it can be said that the Brazilian government has been an indirect player in the overall industrial development effort, except (1) by providing policy guidance by means of legislation, subsidies, and other financial incentives for export and (2) by creating a technological infrastructure. The political pragmatism of the Brazilian government in the international arena enabled the Brazilian defense firms to operate in an extremely open international arms market, allowing them to compete in some instances even against U.S. and Soviet defense equipment.

The Brazilian armed forces have provided intense technical assistance to private firms in the development of defense products, creating an effective internal technology generation and transfer process. The research institutes created in the early 1960s have been instrumental in the generation of domestic technology and the assimilation of foreign technology. However, the main source of advanced technology has been licenses acquired from industrialized countries, particularly for the shipbuilding industry, which has been the least developed of all. The intensive use of the acquired technology, as well as the development of domestically designed products, indicates that foreign technology for systems design and production has been adequately transferred and assimilated, reflecting the existence of a solid technical base and human expertise. The research and development effort to develop defense equipment has been financed not only by the armed forces, some international customers, and the private firms involved but also by funds from the overall federal budget for the development of science and technology. We can thus infer that in Brazil defense technology is considered to be among the driving forces of the industrial development effort.

Brazilian defense firms looked to the international market when deciding to manufacture their products, not restricting themselves to domestic operations. Even though some small firms had been operating in the Brazilian defense industry for many years, the opening of the industry toward the global market allowed growth beyond what the internal market allowed.

The most important civilian industry segments that can be clearly identified in the Brazilian defense industry are metal fabrication, electronics, automotive, and aircraft. Heavy reliance on the early advancement of these industries seems to have been essential for the emergence of the indigenous Brazilian defense industry. The armed forces' preference for private over state-owned firms in the acquisition of defense equipment has allowed the growth of many small, privately owned firms operating in the defense industry.

Large numbers of the locally produced parts utilized in the defense equipment were obtained from firms manufacturing civilian-use products, achieving a very high degree of integration at the firm level and indicating a strong capability in the adaptation of civilian technology to the manufacture of weapons systems. Most of the larger and more expensive weapons systems are manufactured with a national industrial base of quite conventional technology, but their performance relies heavily on sophisticated foreign components and parts. This indicates that defense technological self-sufficiency at higher levels of the technology spectrum remains very difficult to achieve, since more than two decades were needed to master the fabrication of some sophisticated parts and components.

The products offered by the Brazilian defense firms have been able to fill an operational gap between the more advanced products offered by industrialized countries and the small arms that are able to be manufactured by almost all developing countries. In fact, this "niche" marketing strategy focused on middle-range, middle-sized, and middle-priced military systems. The market failure of the Osorio main battle tank can be attributed to a deviation from this niche strategy, because it started competing in price and operational performance with tanks offered by industrialized countries.

The heavy reliance on a limited number of important customers—in particular, Iraq, Libya, and Saudi Arabia—has become the main problem that the Brazilian defense industry is now facing. However, these customers have been Brazil's major oil suppliers, increasing the importance of defense exports beyond the mere financial rewards and further increasing the strategic significance of the defense industry. This enhanced strategic importance contrasts with the apparent pragmatism of the Brazilian government with respect to the survival or bankruptcy of some key companies such as Engesa.

The main barriers to further development of the Brazilian defense industry have been (1) the lack of adequate financing, limiting the addition of more sophisticated equipment to production lines and (2) technological dependence that still persists for the most advanced parts and components, requiring export licenses to be granted by other industrialized countries competing in the same product lines.

4

The Defense Industry
of Argentina

In this chapter a detailed description of the defense industry of Argentina is presented. Many different kinds of weapons are produced by Argentina in the vast state-owned defense industrial complex. The 1970s and 1980s saw intense activity in this area, when major battleships, tanks, missiles, and fighter aircraft were produced with a strong component of indigenous technology.

4.1 THE EMERGENCE OF THE ARGENTINEAN DEFENSE INDUSTRY

Argentina is one of the Latin American countries that has shown sustained military industrial activity over a number of years, providing for its own defense needs by stimulating and supporting the local manufacture of arms (Varas, 1989). Early in this century the arms industry in Argentina was considered an important driving mechanism of the national industrialization process and also part of the overall economic development strategy adopted by many Argentinean administrations. The main objective of Argentinean arms production was to increase political independence, and the creation of an arms industry was regarded as part of the development strategy adopted by Argentina in the 1930s (Millán, 1986; Landaburu, 1986). Self-sufficiency in arms production was seen as an extension of general import substitution policies, and it was hoped that a national arms industry would create spin-offs for the nascent heavy industry (Millán, 1986).

The first decisions to manufacture weapons in Argentina date from the 1920s (Varas, 1989; Porth, 1984; Landaburu, 1986). Then in 1941 the Dirección General de Fábricas Militares (DGFM, General Directorate for Military Factories) was established, strengthening government activity in this sector by linking it to the overall industrialization effort (Landaburu, 1986). This early government involvement in the arms production effort was characteristic of most Latin American arms industries.

In the 1950s, Argentina and North Korea were considered the most important Third World arms producers (Brzoska and Ohlson, 1987, p. 117). From 1950 to 1955 Argentina was the leading Third World arms producer, ranked fifth for the period from 1980 to 1984, and ranked seventh for the overall period between 1950 and 1984 (Brzoska and Ohlson, 1986, pp. 10–11). Kolodziej (1987b, p. 313) indicates that between 1970 and 1980, 18 different weapons systems (aircraft, ground equipment, missiles, and naval vessels) were produced either under license agreements or as nationally developed systems in Argentina.

Owing to Argentina's neutrality during World War II, the United States imposed an arms embargo. This prompted the first spur for indigenous development and production of arms. As a consequence of this early start in defense production—with the manufacturing of the Nahuel tank in 1943—Argentina was recognized as the first Third World country to start an independent project for the production of main battle tanks (Brzoska and Ohlson, 1986, p. 20; Landaburu, 1986). In 1956, Argentina sold Nahuel tanks to Paraguay in one of the first recorded exports of domestically produced major weapons from the Third World (Brzoska and Ohlson, 1986, p. 30).

With the lifting of the U.S. embargo in 1947, cheap World War II surplus weapons were made available to Argentina, bringing about a change in the economic development strategy away from a state-oriented economy. This led to a decrease in defense production activity in the late 1950s and early 1960s (Millán, 1986).

During the years 1940 through 1960, the Argentinean Air Force, with the assistance of German engineers, began the design and manufacture of military planes such as fighter bombers and transport aircraft. Production began in 1956. Likewise, the Argentinean Navy has designed and built naval vessels since 1938 at the Rio Santiago shipyards, where patrol boats and corvettes were later built. The army, with German assistance, produced heavy artillery, machine guns, and various types of ammunition. In 1940, the Rosario plant developed and manufactured a series of machine guns that are still in use today (Varas, 1989; Landaburu, 1986).

During the mid-1960s, the Argentinean armed forces analyzed the available alternatives for the modernization of their arsenals. They formulated three options: (1) to satisfy their requirements through acquisitions in the international arms market, (2) to obtain arms from the United States through the Mutual Aid Pact (Pacto de Ayuda Mutua), and (3) to manufacture arms in Argentina. The Argentinean armed forces concluded that the best alternative was the domestic production of arms. This decision was implemented in a national production program known as the Plan Europa (Europe Plan) because the main thrust was going to come from the assimilation and local production of European arms and technology. The Plan Europa was intended to utilize the existing arms production capacities through transfers of technology from abroad. Contracts were signed with French firms for ship and tank production; with a Spanish-Swiss firm for the manufacture of machine guns, ammunition, and air-to-air missiles; and with FR Germany and British companies for work on warships (Millán, 1986; Sohr, 1990, p. 13).

The Plan Europa was expected to be carried out in four stages (Sohr, 1990, p. 15):

1. coproduction, the assembly of foreign arms with a small proportion of national components;
2. advanced coproduction of foreign arms with a minimum 30 percent integration of national products;
3. domestic production with 80 percent of national integration; and
4. indigenous conception, design, and fabrication of arms.

As will be shown later in this chapter, up to the early 1990s varying degrees of integration had been achieved in different kinds of weapons, most of them already having progressed beyond stage two.

Between 1950 and 1964, only 11 percent of the weapons purchased by the Argentinean armed forces came from local production. This percentage increased to almost 17 percent between 1965 and 1979, jumping to around 30 percent for the period 1980 to 1984 (Brzoska and Ohlson, 1986, p. 28). These figures indicate that Argentina has steadily built up an indigenous defense capability, with a marked increase in the local production of arms during the 1980s, supposedly as a result of Plan Europa. It can be argued, however, that the ratio of local production of arms to imports between 1980 and 1984 could have been much higher, because this period coincides with the 1982

South Atlantic war against Great Britain and the subsequent large volume of Argentinean defense imports in 1983 undertaken to recover the material lost during that war. This situation would explain in part the relatively low ratio of local production to imports in spite of the strong efforts to reduce foreign technological dependence.

It is interesting to note that the major spurs for the advancement of the Argentinean arms industry were provided in the form of three arms embargoes by the United States, first during World War II, later during the mid-1960s (Millán, 1986), and again in the mid-1970s because of human rights considerations (Porth, 1984). This finding about Argentina is similar to the finding presented in the previous chapter about Brazil and is also true for Chile, as will be shown in the following chapter. All these findings support the hypothesis of Chapter 2 that the more restricted the access to defense equipment in the international arms market, the more advanced would be the local defense industry.

It has been argued (Waisman, 1986) that the arms production capability of Argentina contributed to the belligerence toward Chile in the late 1970s and the conflict with Britain in the early 1980s. From a psychological perspective, it is well possible that the capacity to locally produce many different kinds of weapons of moderate sophistication could have made the Argentinean military leaders extremely confident of their technological and productive capabilities.

4.2   STRUCTURE OF WEAPONS PRODUCTION IN ARGENTINA

At the center of the Argentinean defense industry with its across-the-board production are the state-owned factories (Waisman, 1986). Private industry functions as the supplier of raw materials, spare parts, components, and machinery (Millán, 1986), indicating that Argentinean private industry does not strongly participate in the final production of defense goods, this activity being left solely to the state-owned factories. Thus, no effective transfer of technology and enhanced production experience can be expected to take place between both sectors of the economy, leading to a technological stratification of the defense production process, with the state-owned arms factories having the most advanced production capabilities.

The Argentinean Army has had the leading role in domestic arms production via the DGFM. Founded in 1941, DGFM is a conglomerate that runs 14 military factories scattered around the country that produce arms, communication equipment, chemicals, and steel, among other equipment and commodities. DGFM has a majority share in at least 7 other companies in the steel, iron ore, petrochemical, timber, and construction sectors, as well as significant shares in a further 10 companies, including the Bahía Blanca petrochemical complex, another petrochemical plant in La Plata, a ball-bearing plant (built at a cost of over $500 million), and Argentina's biggest steelworks, SOMISA. DGFM also supervises the aircraft industry run by the air force and the yards run by the navy. However, not all of the production at DGFM is weapons oriented. Much of the production of basic materials and components is sold to civilian customers and shipped on to the plants producing weapons as end products (Millán, 1986; Waisman, 1986; Landaburu, 1986). At the end of the 1980s, various state-owned defense firms were targeted for privatization. Most of these firms were operating in related areas such as petrochemicals, with the most important being Fábrica Militar de Aviones (FMA) (*Tecnología Militar*, no. 12, 1987, p. 67). Figure 4.1 shows the structure of Argentina's arms industry as described by Millán (1986).

DGFM employs an estimated 40,000 people directly and a further 16,000 work in associated companies. About 1 percent of its employees are military officers, primarily engineers, and the remainder are civilians. At the end of the 1970s, the annual turnover at DGFM (including its associated companies) was reportedly more than 2 percent of the country's gross domestic product (GDP), or $2.2 billion in 1986 dollars, representing approximately 14 percent of manufacturing GDP (Waisman, 1986; Porth, 1984; Landaburu, 1986). Tanks are produced with German assistance by a newly created state-owned corporation Tanque Argentino Mediano Sociedad del Estado (TAMSE), under the jurisdiction of DGFM, which employed around 400 engineers and technicians in the mid-1980s .

The Argentinean Navy manages and operates the most important local shipyard, Astilleros y Fábricas Navales del Estado (AFNE), which employed around 4,500 people during the early 1980s. Another shipyard, Astilleros Domeq García (ADG), partly owned by AFNE and dedicated to the production of submarines, employed another 1,000 people in the mid-1980s.

Figure 4.1

Structure of Arms Production in Argentina

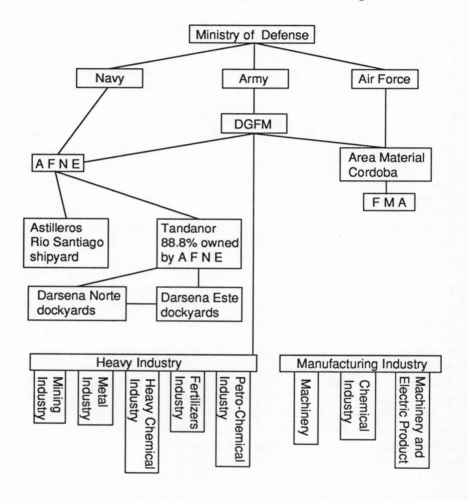

Source: V. Millán, "Argentina: schemes for glory," in SIPRI, M. Brzoska and T. Ohlson (eds), *Arms Production in the Third World* (Taylor & Francis: London, 1986), chapter 3, figure 3.1, p. 38.

Table 4.1

Employment of Major Defense Companies in Argentina

Defense Firm	Employment circa 1985
Dirección General de Fabricaciones Militares	40,000 direct 16,000 associated companies
Fábrica Militar de Aviones	5,300
Tanque Argentino Mediano Sociedad del Estado	400
Astillleros y Fábricas Navales del Estado	4,500
Astilleros Domecq García	1,000
Total Direct Employment	66,200

Aircraft production is concentrated in FMA, which had approximately 5,300 employees during the early 1980s. Table 4.1 summarizes the number of employees of the most important Argentinean defense firms. According to the figures presented in Table 4.1, the direct employment generated by these main contractors is around 66,200 people.

The overall description of the Argentinean defense industry presented here clearly indicates an important economic impact: annual production equivalent to 2 percent of the GDP, approximately $2.2 billion in turnover a year, 66,200 employees, large involvement in civilian industries producing commodities, a strong government influence and participation in the defense industry, and a technological stratification of defense production that favors state production over private production.

4.3   DEFENSE RESEARCH AND DEVELOPMENT IN ARGENTINA

The Argentinean arms industry has benefited greatly from civilian scientific education as well as from civilian research.   The armed forces have in the past dominated practically all government organizations and most important centers of research (Waisman, 1986). Defense-related R&D activities in Argentina have been coordinated and directed by the Council of the Armed Forces for Research and Development, under the Ministry of Defense.   The Instituto de Investigaciones Científicas y Técnicas de las Fuerzas Armadas (CITEFA, Scientific and Technical Research Institute of the Armed Forces), founded in 1954, carries out basic and applied research as well as production of missiles.   A law passed in 1969 created in Argentina the Military System for Research and Development, making CITEFA the centralized body for the research and development of new weapons.   The Institute of Aeronautical and Space Research (established in 1957 and strongly related to the state-owned aircraft manufacturing factory FAMA), under air force control, deals with research related to space, rockets, and missiles.   SENID (Naval Research and Development Center), under the control of the navy, deals with naval technology and engineering.   DGFM research departments are responsible for the design and development of small arms, ammunition, and explosives (Millán, 1986; Landaburu, 1986; Porth, 1984; Waisman, 1986).   Around 900 people work in research-related activities at the state-owned aircraft manufacturing factory (*Tecnología Militar*, no.7, 1984, p. 78).

The identifiable portion of science and technology funds allocated for military R&D has varied sharply, following the political changes in the country.   In 1976, of the total federal budget allocated to science and technology, 6.9 percent was explicitly devoted to defense activities.   In 1978 this percent allocation increased to 17.94 percent assigned for the Ministry of Defense, plus an additional 0.20 percent for the navy and 1.72 percent for the air force (Roper and Silva, 1983, p. 6).   In 1983 the official share of the Ministry of Defense had dropped to only 4 percent (Millán, 1986).   The actual share of funds for military scientific and technological research in Argentina is unknown.

Figure 4.2 illustrates the comprehensive scope of the Argentinean defense-related R&D effort.   Also the centralization of the research process by the Ministry of Defense is noteworthy, as well as the early consideration (1954) given to these activities.   With a special

Figure 4.2

Structure of Defense Research and Development in Argentina

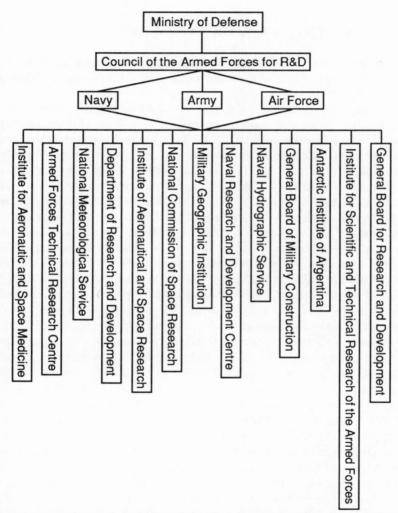

Source: V. Millán, "Argentina: schemes for glory," in SIPRI, M. Brzoska and T. Ohlson (eds), *Arms Production in the Third World* (Taylor & Francis: London, 1986), chapter 3, figure 3.2, p. 39.

percentage of the overall national science and technology development budget reserved for the Ministry of Defense, the development of defense technology in Argentina is considered to be one of the top national technological priorities. However, dependence on foreign technology and licensing agreements shows no sign of decreasing (Millán, 1986).

4.4 THE ARGENTINEAN AIRCRAFT INDUSTRY

From the military, technological, and industrial points of view, the aircraft industry has been Argentina's most important arms production sector.

Airplane manufacturing in Argentina can be traced back to 1909, when the first locally designed monoplane was built (Millán, 1986). Founded in Córdoba in 1927 as the central organization for aeronautical research and production, the state-run factory for the production of military aircraft is the oldest of its kind in Latin America. Now known as FMA, it has dominated the Argentinean aircraft industry. Since its creation, FMA has worked on 56 different aircraft types, of which 24 (including civilian models) have entered production. FMA also controls the Flight Test Center, to which all civilian and military aircraft produced in Argentina are sent for certification tests. During the mid-1950s and 1960s, FMA employed almost 10,000 people. In the early 1980s, FMA employed about 5,300 people, of whom about 2,300 were in aircraft manufacturing, but their numbers were expected to rise with the production of the IA-63 Pampa jet-trainer (Millán, 1986; *Tecnología Militar*, no. 7, 1984, p. 80). Fábrica Militar de Aviones is currently owned by the Argentine Air Force (46 percent), Aeritalia and Agusta (22 percent each), and the national industrial company Techint (10 percent) (*Jane's All the World Aircraft*, 1990). However, up to the mid-1980s there were nearly 30 privately owned firms that provided services, components, spare parts, and manufacturing for the Argentinean aircraft industry (Millán, 1986; Landaburu, 1986).

Licensed production at FMA started in 1928 with Avro 504R Gosport trainers (United Kingdom), followed by manufacture of the Dewoitine D.21-C1 fighter (France) and the Bristol F.2B Mk 3 observation aircraft (United Kingdom). Approximately 180 aircraft of each of these types were built before World War II. In 1937, FMA acquired licenses to produce 500 Focke-Wolf FW 44J Stieglitz primary trainers (Germany) and 200 Curtis Hawk 75 (United States). After

World War II, in particular during the Perón era (1945–1955), efforts were directed toward local manufacturing, with a proliferation of aircraft designs for domestic production, ranging from small utility aircraft to jet transports and fighters. At the end of the 1950s, FMA resumed production of foreign aircraft: 25 Beechcraft T-34 trainers were assembled after 1957. A year later, assembly of MS-760 Paris twin-jet-trainer/liaison aircraft (Morane Saulnier, France) was started (Millán, 1986).

The origins of the technology employed in Argentina for aircraft production can be traced back to France, Germany, the United Kingdom, and the United States. The production of jet planes assembled under license in Argentina in the late 1950s is a technological prowess worth being highlighted, especially at a time when propellers were still widely used, in particular for commercial airplanes. As will be explained below, the local production of jet airplanes at the end of the 1940s allowed the assimilation of this new technology.

Immediately after World War II, Emile Dewoitine, a well-known prewar French designer, drew the plans for the IA-27 Pulqui-1 jet-propelled aircraft, which first flew in August 1947. This was the first jet fighter to be designed, built, and flown in a Third World country. However, it proved unsuccessful and was canceled at the prototype stage. In 1950 Dr. Kurt Tank (a designer of Focke-Wolf aircraft of Hitler's Luftwaffe) introduced his swept-wing jet fighter, the IA-33 Pulqui-2, which incorporated the latest developments in the field of high-speed aerodynamics. It flew for the first time in June 1950. The IA-33 Pulqui-2 closely resembled an early Focke-Wolf design. The engine and most components were also European. Although the IA-33 Pulqui-2 proved technically successful after some initial problems, only six aircraft were built (Millán, 1986; Landaburu, 1986).

After 1950, only a few more aircraft were built in Argentina. The DINFIA IA-35 Huanquero, which first flew in September 1953, was originally a trainer aircraft. Later, the Huanquero was converted to a bomber and ground-attack unit, of which 47 airplanes were built. The Huanquero can be considered the precursor of one of FMA's most important designs, the IA-58 Pucará, described below. The DINFIA IA-38, an experimental tailless cargo aircraft that closely resembles the Stealth bomber of the United States because of its wing shape, flew for the first time in December 1960 (*Jane's Encyclopedia of Aviation*, 1980).

The stage in the Argentinean aircraft industry between the end of World War II and 1960 can thus be categorized as a technology transfer and assimilation period, with know-how provided by foreign engineers and strong national-political support. Again, the fast start in the indigenous development of jet propulsion technology with foreign assistance is one of the main milestones of this period. The production decline at the end of the 1950s coincides with the renewed supply of defense equipment by the United States and, as was already indicated, by a change in the Argentinean economic development strategy.

Argentinean policy toward the aircraft industry changed again in the early 1960s, when design of the IA-58 Pucará (counterinsurgency) aircraft began. Due to many design changes and political infighting between the services, production began more than a decade later. The delay also derived from the difficulty of putting different components together. Although the Pucará is considered domestic, the design is U.S.-inspired (Rockwell OV-10 Bronco), and components from the United Kingdom, FR Germany, the United States, Belgium, Switzerland, Australia, and Sweden are incorporated in the aircraft (Millán, 1986). The Pucará was first delivered to the Argentinean Air Force in 1974, and since then it has undergone several modifications in order to improve its operational characteristics (Landaburu, 1986; *Tecnología Militar*, no.5, 1983, p. 126).

The Argentinean Air Force decided in 1979 to commission from FMA the design of a new-generation jet-trainer. In 1979, FMA, with technical assistance from Dornier (FR Germany), initiated the IA-63 Pampa program with a budget of $200 million to meet this requirement. The introduction of 100 IA-63s into service was to begin in early 1986. The new trainer, basically similar to the French/West German Alpha Jet,[1] is powered by a U.S. Garret turbo-fan engine. The wings would be built first in FR Germany and later by FMA, and several other components would be supplied from the United States, FR Germany, France, Spain, and Israel (Millán, 1986; *Tecnología Militar*, no. 4, 1985, p. 93). The first locally produced IA-63s were actually handed to the Argentinean Air Force in May 1988 (*Tecnología Militar*, no. 3, 1989, p. 11).

During the 1970s, the Argentinean Air Force was interested in buying a medium-sized passenger and cargo aircraft for entry into service in the late 1980s. Thus, FMA started working on a light twin turbo-prop transport, known as project ATL (Avión de Transporte

---

1. Dornier built over 200 of these aircraft.

Liviano, or Light Transport Aircraft), and has discussed a joint venture for the ATL with Perú (Millán, 1986).

Most of Argentina's domestic aircraft have been designed to be powered by U.S., British, or French engines, either imported or assembled locally. Despite the lack of production capability for making large metal castings or specific types of turbine blades for jet engines, the Argentine aircraft industry has managed to produce some piston engines locally (Millán, 1986).

In 1973 RACA S.A. (Representaciones Aero-Comerciales Argentinas S.A.) was founded in response to an international bid by the Argentinean Air Force, with the aim to build a helicopter assembly plant financed by private capital. RACA began production, under license of Hughes (United States), of Model 500-D helicopters for military and civilian use (Millán, 1986; *Tecnología Militar*, no. 6, 1984, p. 106). According to Brzoska and Ohlson (1987, p. 282), during the mid-1980s the production of the Model 500-D helicopter was the only licensed production in the aircraft industry of Argentina. In 1988, licensed production was further expanded to include Italian helicopters, with the denomination of the A-109 Hirundo (SIPRI, 1990, p. 304). Having been given funds to develop and manufacture small aeroengines and light helicopters, Cicaré Aeronautica J.C developed the CK-1 Colibri, an experimental helicopter. Neither this nor the RACA Hughes Model 500-D were bought in large numbers by the Argentinean armed forces (Millán, 1986).

Even though the Argentinean aircraft industry had an early start in the late 1920s, with significant activity in the late 1940s and early 1950s, it does not seem that the economic results can be considered successful, particularly in respect to the commercialization of its most advanced production model, the IA-58 Pucará. Brzoska and Ohlson (1987, pp. 150-279) report that, according to the SIPRI data base, the following were the orders for Argentina's IA-58 Pucará:

- Central African Republic: 12 units being negotiated in 1986;
- Iraq: 20 units ordered in 1986;
- Kuwait: 20 units ordered in 1985, at a total cost of $120 million; with an option for 40 more units;
- Morocco: 20 units ordered in 1985; and
- Uruguay: 8 units ordered in 1980 and delivered in 1981.

This list gives a total export number of 80 units at an overall price of $480 million, considering the Kuwait price as a reference, with the potential to sell an additional 40 units ($240 million more).

Unfortunately, with the exception of the Uruguayan sale, the rest were unconfirmed at the time Brzoska and Ohlson reported these figures; thus, these sales cannot be considered as final.

In the list of trade in major conventional weapons published by SIPRI (1990), the following countries are identified as placing further orders for the IA-58 Pucará:

- Colombia: 2 units ordered in 1989; and
- Egypt: 50 units ordered in 1988.

According to Sohr (1990, p. 20), the Pucará did not have good acceptance in the international arms market. Since it came out of the assembly lines in 1974, only 105 units have been manufactured; 99 were incorporated into the Argentinean Air Force, and only 6 units were exported to Uruguay, in this latter case at a sale price of only $1.8 million each, well below its manufacturing cost of $3 million (Porth, 1984). This indicates that most of the orders placed, according to Brzoska and Ohlson and to the SIPRI 1990 information, were not finalized. However, the list of countries placing orders indicates that for Third World countries the Pucará seemed to be a good option. The difference in the price of the Pucará offered to Kuwait at $6 million and to Uruguay at $1.8 million is noteworthy, and no explanation for this discrepancy was found in the literature. Most probably, the price difference was due to a marketing strategy that discriminated between a rich oil-exporting country far from the Argentinean sphere of influence and a low-income country in the core of the sphere of influence. However, the difference is too large and would indicate a failure in the marketing effort for this aircraft.

No indications about the economic and technical success of Argentina's most advanced aircraft model, the IA-63 Pampa, have been found in the literature. Brzoska and Ohlson (1987, p. 151) report that in 1986 Bolivia had placed an unconfirmed order for 12 units of the Pampa. This was the first export order for this aircraft, and there is no reference to price for this sale. Varas (1989) indicates that the IA-63 Pampa was mass-produced in 1985, and according to *Jane's* (*Jane's All the World Aircraft, 1991*, 1990), at the end of 1989 the production rate for the Pampa was 1 per month, with a version for the Argentinean Navy being currently under development.

As can be seen, during the period 1970 to 1990, Argentina demonstrated an increased capacity to design, develop, and manufacture indigenous aircraft. At the end of the 1980s the overall manufacturing process can be considered to have been mastered by

Argentina, this being particularly evident in the case of the structural and aerodynamic parts of the design. However, Argentina still lacks some industrial capabilities in highly sophisticated areas and, up to now, is unable to attain a self-sufficiency level in most of the advanced technologies of avionics and engine systems.

In Argentina, the lack of early integration between civilian firms and military aircraft factories can be considered a consequence of the strong government participation in the industry, hampering the civilian involvement in the production of military aircraft and parts. The latest attempts in the helicopter assembly plant to incorporate the civilian sector indicate a change in policy, probably driven by economic considerations because of reduced defense budgets.

As can be seen, the Argentinean aircraft industry has a long-standing tradition, with a very wide scope reflected in the number of different aircraft manufactured, the capacity to test its own planes, and involvement in aerospace research.[2]   This long process of technology assimilation and indigenous development helped the Argentinean aircraft industry in the establishment of a strong technical base and knowledgeable professional labor force, the most important in Latin America until the late 1960s.

4.5   ARGENTINEAN ARMORED VEHICLES

The first armored vehicle domestically designed and manufactured by the Argentinean military-owned industries was the 35-ton Nahuel DL-43 tank, built in 1943. Like many weapons of that era, it was produced in only limited quantities (reportedly 16 vehicles). The main armament of the Nahuel DL-43 was a German 75-mm cannon. Production was abandoned because cheaper war surplus tanks were available, in particular the U.S. M-41 Sherman (Millán, 1986; Landaburu, 1986). Again, as in the case of the aircraft industry, readily available and abundant imported war equipment hampered the local production of armored vehicles. From the late 1940s to the late 1960s activity concentrated on maintenance and overhaul of vehicles bought elsewhere (Millán, 1986).

As part of the Plan Europa, the French AMX-13 light tank (armed with a 105-mm cannon) and the infantry combat vehicle AMX-VCI

---

2. During the mid-1980s, because of its aerospace research capability, Argentina was included in a worldwide technological program led by France, known as "EUREKA."

were assembled. During the 1970s the AMX-13 was modernized by TENSA (Talleres Electrometalúrgicos Norte), a private engineering company. The original engine was replaced by Deutz diesels in more than 100 AMX-13s manufactured in Argentina under license from Klockner-Humboldt-Deutz of the FR Germany (Millán, 1986; Sohr, 1990, p. 16).

In 1973 the army commissioned the West German company Thyssen-Henschel to design and develop a new medium tank for Argentine production under the designation TAM (Tanque Argentino Mediano) to replace its obsolete M-41 Sherman tanks, as well as an infantry combat vehicle called VCTP (Vehículo de Combate y Transporte Personal). Prototypes were delivered for trials in 1977. Twenty-four months later the first tanks manufactured at the Fábrica Militar San Martín left the production hall (Millán, 1986; Sohr, 1990, pp. 16–17; *Tecnología Militar*, no. 1, 1984, pp. 93–94; Landaburu, 1986).

In March of 1980 a new state-owned defense company—TAMSE (Tanque Argentino Mediano Sociedad del Estado)—was established under the jurisdiction of DGFM for the production of TAM, VCTP, and other similar vehicles. TAMSE employs about 400 people, of whom 10 percent are engineers and 25 percent are technicians (Piñeiro, 1984; Millán, 1986; Landaburu, 1986).

Currently, more than 70 percent (85 percent according to Landaburu, 1986) of each armored vehicle belonging to the TAM series is composed of locally manufactured components, including the armament, which consists of a 105-mm cannon and a 7.62-mm machine gun (manufactured under license from FN of Belgium). Imported parts include the engine—the MTU MB-83, manufactured in FR Germany—the gearbox, and parts of the optical and fire control systems (Millán, 1986; Sohr, 1990, p. 17).

According to Sohr (1990, p. 17), the imported parts of the TAM tank may be more than what Millán (1986) suggests. Sohr indicates that even though the tank turret is manufactured at the FM Rio Tercero in Argentina, German firms provide several critical materials and components: Thyssen, the steel for the body and the chassis; Turbo-Union, the diesel engine; Renk, the transmission; Diehl, the caterpillars; AEG, the electronics; and Carl Zeiss, the weapons control systems. Most probably the degree of integration has increased with time, as indicated in the objectives of the Plan Europa and the successive stages of indigenous technology envisioned for each of the weapons systems.

In the international arms market, the TAM came to compete with first-rank tanks of a superior class such as the French AMX-30 or the German Leopard I. In an international 600-km cross-country competition in Ecuador, the TAM defeated several other tanks of industrialized countries: the United States competed with the Stingray of the firm Cadillac Gage; France, with the AMX-13 of Creusot-Loire; and Austria, with the Coracero of Stayer-Daimler-Puch (Sohr, 1990, p. 19). Ecuador's order for 56 units, with a purchase price of more than $100 million, was canceled because of internal Ecuadorian political reasons (*Jane's Armour and Artillery, 1991-92*, 1991, p. 1).

Since the TAM is an expensive machine ($1.5 to $1.7 million for each unit), it requires sophisticated maintenance. The fact that Argentina has not developed an important volume of military exports makes acquisitions from this country more risky. This, plus its technical characteristics, made the TAM noncompetitive for the armies of developing countries. For the price of one TAM, it is possible to purchase almost six Brazilian "Cascavel" light tanks, good for all-terrain and efficient for internal control (Sohr, 1990, pp. 17–18).

Besides these drawbacks, political interference from some governments—in particular, FR Germany, which apparently still has some licensing power—has impeded the sale of TAMs to several countries, such as Malaysia, Iran, and Saudi Arabia (Sohr, 1990, p. 18). Thus, even though some degree of technical self-sufficiency has been achieved, political pressures have inhibited the full autonomy sought by Argentina with Plan Europa.

Fabricaciones Militares (Military Factories) forecasted the production of 1,500 TAMs (Sohr, 1990, p. 18), but only around 350 units have been completed (*Jane's Armour and Artillery, 1991-92*, 1991, p. 1). It has been reported that Perú had purchased 80 TAMs, and Panama another 60 TAMs (Sohr, 1990, p. 18). However, *Jane's* (*Jane's Armour and Artillery, 1991-92*, 1991, p. 1) indicates that these two orders were canceled because of budgetary reasons in the recipient countries.

As already mentioned, the TAM was manufactured under German license, giving the latter country strong international political leverage. It competed head-to-head with similar products of industrialized countries, increasing the pressure on Germany not to authorize the sales to potential customers. The TAM's high price also made it unattractive to Third World countries. All of these factors negatively affected Argentina and its possibilities of securing orders for the TAM in the international market. However, the good performance of the

TAM tank demonstrated in the Ecuadorian competition indicates that the tank's design and fabrication are among the best in the world for its characteristics and price.

4.6   MISSILES IN THE ARGENTINEAN DEFENSE INDUSTRY

Brzoska and Ohlson (1986, p. 20) indicate that missile production "requires advanced capabilities in the making and handling of propellants, explosives, sensors, guidance systems, fuses and system integration." Thus, if a Third World country is able to indigenously design and manufacture successfully this kind of sophisticated weapon, this success indicates advanced defense technological self-sufficiency. According to Brzoska and Ohlson (1986, p. 20), attempts at licensed production of less sophisticated missiles have been made in countries without such advanced capabilities, among which it is possible to mention Argentina, Brazil, Pakistan, and South Africa, but so far without much success.

Having some previous experience with rocket artillery, in the early 1970s CITEFA started to work on missiles. In 1974, the Mathogo antitank missile emerged as the first successful rocket project. Resembling the German-designed Cobra rocket produced under license in Brazil, the Mathogo incorporates foreign technology most probably from the FR Germany, and it is the only antitank rocket produced by a developing country. Research and design work then extended to more sophisticated air-to-surface missiles (ASMs) and surface-to-surface missiles (SSMs), in particular after the South Atlantic war of 1982. These research and development efforts resulted in the Martín Pescador air-to-surface naval missile, the Albatros surface-to-surface naval missile, the Pampero air-to-surface and surface-to-surface rocket system, the surface-to-air Halcón missile system, and the surface-to-surface SAPBA rocket system (Millán, 1986; Landaburu, 1986, *Tecnología Militar*, no. 6, 1983, p. 118; no. 11, 1986, p. 97; no. 4, 1983, p. 33).

For more than five years the Argentinean Air Force, through FMA, worked on the development of a missile capable of transporting a useful load to the atmosphere (*Tecnología Militar*, no. 9, 1989, p. 87; no. 7, 1984, p. 78). Klare (1990) mentions that Argentina collaborated with Egypt and Iraq in developing the Condor II ballistic missile. SIPRI (SIPRI, 1990, p. 239) reported that at the end of September 1989 Egypt withdrew from the Badr II/Condor program pursued in conjunction with Argentina. However, both Argentinean and

Egyptian officials continued to insist that this had been a satellite launch vehicle program and not a missile program. The main obstacle for the continuation of the Condor II program was considered to be financing (*Tecnología Militar*, no. 9, 1989, p. 87).

Even though the Condor II program seemed not to have been successful, the international effort of Argentina in conjunction with Egypt and Iraq indicates the existence of a technological capability sufficient to start a development program. Of the three countries participating, clearly it was Argentina who possessed the most advanced capacity.

4.7   NAVAL SHIPBUILDING IN ARGENTINA

Argentina has a long history of naval shipbuilding, with a tradition not only of repair and maintenance but also of local construction of vessels. Argentina's entire shipbuilding industry consists of two dozen major shipyards and about 100 small facilities producing mainly merchant and fishing vessels. The capacity of the major shipyards is currently sufficient to construct some 200,000 tons of new vessels annually. The Argentinean shipbuilding industry employed about 10,000 people in 1982 (Millán, 1986).

Today the major warship-building enterprise in Argentina is the state-owned company Astilleros y Fábricas Navales del Estado (AFNE). Established in 1953 as a state enterprise, AFNE's major production facility is the Rio Santiago shipyard, and it has some 4,500 employees (45 percent of the industry work force). The second-most important naval shipyard is Astilleros Domecq García which produces submarines. With a shared ownership by AFNE and private companies, ADG has around 1,000 employees. The Argentinean Navy warships are repaired and maintained at the state-owned Talleres Navales Dársena Norte Sociedad Anónima (TANDANOR) shipyard (Millán, 1986; Landaburu, 1986).

The Argentinean Navy has on at least three occasions launched modernization programs. The first occasion was the 1926 modernization plan. The plan was fulfilled in spite of the depressed economic conditions of the late 1920s and early 1930s. Under this first plan, corvettes and minesweepers were built in Argentina in the late 1930s (Millán, 1986; Landaburu, 1987a).

The second naval construction plan came after World War II, when warships of different types were acquired from Europe and the United States, often through U.S. military aid. Domestic production during that time consisted of several river patrol boats, corvettes, and the masted training ship Libertad (Millán, 1986; Landaburu, 1987a).

The third period of modernization in the 1970s and 1980s involved both domestic production and overseas acquisition of naval vessels. It began in 1968 with the order of two Type 209 submarines from Howaldswerke Deutsche Werft A. G. (FR Germany), to be assembled at the TANDANOR shipyard (Millán, 1986; Landaburu, 1986). According to the SIPRI data base (Brzoska and Ohlson, 1987, p. 145), the two Type 209 submarines were manufactured in Germany by sections and then shipped to Argentina for their assembly.

In 1970 Argentina signed a contract with Vickers Ltd. (United Kingdom) for two Type 42 destroyers, one to be built at Barrow-in-Furnesss (United Kingdom) and the second at AFNE's Rio Santiago shipyard, with British assistance. The British-built *Hercules* was commissioned in 1976, while the Argentinean-built *Santísima Trinidad* was considerably behind schedule when the Argentinean Navy took delivery in 1981 (Millán, 1986; Landaburu, 1987a).

In 1977 a contract was signed with Thyssen Nordseewerke (FR Germany) for the licensed production of four Type TR-1700 submarines, to be built at Astilleros Domecq García, with assistance from Thyssen. For this purpose, Astilleros Domecq García had to be rebuilt in the late 1970s almost from scratch, being reinaugurated in March 1982. Besides the four TR-1700 submarines to be built in Argentina, another two were delivered directly from Germany. Of these submarines, Germany gave permission to sell two of the locally built units abroad (*Jane's Fighting Ships, 1990-91*, 1990).

Another contract was signed with the FR Germany shipyards Blohm and Voss for four Meko-360 frigates. The Meko-360 frigates built in FR Germany are equipped with Olympus turbines manufactured by Rolls Royce of the United Kingdom (Sohr, 1990, p. 22), rendering them liable to the political embargo of spare parts in case of further conflicts with the United Kingdom. In fact, the construction of the Meko-360 frigates was halted by FR Germany during the South Atlantic war in 1982. In addition, production of six Meko-140 corvettes began under license from Blohm and Voss at the AFNE Rio Santiago shipyard, the first of these being commissioned in 1985 and the second in 1986. Of the six Meko-140 corvettes, two would be available for export (Millán, 1986; Landaburu, 1986).

In 1983, after the South Atlantic war, the Argentinean Navy announced its plans to build a nuclear-powered submarine (*Tecnología Militar*, no.3, 1983, p. 97), and an enlarged version of the TR-1700 has been considered for such purposes (*Jane's Fighting Ships, 1990-*

91, 1990). There are also plans to build an aircraft carrier of about 30,000 tons. However, the financial situation and some pressure from abroad have raised doubts as to whether these projects are realistic (Millán, 1986).

The existence of defense technology transfer agreements tied to large sales is clearly visible in this industry:

- purchase of four Meko-360 frigates to acquire the capability to build six Meko-140 corvettes;
- purchase of two TR-1700 submarines in order to be able to construct four more in Argentina; and
- purchase of one Type-42 destroyer in the United Kingdom in order to be able to build a similar one locally.

Sohr (1990, p. 20) reports that the overall price of the German contracts for naval vessels to be built in Argentina was nearly $2 billion. It can be assumed that this figure represents the acquisition cost of the readily available vessels, plus the license costs associated with the technology transfer agreements. Spread over a period of 10 years, this would mean transfers to FR Germany of approximately $200 million a year. This indicates the order of magnitude of the price to be paid for heavy defense technology transfer from industrialized countries.

The Argentinean program for the licensed production of warships has been bedeviled by shortages of skilled labor and facilities, creating delays. However, it has also led to a large inflow of know-how and expertise to the Argentine shipyards (Millán, 1986). In general, the production of naval vessels in Argentina enjoys a strong position, in particular because of the heavy transfer of technology from Germany since the late 1960s. Just as in the aircraft industry, Argentina still lacks the capability to manufacture critical components for its most advanced units, and all its production is done under German licenses, leaving it exposed to political blockades of international sales, as in the case of the TAM tanks. Nonetheless, in Argentina there exists the manpower and manufacturing capabilities for the construction of submarines, destroyers, and corvettes.

4.8   OTHER WEAPONS

The Argentinean military factories produce several kinds of minor weapons like pistols, rifles, submachine guns, machine guns, grenade launchers, mortars, and the like, as well as the ammunition for those weapons. Some of these minor weapons have been exported to Perú and Central American countries in shipments worth millions of dollars. Most of these small weapons are fabricated under licenses from Belgium (FN), Switzerland (Oerlikon), and France (Hotchkiss-Brandt) and also from indigenous designs. The majority are reverse-engineered from the licenses available and from the manufacturing experience gained with previous models. Fábrica Militar General San Martín produces communication equipment, under Dutch and French licenses (Millán, 1986; Landaburu, 1987b; Porth, 1984).

4.9 CHAPTER SUMMARY

As we have shown, the Argentinean defense industry is highly capable in several of the major segments of this industry. However, Argentina does not export arms on a large scale principally because of the noncompetitive prices of the weapons produced (Waisman, 1986) and the lack of marketing capability on the part of the military people who run the production plants (Porth, 1984). Although Argentina's arms industry can be said to be technologically on a par with, for example, Brazil's, it has been devoted to national requirements rather than to attracting Third World buyers (Millán, 1986). This is consistent with the low historical export figures reported by ACDA (1990).

Argentina's main defense export products are the TAM tank and the Pucará aircraft. Both were designed to meet local needs, but the first is highly priced and in head-to-head competition with tanks produced by industrialized countries, and the second has not been widely accepted due to its high price and outdated technology. Therefore, these two drawbacks have reduced the international market penetration of the Argentinean defense industry. Thus, it may be concluded that the main economic effect of the arms production in Argentina has been through import substitution, with a high reliance on transferred know-how through licenses, in particular from FR Germany. This heavy reliance on foreign licenses to produce advanced defense systems showed its drawbacks when FR Germany blocked some sales because of international political reasons.

During the South Atlantic war of 1982, the weapons fabricated in Argentina performed poorly, possibly because they had been designed for a land war (in particular, against Chile during the late 1970s) and not for an amphibious or aeronaval conflict with an industrialized nation.

In terms of employment, the overall large figure of 66,200 defense workers was obtained by totaling all the employment figures for companies presented here. The large percentage of defense workers in some segments (45 percent in the shipbuilding industry) makes the defense industry very important not only strategically for the military but also economically for the country, with 2 percent of the GDP, $2.2 billion in turnover a year, and almost 14 percent of manufacturing GDP.

The 1978–1988 average dollars-per-soldier expense of Argentina, obtained by dividing the after-imports defense budget by the total number of soldiers of the armed forces, is the largest of the Latin American region. This indicator is representative of the structure of defense expenditures and of the efficiency in the use of resources. The large value of this indicator for Argentina may indicate that the local production of arms and weapons systems is very expensive, at least in the short run, when all the capital investments need to be made. In spite of its high capability to locally produce weapons systems and weapons in general, during the late 1970s and early 1980s Argentina relied heavily upon defense imports to equip its armed forces. The shipbuilding contracts with FR Germany can be considered a large component of these expenditures.

The large investments in plants and infrastructure, such as a bearings factory for $500 millon and a fully redesigned and rebuilt shipyard for the construction of submarines, illustrate the heavy economic burden that this industrialization process has created. It can be argued that a share of the enormous Argentinean external debt can be in part due to the heavy investment in the state-owned defense industry and defense imports during the 1970s and 1980s.

The strong state involvement in the defense industry is starting to yield to higher participation of private firms, as the helicopter plant indicates, as well as the shared ownership of the aircraft factory FMA and some of the shipyards.

As was mentioned, the three embargoes imposed by the United States can be considered as Argentina's main incentives for expanding its domestic defense capability.

5

The Defense Industry of Chile

According to ACDA (1990), Chile was ranked fifteenth in world arms exports in 1988. The surprising fact about this significant level of military exports is that as recently as 1980 Chile had a highly unknown defense industry and no previous record of military export capability. The reasons for this change from net importer of weapons to a net exporter in less than ten years and the way this world status was achieved will be presented in this chapter.

5.1 THE EMERGENCE OF THE CHILEAN DEFENSE INDUSTRY

Military production in Chile can be traced back to the last century, after it achieved its political independence from Spain, but with significant capabilities in some areas starting to emerge only in the 1960s (Sohr, 1990, p. 47). Varas (1989) argues that the emergence of a defense industry in Chile was in response to the international political situation originating in 1973, when a military government was established. After that year, Great Britain, FR Germany, and more significantly, the United States in 1977 embargoed the sales of new weapons as well as military resupplies to Chile (Brzoska, 1986).

International tensions with Perú during the mid-1970s, and with Argentina during the late 1970s and early 1980s, together with the weapons' embargo, encouraged the Chilean armed forces to develop further the local arms industry, resulting in a substantial effort of arms import substitution (Varas, 1989).

According to Brzoska (1986), the most important activity in the Chilean defense industry has been the one carried out by Astilleros y Maestranzas de la Armada (ASMAR, Navy's Shipyards and Workshops), since its inception in 1960 as an independent government company under the management of the Chilean Navy, with shipyards in Talcahuano, Valparaíso, and Punta Arenas, this last one on the shores of the Magellan Strait.

The activities of ASMAR during the 1970s were guided by the objectives stated in its first ten-year plan covering 1967 to 1976. According to Sohr (1990, pp. 71–72) these objectives were:

- Provide better service to the Chilean Navy and to the Merchant Marine.
- Increase the return on investment and benefit the national economy by reducing the hard currency expenditures abroad for the construction and repair of ships and by demanding products that could help several local private and state-owned firms.
- To create work opportunities that could also help to solve the critical socioeconomic problem of unemployment.

Besides the goal of increasing the quality of service provided, in these broad objectives we can observe the two core economic concepts delineated in the defense industry model presented in Chapter 2: (1) the substitution of imports through direct purchases or repair services and (2) the economic (and social) impact of the defense industry activity. ASMAR's first plan contemplated an investment of $27.5 million for the first ten years, with a gross return of $25 million annually, the saving of $14 million in hard currency, and the provision of employment for 1,000 people.

The production of small weapons in Chile can be traced back to the last century, and since then it has been carried out under the direction of the Chilean Army. During this century, different military production capacities in the areas of small guns, ammunition, artillery shells, and explosives were integrated into a single state-owned organization managed by the Chilean Army, the Comando de Industrias Militares e Ingeniería (CIMI).

In a promotional brochure provided by FAMAE, the Chilean Army's largest military factory under CIMI's supervision, the relationship between the military and the civilian industry is explained as follows (Sohr, 1990, p. 54):

With its technology and production, the military industry not only supports the military defense capabilities, but also offers to the private industry a whole range of products, that allow the supply of raw materials of prime quality and competitive prices to important productive sectors such as construction, health, education and agriculture.

The close integration of military production and civilian production capabilities indicated here should be stressed, particularly coming from the strategy of a military-run factory, signaling the spirit of commercial rather than just autarkic principles in the production of defense goods.

In 1953 a domestic aircraft factory[1] was established in Chile but was closed down in 1960 for commercial reasons (Varas, 1989). FANAERO (Fábrica Nacional Aereonáutica) produced only flying prototypes made of wood that never reached the stage of production in series (Boisset, 1991). No aircraft production was reported until 1977 when Industria Aeronáutica (INDAER, Aeronautics Industry) was created under the supervision of the Chilean Air Force. It was later chartered in 1984 as an independent government enterprise with the name of Empresa Nacional de Aeronáutica (ENAER, National Aeronautics Company). Currently this firm also provides small parts manufacturing and repair services for the aeronautical equipment in use by the two local airlines (Sohr, 1990, p. 94).

Among the reasons for the current state of underdevelopment of the Chilean defense industry, when compared with Argentina or Brazil, for example, Martínez and Pérez (1990) recognized the following:

- the monopolistic nature of the state involvement in the industrial development of the Chilean defense industry that has resulted in economic inefficiencies;
- low demand for defense items, which resulted in higher costs because of the inefficient size of the manufacturing plant and the necessity to resort to the production of civilian items to increase plant utilization; and
- extensive use of autarkic principles, based on import substitution policies that omitted critical concepts such as costs, technological

---

1. FANAVE according to Varas (1989), and FANAERO according to Boisset (1991).

progress, and the advantages of participating in the international market.

Another very important aspect that Martínez and Pérez have failed to recognize was the widespread availability of cheap, and sometimes obsolete, defense equipment that was available to Chile in the international defense market after World War II. As Molero (1988) points out, this glut in the defense market can reduce the defense manufacturing capabilities of a country because of insufficient internal demand.

During the late 1970s a substantial private arms industry emerged in Chile (Brzoska, 1986). Among the reasons for this emergence is the free market economy policy that was implemented in Chile at that time, as well as the international arms embargo. The introduction of free market principles helped to reduce some of the imperfections introduced in the defense market by the monopolistic position of the state as mentioned by Martínez and Pérez (1990). Hewish and Luria (1992) indicate that several operations that were formerly integral parts of the armed forces are now wholly or partially organized on a commercial basis. The arms embargo eliminated the abundance of readily available inexpensive defense equipment, increasing internal demand. These two elements positively reinforced each other and helped Chile to break free of the vicious circle of technological dependence.

5.2   STRUCTURE OF ARMS PRODUCTION IN CHILE

Martínez and Pérez (1990) indicate that the Chilean defense industry has substantial capabilities in the basic sector (clothing, leather, and blacksmith items) and light manufacturing sector (light weapons and ammunition, simple explosives, parts manufacturing, and repairing of heavy vehicles) of the defense industry. This industry has some capabilities in the heavy manufacturing sector (large ammunition, automatic weapons, optical systems, training aircraft, transport vessels, light armored vehicles) and only limited capabilities in the advanced sector (tanks, large-caliber weapons, fighter aircraft, warships, missiles).

ASMAR has commercial joint ventures with a Spanish shipyard for the operation of a floating dock in the port of Valparaíso; with Ferranti of the United Kingdom for the development of electronic systems through the firm SISDEF (Sistemas de Defensa Sociedad

Limitada); and with a South African firm for the operation of another shipyard in Punta Arenas, which provides maintenance and repair services to the oil industry and other maritime companies that operate in the area. The Punta Arenas project had a cost of $12.8 million and provides employment to 125 people (Chales de Beaulieu, 1990). Associated with a Chilean engineering firm, ASMAR also participates in the design and construction of offshore crafts and small support units for the oil industry that operates in the Magellan Strait (Tromben, 1989, p. 324; Sohr, 1990, p. 74).   In 1983 it was estimated that ASMAR had a total capital of $100 million, with a total employment of 4,500 people, including electronic engineers and naval construction technicians (*Tecnología Militar*, no. 4, 1983; Varas, 1989).

Weapons production and some other commercial services provided by the Chilean Army are grouped together in the Comando de Industrias Militares e Ingeniería (CIMI, Directorate for Military Factories and Engineering), which claims to be Chile's largest weapons production corporation.   It is composed of five industrial organizations: Fábricas y Maestranzas del Ejército (FAMAE, Army's Factories and Workshops), chartered in 1953 as an independent government enterprise and located in Santiago; Complejo Químico Industrial del Ejército (CQIE, Army's Chemical and Industrial Complex); Instituto de Investigaciones y Control (IDIC, Institute for Research and Control), which acts as the national test facility for all kinds of arms, ammunition, and explosives manufactured locally or imported; Instituto Geográfico Militar (IGM, Military Geographic Institute); and the Centro de Cohetería del Ejército (CECOE, Army's Rocketry Center).   According to an ex-director of FAMAE, the military factories provide no more than 18 percent of the needs of the Chilean Army, with the remaining provided by private firms (Sohr, 1990, pp. 53, 56).

FAMAE is CIMI's largest division, employing around 3,000 people, of which 2,800 are civilians, with around 40 military and civilian engineers.   It has several plants distributed throughout the country, with the largest one in Santiago for the manufacturing of heavy and light weapons. A steel workshop for the manufacture of armored vehicles and construction equipment for civilian use is located near Santiago. FAMAE has been licensed to produce Swiss SIG rifles and MOWAG armored vehicles and manufactures under license from Thomson Brandt almost all the ammunition and explosives needed by the Chilean Army: grenades, mines, small weapons, and armored structures, as well as a large variety of aircraft bombs and military explosives. A Systems Division was created for the development of indigenous technology in the areas of missile guidance, command and control systems for artillery and artillery rockets, and radars (Letelier, 1991).

FAMAE opened new production facilities in 1983, installing modern computer-controlled machine tools. With its installed capacity, FAMAE manufactures several products for civilian use, such as agricultural equipment and hand tools, and had plans for other civilian ventures starting in 1992 (Letelier, 1991). In a second plant located in the northern part of the country, FAMAE provides heavy metal manufacturing services for the copper mining industry (Sohr, 1990).

ENAER produces subsonic fighters under license from Construcciones Aereonáuticas Sociedad Anónima (CASA) of Spain, training aircraft in cooperation with Piper of the United States, and light civilian aircraft with indigenous technology. Aircraft upgrades are performed with the assistance of Israel Aircraft Industries (IAI). Electronic equipment for aircraft use is currently produced with assistance provided by the Israeli firm Elta Electronics (Hewish and Luria, 1992). Today, the number of employees of ENAER is approximately 1,600, having reached levels of 1,700 employees in certain years (ENAER, 1992).

The most important private company that emerged during the late 1970s was Cardoen Industries, established in 1977. Cardoen Industries produces a wide spectrum of munitions, aviation bombs, security equipment, and armored vehicles and even entered the area of helicopter production (El Mercurio, April 12, 1992). In 1985 Cardoen sold $89 million worth of goods (Sohr, 1990, p. 101) and, between 1986 and 1989, sold a total of $500 million in military products, of which $450 million was exported, with $150 million subcontracted to the local industry (Cardoen, 1991). Using imported computerized numerically controlled machine tools, during the last decade Cardoen has been manufacturing, in addition to military supplies, different products for the metallurgical, mining, agricultural, and automotive sectors (Bureau of International Economic Affairs, 1989), as well as parts for ENAER (Brzoska, 1986). According to the president of the company, in 1986 Cardoen Industries had 700 employees (Tecnología Militar, no. 3, 1986).

Encouraged by the government's attitude not to buy exclusively from its own arsenals, and by the success of Cardoen Industries, other producers of mining equipment and machinery have tried to enter the Chilean arms market. One such company is Makina, which, competing against other local firms, won a contract for producing an armored patrol vehicle for the Chilean Air Force (Brzoska, 1986).

From the description above, it is possible to identify the main structure of the Chilean defense industry, shown in Figure 5.1. At the Ministry of Defense level, there is no centralization of the technological development and acquisition processes, as there is in Argentina. In Chile, each of the services is free to acquire whatever weapons systems best meet its needs from an economic and technical perspective. This indicates a much lower pressure for domestic supplies, allowing for a better allocation of resources and the possibility of choosing the best technologies available. In fact, the Pillán trainer aircraft manufactured locally by ENAER is neither in use in the army nor in the navy for their pilot-training activities, indicating that in Chile domestic production is not assumed to imply autarky. In the long run, as will be shown in Chapter 8, this pragmatic approach has increased the efficiency of the Chilean defense industry.

From the employment figures presented for the different arsenals and factories (see Table 5.1), it can be estimated that the prime contractors of the defense industry in Chile directly employ around 9,800 people.[2] Using an indirect labor multiplier of 1.6 (in the lower range of the employment multiplier suggested by Mosley [1985]), the total number of people employed directly and indirectly by the Chilean defense industry can be estimated at approximately 15,680 workers.

5.3 DEFENSE RESEARCH AND DEVELOPMENT IN CHILE

Data on the research and development expenditures of the Chilean defense industry are not available. In an official publication of the Chilean National Commission of Scientific and Technological Research (CONICYT, 1990), no defense R&D expenditures are reported. This means that all the defense-related research and development activity is financed either by the respective services, by associated weapons production corporations (ASMAR, FAMAE,

---

2. At the National Defense Industry symposium, Francisco Bertolucci (1991) mentioned that the defense industry provides directly more than 7,000 jobs, the indirect effect being difficult to estimate.

Figure 5.1

Structure of Arms Production in Chile

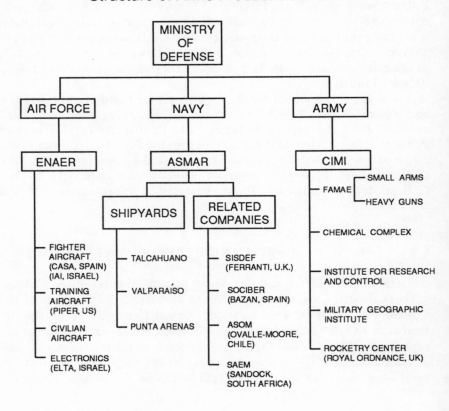

Table 5.1

Employment of Major Defense Companies in Chile

DEFENSE FIRM	EMPLOYMENT CIRCA 1985
ASMAR	4,500
FAMAE	3,000
ENAER	1,600
CARDOEN	700
TOTAL DEFENSE EMPLOYMENT	9,800

ENAER), or by private firms. In 1991, at the National Defense Industry symposium held in Valparaíso, the Chilean Minister of Economic Affairs indicated that defense firms could also participate in the requests for funds available through the national science and technology program for the execution of research projects (Ominami, 1991). This statement indicates a change in the existing policy with respect to the access of the defense industry to these funds. As a consequence, it might be expected that in the future defense research and development expenditures in Chile will increase.

Hewish and Luria (1992) indicate that the Chilean defense firms have adopted the classical combination of domestic development, reverse engineering, licensed production, and joint ventures to advance their technology. During the 1980s, in support of their weapons development effort, the Chilean armed forces started looking for technological capabilities at the local universities and, together with their internal R&D organizations, pursued joint research programs (Maldifassi, 1990). Montoya (1989) reports that retired officers of the Chilean Navy with their extensive technical expertise and up-to-date knowledge of the organizational environment, and motivated by the new economic conditions, started their own companies, providing technical services to the Chilean Navy in the areas of electronic warfare and gunfire control.

In 1987 the First Congress of Defense Engineering was held at the Chilean Air Force's Polytechnic Academy in Santiago, with the assistance of several universities and private firms (FACH, 1987). In November 1990 a symposium on "Rocketry and Missiles" was held in Santiago (*El Mercurio*, November 21, 1990), and another symposium entitled the "National Defense Industry" was held in Valparaíso in November 1991, where representatives of the local armed forces, state- and privately owned defense firms, House representatives, senators, and ministers discussed the actual situation and political aspects of the Chilean defense industry (ASMAR, 1991).

As can be seen, increasing industrial, institutional, and political support is being given to the development of defense technology in Chile, with broad participation of the several parties involved. This means that in Chile increased levels of domestic defense production and enhanced embodiment of technology in the weapons produced can be expected in the future.

5.4   THE CHILEAN AIRCRAFT INDUSTRY

Exploratory studies for aircraft manufacturing were begun in Chile in 1979, with the assembly of the PA-28 Dakota basic training aircraft, in close collaboration with Piper of the United States. This was done at the Chilean Air Force's Maintenance Wing near Santiago (Brzoska, 1986; Sohr, 1990, p. 87).

In March 1980 the first prototype of the basic trainer T-35 Pillán—a follow-on development of the PA-28—was flown in the United States. The Pillán was designed by Piper, integrating elements from various other Piper aircraft, with Chilean engineers participating in the conceptual design stages. The development program cost $8 million and was completely financed by the Chilean Air Force. Production of the Pillán began in 1982. Only 56 of the more than 1,500 parts that are used in the Pillán are imported. Included among the imported parts are the engine and the wings, these being the most sophisticated elements of the aircraft (Sohr, 1990, pp. 86–88). This would indicate that Chile possesses a substantial capability for the production of domestic aircraft parts at the middle to lower levels of the technology spectrum.

In May 1987, the first 12 units of the T-35 Pillán were finished. These aircraft are currently being used for training purposes at the Chilean Air Force Academy. Another 68 T-35 Pillán units have been ordered by the Chilean Air Force at a cost of nearly $150,000 per unit (Sohr, 1990, pp. 86–88; Brzoska, 1986). General Caupolican Boisset of the Chilean Air Force (1991) indicates that ENAER took over the responsibility for the production-engineering development phase of the Pillán, as well as the optimization of the prototype, and was able to reach production levels of 4 planes per month. Boisset also reports that 102 units of the Pillán have been produced, of which 41 were exported to Spain and 10 to Panama. According to the same officer, a turbo version of the Pillán already underwent prototype tests, with a full commercial version expected to be marketed during 1992. Hewish and Luria (1992) indicate that besides the sales reported by Boisset, 15 Pillán have been sold to Paraguay, making a total of 127 units produced up to 1992.

In July 1984, a contract was signed between ENAER and the Spanish aircraft firm CASA for the coproduction and assembly in Chile of the C-101-BB Aviojet aircraft. Chilean engineers participated in adapting the Spanish C-101-AA version of this aircraft, and Spanish and Chilean designers went on to develop a ground attack version, called T-36 Halcón. The Chilean Air Force ordered 21 units of this aircraft. The first Halcón assembled in Chile rolled out in October 1986. In an offset agreement, the Spanish Air Force ordered 40 Pillán to be used for training purposes.

According to Sohr (1990, p. 90), perhaps the most ambitious technological development project undertaken by ENAER to date has been the modernization of the fleet of French Mirage-50 aircraft. The project to improve these jet fighters started in 1986 with the installation of "canard" winglets in the front of the aircraft. This work was done with the technical assistance of Israel, through the firm Israel Aircraft Industries. This modification has been severely criticized by Dassault, the original manufacturer of the Mirage. After the canards were installed, the full set of cables of the Mirage was replaced, a new target acquisition radar was installed, and much electronic equipment was also renewed. The operational performance of the aircraft changed so dramatically that the Chilean Air Force renamed the aircraft "Pantera." The original cost of the modernization program has been reported to be close to $40 million, covering the whole fleet of 16 Mirage actually in service at the Chilean Air Force.

To meet requirements of the Chilean Air Force, in 1986 ENAER reached an agreement with the German firm Messerschmitt-Bolkow-Blohm (MBB) for the coproduction in Chile of 30 helicopters model BO-105. After the agreement was reached, budgetary constraints forced the Chilean Air Force to reduce the number of units ordered to about 15. Because of this, MBB considered that the reduced number of units did not warrant a technology transfer agreement, and the contract was finally signed only as a direct purchasing order (Sohr, 1990, p. 91).

In 1985 Cardoen Industries also contemplated the production of a combat helicopter. This firm displayed a mock-up of the unit intended to be produced at Santiago's International Air Fair in 1986. Cardoen tried to reach a contractual agreement with MBB for the development of a combat version of the BO-105, which in the end was rejected by MBB (Sohr, 1990, p. 103). After a failed attempt to produce the German helicopter, around 1989 Cardoen was able to obtain the manufacturing license for the Bell 206 L-III helicopter in the United States at a cost of $1 million. The Federal Aviation Administration of the United States had agreed to give the required certification for the civilian version of Cardoen's helicopter. The combat version of the Bell 206 to be manufactured by Cardoen includes a crew of one pilot, a gunnery officer, and three passengers, one of which can operate a heavy machine gun. The aircraft will be equipped with a Chinese periscopic aim and a 20-mm cannon fixed to the fuselage. The development costs amount to $3 million (Sohr, 1990, pp. 103–106).

In 1986 ENAER initiated the indigenous development of a lightweight two-seater single-engine civilian aircraft, made of composite materials, targeted for flight clubs. This same firm also manufactures electronic aircraft systems used by the Chilean Air Force (*Tecnología Militar*, no. 11, 1985) and, as was mentioned above, provides maintenance and repair services for the two local airlines. It also provides engineering services for other firms in the manufacturing industry (Sohr, 1990).

5.5 CHILEAN ARMORED VEHICLES

In 1981 Cardoen Industries produced under license the first MOWAG-Piraña armored vehicles manufactured in Chile (Brzoska, 1986). Cardoen Industries produced 220 units of the 6×6 version of these vehicles for the Chilean Army, the last 20 units in 1987, with FAMAE manufacturing the armored bodies.

FAMAE has also been licensed by the Swiss firm MOWAG to produce the Piraña 8×8 amphibious armored vehicles. Currently FAMAE is producing the 8×8 version for the Chilean Army, with the Chilean Navy's Marines proposing to acquire some units because of their amphibious capabilities (*Tecnología Militar*, no. 3, 1986).

Cardoen Industries also tried to market other models of armored vehicles, building three prototypes: the 18-ton Orca VTP-1 armored personnel carrier (APC), based on the West German Unimog chassis; the Escarabajo VTP-2 4×4 for transporting personnel; and the multiple-use half-track BMS-1 Alacrán armored vehicle, one of the few half-track vehicles offered in the international defense market. The Chilean Army showed no interest in these vehicles, and none of these models reached the production stage (Sohr, 1990, p. 98).

In 1989 Cardoen Industries, in a contractual agreement with the South African firm ARMSCOR (Arms Corporation of South Africa), produced an armored self-propelled cannon of 155 mm known as G-6. The cannon has a maximum firing range of 40 km, and the unit is able to speed up to 90 km/h on roads and 30 going cross country. This is the most advanced artillery unit ever built in Chile, and its firing power and self-propulsion make this unit a very powerful artillery weapon (Sohr, 1990, p. 111; *Jane's Armour and Artillery, 1991-92*, 1991, p. 607).

The firm Makina, at the request of the Chilean Air Force, developed the lightweight armored open vehicle Carancho for base patrol duties. The vehicle can transport up to ten soldiers and comes equipped with three machine guns. Makina's armored vehicles are based on a commercial truck chassis and use a commercial Chrysler engine. The Carancho is able to drive at speeds up to 130 km/h, but with a much lower performance in cross country. Around 50 percent of the parts and components of the Carancho are imported, but, because of their civilian nature, they are not subject to military export controls. The price of each unit was less than half the price of similar units offered by foreign companies. No more than 20 Caranchos were produced, all of them purchased by the Chilean Air Force (Brzoska, 1986; Sohr, 1990). Thus, as in Brazil, Chilean defense firms have started adapting civilian-use parts for use in defense equipment, increasing their technological capabilities and know-how.

5.6 ROCKETS MANUFACTURED BY THE CHILEAN DEFENSE INDUSTRY

No missiles have ever been produced in Chile, and there are no indications in the literature about such intents. However, an advanced rocket system has been developed during the last two years.

In 1988 a Chilean newspaper reported that according to a Chilean Army general, FAMAE had the intention of manufacturing rockets and missiles. The news article indicated that the rockets would be of tactical use, with a range of 30 km. According to the news article, the rockets could be further developed for the production of missiles. Information about this project was further clarified in 1990, when at the International Air Fair in Santiago a mock-up of a 2-m green rocket was displayed. The project at that time was shown to be carried out as a joint effort by FAMAE and British Royal Ordnance, a division of British Aerospace (Sohr, 1990, pp. 65–66).

The rocket program of the Chilean Army was called "Rayo" (Ray), consisting of tactical rockets with an effective range of up to 40 km. According to Sohr (1990, p. 65), some rockets had already been fired in a northern region of Chile in 1990. The contract for the marketing of the Rayo rockets was supposed to be of a joint nature, with Chile being the first buyer and the intention of the British firm being to convince its government to do the same.

In 1991 another newspaper (*El Mercurio*, October 12, 1991) reported that in an official launching demonstration two Rayo rockets of 160 mm had been successfully tested, reaching a distance of 40 km. In an on-site interview with the director of FAMAE it was revealed that 12 nations of Latin America, the Middle East, and Africa had expressed an interest in acquiring the rocket system. Each rocket would sell for a price of $7,000; a full unit might consist of a launching platform along with 12 rockets.

For the production of the Rayo rocket system, a joint-venture company has been established between FAMAE and Royal Ordnance of the United Kingdom, with the former providing between 60 and 70 percent of the needed capital. All the development costs of the project up to 1992 have been paid for by the Chilean Army, with Royal Ordnance providing the technology and also taking care of the worldwide marketing effort of the weapon system (Hewish and Luria, 1992).

5.7   NAVAL SHIPBUILDING IN CHILE

The first battleship built in South America was launched in Valparaíso, Chile, in 1851, with a total displacement of 644 tons (Volker, 1991). Currently the shipbuilding industry in Chile consists of 21 small repair shipyards plus 32 naval repair shops. Additionally, there are three private shipyards that build oceangoing fishing vessels (Volker, 1991) and one corporation engaged in the construction of warships. This last concern, known as ASMAR, was created in 1960 as an autonomous government company managed by the Chilean Navy.

The first naval craft produced by ASMAR for the Chilean Navy were completed in the late 1960s and early 1970s. They consisted of a small landing craft in 1968 and the assembly of a small submarine-hunter ship sold by the United States in 1971 (Tromben, 1989, p. 304; *Jane's Fighting Ships, 1991-92*, 1991). The reduced tonnage of these vessels comes from the fact that until 1979 ASMAR did not have a slipway to build larger units.

In April of 1979 at ASMAR's Talcahuano plant, a slipway was inaugurated for the local construction of naval vessels and other naval craft up to 60,000 deadweight tons (DWT), a length of 161 m, and a width of 34 m. This enhanced manufacturing capability, together with the automation of the slipway's workshops, made it possible for ASMAR to win an international contract for the construction of an oil-drilling platform. This was the first construction to come out of the new manufacturing facilities (Tromben, 1989, pp. 321–322; Sohr, 1990, p. 72).

With the enhanced production capacity provided by the new slipway since 1979, ASMAR has been able to engage in the construction of larger naval craft. The next units built were three landing ships of the Batral type. These units were built from a French design and with technical support provided by French firms.

After the construction of the Batral units, ASMAR built its largest naval craft, a floating dock of 10,000 DWT finished in 1985 and currently operational in Valparaíso.

In 1988 the Chilean Navy added to its fleet the *Aquiles*, the largest ship built in the country. The *Aquiles* is a transport ship of 4,550 DWT, and its construction was one of the most important projects undertaken by ASMAR since its inception (Tromben, 1989; Sohr, 1990; *Jane's Fighting Ships, 1991-92*, 1991).

According to Sohr (1990, p. 76), the Chilean Navy congratulates itself for not making the same mistake that the Argentinean and Peruvian navies made when they embarked on the local construction of warships. This observation comes from the fact that the Argentinean Navy had several problems during the construction in Argentina of the British-designed "Santísima Trinidad" Type 42 destroyer, which was delivered substantially behind schedule. Perú had its own problems and delays when building two Italian Lupo-type frigates during the late 1970s and mid-1980s. As already mentioned in Chapter 3, the Brazilian naval construction program also had some difficulties, further reinforcing Sohr's statement.

In fact, the largest units that the Chilean Navy has operated had been acquired secondhand from the United States in the 1950s, Sweden in the late 1960s, and the United Kingdom in the 1980s. Some of these ships, in particular the U.S.-built units, have reached operational lives of up to 50 years. Thus, more than an important capacity to build warships, ASMAR developed a substantial capacity and expertise in the maintenance, repair, and modification of existing units that were purchased secondhand from industrialized countries. According to Montoya (1989), in the 1970s and 1980s the Chilean Navy bought British ships largely because of the reluctance of the United States to sell newer warships after its World War II surplus of old used ships disappeared.

Whereas the Peruvian Navy had to pay $120 million to the Netherlands' government for the modernization of the cruiser *Aguirre* in 1984 (Sohr, 1990), the Chilean Navy purchased four secondhand British destroyers during the 1980s at a substantially lower overall price. Two of these destroyers have already been transformed at ASMAR's Talcahuano shipyard into helicopter carriers to be equipped with French Super Puma and Dauphine helicopters (*Jane's Fighting Ships, 1991-92,* 1991). Another example of how ASMAR is able to repair and overhaul secondhand ships is the purchase by the Chilean Navy of another British unit, in this case a Leander frigate, that was brought from the United Kingdom to Chile on board a transport ship because of its poor condition. The frigate was completely overhauled in Talcahuano at a cost substantially lower than what it would have cost to do the same repairs in the United Kingdom (Mann, 1991).

ASMAR is also able to perform major overhauls on the British Oberon and German U-209 submarines in service in the Chilean Navy (Sohr, 1990, pp. 76–77), whereas the Peruvian, Ecuadorian, and Colombian navies need to take their similar submarines to Germany to be overhauled.

ASMAR has also signed licensing contracts with the French firm Chantier Mécanique de Normandie for the construction of small (400 DWT), 54-m-long fast-attack boats and with the British firm Fairley Brooke Marine for the fabrication of small 33-m-long boats (Sohr, 1990, pp. 77, 81).

With respect to submarines, *Jane's* (*Jane's Fighting Ships, 1991-92,* 1991) reports that as of 1988, according to a five-year plan, two U-209 German submarines could be assembled in Talcahuano in the future. In 1989 the commander in chief of the Chilean Navy indicated to a Chilean newspaper that no more purchases of submarines would be effected but that in the future submarines would be built in Chile

(*El Mercurio*, June 25, 1989). The construction of submarines in Chile depends to a large extent on the availability of funds to carry out the program (Hewish and Luria, 1992).

Cardoen Industries has also been considering the fabrication of midget submarines in Chile, either to be exported or for the Chilean Navy's use. The unit that Cardoen has in its plans is produced by the firm Cosmos of Italy, and the particular model has a displacement of 110 DWT and is 27 m long. It is not clear yet if these units would be built on Cardoen's premises in the northern part of Chile or in Talcahuano-ASMAR (Sohr, 1990, p. 109).

For the near future, ASMAR has been considering the local production of 1,000-ton patrol ships, in particular for the export market (*Revista de Marina*, no. 4, 1992, p. 426).

5.8   OTHER WEAPONS

Similarly to Brazil and Argentina, the Chilean defense industry manufactures several small arms as well as the ammunition needed to use them. FAMAE is perhaps the company that produces the largest number of small weapons, for example, rifles under license by Swiss and Belgium firms, aviation bombs, grenades, and several types of mines.

In cooperation with the Chilean Air Force, ASMAR developed a radar system with civilian and military applications (*Tecnología Militar*, no. 4, 1983). Other electronic systems in the areas of detection and fire control have been developed in ASMAR with the help provided by Ferranti in its joint venture SISDEF (Hewish and Luria, 1992).

5.9   CHAPTER SUMMARY

The Chilean defense industry has been building its domestic production capabilities since the 1960s, but its most important achievements took place in the 1980s, mostly because of the need to overcome the international arms embargo that the country faced after 1977. The arms embargo imposed on Chile by its major suppliers created the need for the development of domestic defense technology. This embargo, the increased industrialization of Chile since the mid-1970s based on a free market economy, and international tensions with

Argentina and Perú can be considered the main circumstances that prompted the emergence of a modern Chilean defense industry.

The appearance of some private companies is consistent with the new economic policy adopted since the late 1970s. This new economic policy strove to reduce the size of the state's involvement and to rely more on the private sector by developing a market economy.

The Chilean defense industry is still in a state of flux, and recently the defense minister of Chile has indicated the need to continue with the development and support of this industry because of its strategic and economic importance (*El Mercurio*, November 17, 1991). During the 1980s the Chilean defense industry was able to supply the local armed forces with defense equipment of some degree of sophistication. This helped to ameliorate the effects of the arms embargo and even to develop products sold in the international arms market.

Perhaps the most important feature of the emerging Chilean defense industry is the fact that increased reliance has been placed on the private sector, with economic criteria being given considerable importance in the later years. The Chilean armed forces have also been instrumental in the institutionalization of the defense industry by means of its productive units, being careful not to embark on projects that are too ambitious or uneconomic.

Even though the scope of the indigenous defense capability in Chile is narrower than in Argentina, and much less than in Brazil, Chile has been able to start producing more complex weapons systems with the technical support of foreign companies. However, the Chilean armed forces have not restricted themselves by attempting to attain an absolute self-sufficiency and have diversified the origin of their weapons. With goals less ambitious than Argentina and with a lower availability of capital, Chile has continued to rely largely on external defense supplies. The Chilean defense industry produces only those items considered within technical and economic reach. Also, Chilean defense firms have exports in mind when they embark on the production of more sophisticated weapons systems. Nonetheless, the Chilean defense industry can be considered to be in an earlier stage of development when compared with the Brazilian defense industry and somewhat less developed than the Argentinean defense industry.

6

Comparative Assessment of the Defense Industries of Argentina, Brazil, and Chile

In this chapter a cross comparison is made between the defense industries of Argentina, Brazil, and Chile in order to identify similarities and differences that would help explain the reasons for these countries' different industrial performances. The comparison is made first in terms of the roles played by the various actors—government, armed forces, local private industry, universities, and foreign companies—and then in terms of the observed characteristics of the different segments of the industry in each country during the mid-1980s.

6.1   THE ROLE OF THE GOVERNMENT IN THE EMERGENCE OF A MODERN DEFENSE INDUSTRY IN SEMI-INDUSTRIALIZED LATIN AMERICAN COUNTRIES

In the three countries studied, each government created a modern defense industry by transforming the maintenance and operational infrastructure of the armed forces into productive units. One of the most important reasons given for this change in emphasis was the political desire for enhanced self-reliance in the supply of arms and defense equipment, in order to reduce foreign political dependency. In fact, Argentina, Brazil, and Chile at some point in time were all subjected to arms embargoes, prompting the decision to embark on a larger scale of domestic defense production.   Three other semi-industrialized countries, Israel, South Africa, and India, were also subject to arms embargoes and developed important defense industries.   This finding supports the argument that in semi-industrialized countries the political decision to expand the local defense industry is made in response to the ways industrialized countries restrict access to the international defense market.

The countries in this study also mentioned the following other reasons for increasing local defense production: import substitution policies aimed primarily at increasing the industrial capacity of the country and reducing hard currency purchases abroad and, to a lesser extent, the possibility of reaping the benefits of foreign defense sales.

These reasons for increasing the domestic capacity to produce more sophisticated weapons indicate that the defense industry is in fact a government tool that can be effectively used to assist in solving some of the problems faced by many developing countries, in particular:

- lack of political self-determination, which made it almost mandatory to become aligned with one of the East-West blocs during the Cold War era;
- reduced capacity and expertise for manufacturing industrial products;
- hard currency drain to purchase highly priced defense items in the international market; and
- lack of products with high value added to be sold abroad.

However, implementing an industrial policy that is aimed at creating a highly autarkic defense industry but does not consider the efficient allocation of resources (such as Argentina, as will be shown in Chapter 8) can be harmful to other related industries. This harm is caused by the high opportunity cost of the resources used: human, financial, and productive. A well-balanced industrial policy in harmony with the technical capabilities of the rest of the economy is essential for reaping the benefits of a modern defense industry.

The armed forces' maintenance and operational infrastructure was further expanded by means of state-owned defense production facilities managed by members of the armed forces, with a later entry of private firms. The charter of these state-owned factories varied somewhat among the countries, with the Brazilian and Chilean establishments operating closer to the charter of private, for-profit corporations. This trend took place earlier in the case of Brazil, and somewhat later in the case of Chile.   In line with the autarkic principles and strong import substitution policies supported historically by the Argentinean government, the Argentinean factories appeared to be less concerned with the profitability of the enterprise and more interested in the ability to produce domestically more sophisticated equipment with autochthonous technology.

According to Dodaro (1991), a country's ability to export depends essentially on its ability to produce products that are competitive on price and quality in world markets. It can be argued that any deficiency in either of these two characteristics would require subsidizing exports as a means for increasing the market acceptance of the exported goods. As will be shown in Chapter 8, the degree of economic efficiency of the defense industry varies considerably among the three countries studied here, with the Chilean defense industry the most efficient of the three. Because of the low level of Argentinean defense exports, there is not much evidence of government subsidies. One exception is the case of the Pucará aircraft exported to Uruguay, where an estimated $1.2 million was discounted from the estimated $3 million production cost: a substantial 40 percent subsidy. Government subsidies to boost exports have also been important in the case of the Brazilian defense industry. No evidence of government subsidies could be found in the case of Chilean defense exports. This indicates that the more efficient the defense industry, the less necessary it is for the government to provide subsidies for its exports.

These military factories, like any other state-owned enterprises, followed to a great extent the overall economic policies adopted in each of these countries. Some of these factories were later rechartered as state-owned corporations, giving emphasis to profitability and economic self-sufficiency only when the economic policies shifted predominantly toward free market systems (first in Brazil and later in Chile). This finding indicates that the defense industry's emphasis on profitability, efficiency, and economic criteria for decision making is contingent upon the governmental policies adopted for the overall economy.

The same argument can be used to explain the late entry of private firms in the defense industry. With strong state involvement in the overall economy, the role of private firms in the defense industry is minimized. All these considerations indicate that from an industrial policy perspective the efficiency and productivity of the defense industry and the role played by private firms in this industry—as in the other industries across the economy—are contingent upon the governments adopting a predominantly free market economy. It can be argued that autarkic principles and closed economies hinder more than favor the efficient allocation of resources in the defense industry.

Some of the other incentives provided by the Brazilian government for the inception of a modern and predominantly privately based defense industry have been (1) soft credits through state or regional banks and (2) heavy financing of research and development activities. Because heavy governmental commitment requires the administration to allocate substantial financial resources in order to attain its objectives, it can be said that the significant financial government support provided to the Brazilian defense industry has been one of the most important factors for its emergence as a world player. This important financial commitment may also help explain the relative technological advantage that the Brazilian defense industry has had in comparison with the Argentinean and Chilean.[1]

Because the defense market is highly contingent upon international relations, the political pragmatism of the Brazilian government helped the local defense industry reach foreign markets and also facilitated the transfer of technology from several sources, mostly European. After 1973, the political scenario for the Chilean government became highly restricted, making it difficult for the Chilean armed forces to acquire arms and defense technology and also for its defense industry to sell weapons abroad. These opposite scenarios, and the better international performance of the Brazilian defense industry when compared with the Chilean, indicate that the local defense industry is favored under certain conditions. These conditions include open international relations, a variety of sources for technology, and access to the overall world arms market.

Another aspect for the emergence of an indigenous defense industry that is sometimes taken for granted is the internal and external political support provided by the government. However, the Chilean government denied FAMAE and another private firm the authorization to export weapons to Saudi Arabia during the Gulf crisis, suggesting that this support is not always granted after a change in administration.

The legislature also plays a role in helping the emergence and activity of the domestic defense industry. A defense budget that includes a substantial component of local currency can also be considered political support for the local defense industry. The legislature determines the hard/local currency ratio of the defense budget and, more important, approves the laws that regulate the local defense industry, including import and export policies. Because the respective shares of hard and local currency in the defense budget are

---

1. See Chapter 7 for an analysis of the degree of sophistication of the respective defense industries.

defined in consultation with the local armed forces, the latter also play a political role.

Government policies, therefore, play a very important role in the operational characteristics, efficiency, level of technological sophistication, industry structure, and size of the market of the defense industry. A free market economy provides the basis for a modern and productive defense industry, as long as other policies provide:

- strong government support for R&D and technological innovation,
- heavy reliance on private over state-owned firms,
- open access to sources of technology from industrialized countries,
- a vision of the defense market as being global in nature with unrestricted access to all buyers, and
- sustained political support by the government.

The government, by means of laws and policies, is responsible for ensuring that all these conditions are met in order for the defense industry to become an efficient and fruitful sector of the economy.

6.2   THE ROLE OF THE ARMED FORCES

Because the armed forces are both users and purchasers of defense equipment, they play an important role in the defense market of all countries. In the case of semi-industrialized countries, the armed forces' role extends to development and manufacture of the defense goods produced locally. This role is even greater when the armed forces become involved in government activities.

It is noteworthy that Argentina, Brazil, and Chile all had military governments when the defense industry was developed beyond the basic maintenance and operational infrastructure of the armed forces. This phenomenon is due to the fact that the armed forces find it frustrating and difficult to operate obsolete secondhand equipment or to be unable to acquire equipment from abroad. This frustration is especially severe when the armed forces need adequate equipment to confront an international crisis but cannot get what they need because of political reasons. During military regimes, this firsthand experience of the armed forces with political and technological dependency on industrialized countries prompts the political decision to foster the incipient defense industry beyond the existing arsenals and factories. Other Latin American countries that have not had military regimes since the 1960s or earlier (in particular, Mexico, Venezuela, and Colombia) but that do have some degree of industrialization capable of supporting some defense production activity have the least developed defense industries of the region. Thus, it can be argued that the existence of a military government can act as a catalytic agent to prompt the emergence of a sophisticated defense industry. However, as will be shown in Chapter 7 and as the failed experience of the Peruvian defense industry illustrates, other factors such as industrial, human, and technological requirements need to be satisfied for this effort to be successful.

The distinction made by Ross (1984, p. 111) between the two groups of armed forces' officers that are either users of defense equipment or militarily active and politically aware becomes important at this point. The users of military equipment will prefer imported equipment with known and proven operational capabilities. The politically aware, on the other hand, will tend to favor the emergence of a domestic defense industry. With the military becoming involved in the country's government, the group of politically aware officers will tend to predominate over the users of defense equipment, further encouraging the emergence of the local defense industry. In Argentina, where during the last 40 years there have been predominantly military governments, the influence of the militarily active and politically aware officers has clearly prevailed, with the Plan Europa being the most clear example of this phenomenon.

In the three countries studied, the armed forces were the original managers of the maintenance and operational infrastructure that evolved later into state-owned defense firms and corporations. As such, the armed forces were also charged with the responsibility of transforming their arsenals and factories into productive for-profit enterprises, a task for which they were ill-equipped because of their lack of business training and expertise, particularly in the areas of marketing and large-scale manufacturing. This lack of experience is evident in the case of the Brazilian arsenals IMBEL, where there was a need to assign a civilian manager to transform the arsenals into a for-profit corporation. This transformation has not yet taken place in the cases of Argentina or Chile. However, in Chile the emergence of an important private defense industry together with the requirements imposed by a market-oriented economy have made this change less important. In Argentina, where neither of these changes has taken place, there is a pressing need to increase economic and market orientations in the defense industry and to transfer the responsibility for production from the armed forces to the private sector.

The armed forces of these countries needed to develop the expertise to translate their operational requirements into technological characteristics of the domestically produced defense equipment and to learn how to trade off one for the other during the design and production phases. Now, members of the local armed forces must specify and perform homologation and performance tests, activities not needed when arms and weapons were purchased abroad. The officers in charge of the new production facilities needed to improve their managerial and business skills in order to improve the quality and productivity of the plants under their management. These skills were traditionally not provided by the military educational establishments, so the military had to resort to the education provided by local and foreign universities. This increased technical expertise has required the armed forces to increase education and training, not only for their officers but also for their enlisted personnel in charge of operation and maintenance. Thus, as a consequence of the emergence of a modern defense industry, the activities of the armed forces have become much more business and technically oriented than before, demanding a structural change in their education and training.

On the operational side, the armed forces of Argentina, Brazil, and Chile have been able to count in their arsenals large quantities of locally produced medium-technology equipment that has increased their operational effectiveness. However, because of their relatively lower expertise and technological capacity, the reliability of some of this domestic equipment has not been able to match the performance of weapons systems of industrialized countries. So, for example, the Brazilian Navy was forced to abandon the idea of equipping new corvettes with domestic missiles and cannons of unproven reliability and effectiveness. This reliability issue can be considered one of the main problems that the armed forces may need to solve—both at the technical and operational level—in conjunction with the local defense industry before embarking on expensive development projects. The struggle between the users of defense equipment and the politically aware officers will continue until the reliability issue is solved once and for all.

6.3 PRIVATE INDUSTRY

Historically, local private firms have played secondary roles in the defense industries of semi-industrialized countries, even though these firms have significant roles in all the industrialized countries. As mentioned, this secondary role has been a result of previous heavy government involvement in the defense industry. This trend was reversed in Brazil in the early 1970s, in Chile during the late 1970s and early 1980s, and in Argentina during the late 1980s, following the trend in the overall economy toward a free market system as dictated by the respective governments.

With the high technological and financial barriers to entry enjoyed by the defense industry, it should be no surprise that private investors in these semi-industrialized countries were reluctant to enter the local defense industries. Private investors decided to embark on the domestic production of defense goods only after the local governments decided to promote local defense industries by securing the national market and by providing financing for the development of more sophisticated domestic defense equipment.

Most of the private firms that entered the defense industries did so with previous experience in either the heavy metalworks, transportation, or electric and electronic civilian industries, indicating that these sectors need to have some degree of development for enabling the creation of a modern defense industry. Also, most of these private firms started by working on modifications and upgrades of existing defense equipment, providing these firms with some experience in arms and defense equipment before committing them to full manufacturing of new or licensed designs.

It can be argued that in Brazil the strong presence of private firms in the defense industry was instrumental in the surge of defense exports during the 1980s. In Chile, the most important exporter of defense equipment was also a private company. The absence of private firms in the Argentinean defense industry can be considered a significant factor for the low volume of defense exports. As one anonymous Argentinean observer indicated, "Military people don't make good marketing people" (Porth, 1984, p. 66). Thus, the presence of private firms in the defense industry can be considered a driving force for increasing defense exports.

The financial difficulties faced by the major Brazilian private defense firms, some of them on the brink of bankruptcy by the end of the 1980s, illustrates the challenges faced by the defense industries when producing major weapons systems. It may take several years to master a certain kind of defense technology and a few more years to develop domestic proprietary products and to establish a dedicated production facility. During this time a firm must invest many millions of dollars of borrowed funds in the enterprise. Because of the long life expectancy of these major defense items (a war notwithstanding), it may take only another two or three years until the local defense market saturates and no more orders are placed by the armed forces. The international markets of other developing countries also saturate after limited sales because of foreign competition and the fulfillment of previously unmet needs. In all, perhaps five to eight years after production starts, the firm will stop receiving orders for its single-most important product. With very high development and retooling costs, in countries where the cost of capital is also high, it becomes extremely difficult for these private defense firms to develop a replacement product able to fill the gap. With no more cash flow and with outstanding debt already incurred for capital investment, layoffs become unavoidable and bankruptcy becomes the only alternative. In industrialized countries this problem used to be solved by means of successive improvements and new generations of weapons systems, rendering existing defense equipment obsolete before it could serve out a normal life cycle. For semi-industrialized countries, this forced obsolescence process is too expensive and almost unthinkable.

This realistic scenario indicates that for private firms in semi-industrialized countries major arms sales are a one-shot deal. It is wrong for a private defense firm to invest in capital and infrastructure and assume a long-term demand for the product. The niche and manufacturing strategy adopted by Brazil for its most successful products—light armored vehicles and dual-use aircraft—can be considered the best product strategy to be pursued by these firms: medium technology derived mostly from civilian components, medium prices, medium volume, use of existing infrastructure, and general-purpose manufacturing equipment.

In Argentina, Brazil, and Chile interfirm competition has been very weak or has not existed at all. Most competition was found in Brazil, where there are many private companies in the defense industry. This competition is more intense at the lower end of the technology spectrum where small items and general-purpose equipment are sold. At the more sophisticated end of the spectrum a single supplier is the norm. The competition for the main battle tank between Bernardini and Engesa, where each of the firms has produced only prototypes, has not been resolved. However, these tanks were developed somewhat exclusively for export, with no clear indication of intent by the Brazilian Army to purchase them. Under these conditions it is not clear which of these two firms will survive in the end.

In Chile a small degree of competition was found except that, unlike Brazil, it occurred mostly between a private and a state-owned firm—Cardoen and FAMAE in the manufacture of armored vehicles—with products not totally comparable. Another firm also produced a small number of simple armored vehicles, but it is difficult to assess this firm's competitive impact. However, in Chile, private companies have not yet been able to match the installed capacity of the state-owned firms and instead of head-to-head competition have achieved some degree of complementarity between state-owned and private companies. Clear examples of this complementarity have been ASMAR-Ferranti in the case of naval electronics by means of a joint venture, and FAMAE-Cardoen in the case of armored vehicles. In the case of FAMAE-Cardoen, both firms acted as subcontractors of each other for some production proceses.

In Argentina, no competition at all was found. All final production was concentrated in state-owned firms.

Latin America does not have a strong tradition of technology-based industrial development, and private firms have seldom been active participants in creating indigenous technology through research and development.[2] This circumstance has required the establishment of stronger links between the armed forces, their R&D establishments, universities, and the private and state-owned firms that participate in the local defense industry. This finding provides support to the hypothesis presented in Chapter 2, stating that increased defense production strengthens the technological infrastructure of the local economy.

6.4 LOCAL UNIVERSITIES

In the three countries studied, local universities have participated with dissimilar degrees in the effort to enhance the production of domestic defense products. Their main role—in addition to educating scientists, engineers, and managers—has been the cooperative effort with the local armed forces and the defense firms for carrying out research and development. Brazil is the country that has most clearly

---

2. The impact that the local capacity to generate technology has had on the defense industries of Argentina, Brazil, and Chile is explored extensively in Chapter 7.

utilized the technological capacity of the local universities. However, in Brazil university participation has been much less than is the norm in the United States and other industrialized countries. One of the reasons for this low participation is the political opposition faced by military governments in the local universities. As mentioned, military governments were the original promoters of the local defense industry. This political situation was strongly repudiated by university communities, reducing their willingness to participate in joint programs of any kind with the armed forces.

Another reason for the low profile of local universities in the defense industries of Argentina, Brazil, and Chile can be found in the emerging nature that graduate education has in these countries (Katz, 1986), particularly in the more technology-oriented areas of engineering and applied sciences. Also, the limited infrastructure and lack of sophisticated equipment for advanced research limit their capacity to provide better services to the local defense industry.

It can be argued that in Argentina, Brazil, and Chile the sometimes inadequate technological capacity of the local universities and their inclination toward more pure than applied science (as will be shown in Chapter 7) have been limiting factors in the development of more sophisticated defense equipment. Thus, local universities are institutions that need to reinforce their capacity to generate domestic technology for the local defense industry. This enhanced technical capacity will increase the technological content of the defense industry's products and services. The research and development projects undertaken by request of the local armed forces and defense firms represent one step in this direction.

6.5   FOREIGN DEFENSE FIRMS

For the defense industries of semi–industrialized countries, foreign defense firms are the most important and expeditious sources of technology. These firms provide licenses, know–how, process technology, and sophisticated components that cannot be produced locally. Such technology helps increase the quality and reliability of the arms and weapons systems manufactured locally. Licensed production has been considered the most important means for promoting and building up domestic defense industrial capabilities (OTA, 1991b, p. 25).

For these foreign defense companies, the weapons systems produced by semi-industrialized countries represent an additional outlet for their components, spare parts, and proprietary technology. This extended market increases the companies' return on investment and prolongs the economic life of technology and defense equipment that are already obsolete in the countries of origin. Such an extended market will indirectly increase the political influence of their respective governments.

Because of the reduction in defense spending in the industrialized countries during the last years, defense firms in those countries have needed to rely more heavily on exports to keep plants open and production costs down. Given the large number of defense firms willing to export, importing semi-industrialized countries have tied defense imports with technology transfer and offset agreements (OTA, 1991b, p. 13). This last circumstance has facilitated the acquisition of more advanced technology by semi-industrialized countries, thereby reducing the development costs of domestic defense equipment. However, Brigagao (1986) argues that this technology transfer process has been inefficient, not achieving the complete transfer of defense technology. As mentioned in Chapter 3, Brazilian-made defense goods combined many foreign-made sophisticated parts and components (Ross, 1984, pp. 260-261). Thus, incorporating large quantities of sophisticated imported parts and components into Brazilian-made defense goods precluded the effective transfer of know-how and manufacturing technology to develop and produce the same components in Brazil.

With the increased capacity that local defense firms have developed for adapting civilian technology for military purposes, foreign nondefense multinational corporations also play a role in producing defense equipment in semi-industrialized countries. As can be seen in the case of Brazil, foreign firms with subsidiaries in the automotive industry are also important suppliers of advanced parts and components for the production of light armored vehicles. In Chile, one private firm produced light armored vehicles using nonmilitary technology adapted from truck parts and components.

The absence of U.S. defense firms providing technology and parts to the defense industries of Argentina, Brazil, and Chile is noteworthy. In the first place, the absence of U.S. firms in the Latin American defense industry can be said to be a consequence of an explicit policy of the U.S. government to restrict defense exports, a selective tool for foreign policy (OTA, 1991b, pp. 3-31; Heinz, 1991, p. 19). In the second place, this absence of U.S. firms is also a consequence of self-imposed restriction on the part of the local defense firms for not using U.S. technology and components in their products, because it could make them liable to U.S. defense export laws. This restrictive policy toward Latin America in particular contrasts with the highly cooperative policy adopted by the United States in the Western Pacific region, where South Korea, Taiwan, and especially Japan enjoy lenient technology transfer agreements (OTA, 1991b, pp. 3–31). Again, this policy further reinforces the need for these semi-industrialized Latin American countries to develop their own defense industries in order to increase their political and technological independence.

Thus, foreign defense firms are very important agents in the emergence of modern defense industries in semi-industrialized countries. However, Germany's ban imposed on Argentina for the export of the TAM tank (on more than one occasion) indicates that an overly heavy involvement of foreign firms in the production of local products may curtail the capacity for marketing those weapons abroad. The same can be said about Cardoen Industries. This firm has the Swiss license to produce in Chile the MOWAG-Piraña family of armored vehicles but is not allowed to export these vehicles. A cautious balance between too much dependence and too much autarky is the recommended strategy.

6.6 COMPARISON BETWEEN DGFM, IMBEL, AND FAMAE, THE ARMY FACTORIES OF ARGENTINA, BRAZIL, AND CHILE

The most important similarity among DGFM, IMBEL, and FAMAE, the three corporations that produce arms and weapons used by the respective armies, is that they are state owned, with substantial industrial infrastructure, and have many plants operating in several parts of each country. The three factories started their productive history with the local fabrication of light weapons, artillery shells, and explosives. With the exception of IMBEL since the early 1980s, the other two firms are still managed by army officers.

Dirección General de Fabricaciones Militares (DGFM) in Argentina was chartered with the responsibility of establishing associated firms that would enable the local production of defense equipment. This very broad charter allowed DGFM to create associated firms in the areas of steel, electrical machinery, communications, petrochemicals, fertilizers, mining, and forestry (Millán, 1986; *Tecnología Militar*, no. 12, 1986, p. 17). This strategy effectively turned DGFM into the largest corporation that operates in Argentina (Porth, 1984). Even though this effort by DGFM certainly helped to industrialize the Argentinean economy of the 1950s and 1960s, it also led to an extremely high overcapitalization and low efficiency of the Argentinean defense industry, as will be shown in Chapter 8. On the other hand, the extensive vertical integration of DGFM resulted in a high degree of logistical depth of the defense industry, allowing for the domestic production of quite-sophisticated defense equipment based on autochthonous technology. No such high degree of vertical integration was found in Brazil or Chile.

The Brazilian counterpart of DGFM, IMBEL, has had a low profile in the overall defense industry, and the fact that it was placed under the management of a civilian indicates that the Brazilian military was not interested in having a centralized defense production process. This low profile also resulted from the early participation of private firms in the Brazilian defense industry and the significant industrial capacity of the civilian industry, which was adapted for the production of defense items. This adaptation made a heavier state involvement unnecessary.

In Chile, FAMAE's participation in the defense industry is more important than IMBEL's but less so than DGFM's. In spite of being a military production company run by the Chilean Army, FAMAE participates in the overall economy by providing engineering and manufacturing services in the heavy metalworks and also by producing items such as plows and hand tools that are sold in local stores. This civilian-oriented market-driven industrial activity increases returns on investment and also provides a higher market orientation in the decision-making process, thereby improving economic efficiency. The increased participation of private firms in the Chilean defense industry has allowed FAMAE to act as prime contractor in some projects, extending its role beyond manufacturing and becoming involved in the overall procurement process.

The large size of the Brazilian armed forces also allowed for the attainment of scale economies, further facilitating the participation of private firms able to reap profits from producing military hardware. Scale economies in the Brazilian defense industry were further increased through large volumes of exports. In Argentina and Chile, given the smaller size of their armed forces and the very low volume of Argentinean defense exports, scale economies in the local production of defense equipment probably have not yet been realized. Thus, these two countries would still require the state to subsidize defense production in the form of direct financing of investment projects and salaries of public workers, further explaining the higher state-ownership of defense firms when compared with Brazil.

The production of tanks and armored vehicles in Argentina is done solely by DGFM, with almost no participation from private industry. In Chile, various armored vehicles are produced by FAMAE and by other private firms. On the other hand, tanks and armored vehicles in Brazil are produced only by private firms, with almost no government participation. The reason for the dissimilar structure of this industrial segment across the countries can be found in the degree of centralization in decision making shown by the defense industry as a whole. In Brazil, the government provides only broad policy guidance and support, with private industry being responsible for production. In Argentina, on the other hand, production and decision making are totally centralized, even having an undersecretary for military production at the Ministry of Defense level. Chile stands in between these two countries, with private industry not strong enough to take all the responsibility for production. The results of the export effort by each of these countries undoubtedly favor the approach and industrial structure adopted in Brazil.

In Argentina, the government made heavy investments in the local defense industry, and DGFM built an extensive infrastructure for the local production of weapons systems. Thus, regardless of the lower prices (when compared with local production costs in Argentina) of defense equipment available in the international market, it may seem unthinkable that arms produced locally in state-owned factories would also be imported. With the very high production costs of items produced under autarkic policies in an overcapitalized Argentinean defense industry, these items could only be exported by means of further government subsidies. In this case, since the government is the financier, producer, buyer, importer, and exporter, autarkic considerations become self-sustaining. Only when the purchaser is not the same as the producer is it possible to break free of the autarkic vicious circle. When the purchaser and producer are two separate entities, the purchaser will not be concerned with the previous investments or financial losses brought about because of economic inefficiencies of the producer. This argument implies that the privatization of the Argentinean defense industry might be an important policy that would help it break free of its heavy autarkic tradition.

Autarky has proven to be a double-edged sword: On the one hand, it truly helps to increase the industrial capability of the country, but, on the other hand, it does so by providing domestically developed and produced goods at higher costs and with outdated embodied technologies. In defense-related terms, autarky increases the logistical depth of the defense industry and the volume of arms produced locally, allowing the armed forces to engage in longer-lasting sustained conflicts. However, the defense goods produced under autarkic principles are of low technological content and are easily outperformed by less numerous but more sophisticated modern weapons systems acquired abroad. In any event, absolute autarky has historically proved impossible even for industrialized countries, and more so for semi-industrialized and developing countries that finally need to resort to foreign technology to improve their products.

6.7 COMPARISON BETWEEN FAMA, EMBRAER, AND ENAER, THE AIRCRAFT PRODUCERS

The three aircraft producers FAMA,[3] Embraer, and ENAER were created by their respective governments with the intent of establishing domestic capability to produce mostly military aircraft. However, since its inception Embraer was conceived as a mixed company, with capital provided by the government and private investors. The company is also run by civilians as a private firm.

Embraer has not concentrated only on military aircraft, and its most successful products—the Bandeirante and the Xingu—had strong dual uses, based mostly on civilian aircraft technology licensed from abroad. With the experience gained in developing and producing these dual-use aircraft, Embraer was able to embark on producing more sophisticated aircraft with purely military applications. The market sought by this company was global, exporting its dual-use products even to industrialized countries.

Argentina's FAMA has had a very different strategy. It has been a state-owned company since its creation, run by the military for purely military purposes. With no dual or civilian use, only a few of its products have been exported. The technology has seldom been licensed but has instead been primarily transferred by foreign engineers, again following strong autarkic guidelines. In spite of its long tradition in the military aircraft industry, FAMA had to request German assistance to design its most advanced aircraft, the jet-

---

3. FMA (Fábrica Militar de Aviones) later became FAMA (Fábrica Argentina de Materiales Aeroespaciales). For simplicity, FAMA is used in this section.

powered IA–63 Pampa. This process for assimilating and developing technology would indicate that previous experience and success with older technology developed with autarkic principles in mind cannot be considered an assurance of success when dealing with new and sophisticated technology.

While Argentina's state-owned FAMA concentrated on producing, at any cost and with indigenous technology, exclusively military aircraft for its air force, Brazil's semiprivate Embraer concentrated on dual-use aircraft produced with foreign technology that could be sold abroad.

ENAER, in Chile, has had the least experience in the field and has also relied on transferred technology from abroad for its products. However, in spite of being managed by Chilean Air Force officers, ENAER is a state-owned corporation run with economic considerations in mind. ENAER concentrated on foreign markets early on, exporting and using offset agreements to acquire foreign technology. Another type of aircraft produced by this company is a small locally designed civilian-use airplane that uses novel composite materials, indicating the company's intent to become involved in civilian aircraft production.

Thus, it can be inferred that aircraft production in Brazil and Chile has been more attuned to commercial success and has relied more on transferred technology than its Argentinean counterpart. Important private participation in the case of Brazil has also allowed for a broader vision of the global market and imposed profit-seeking criteria in its operations, thereby increasing the defense industry's economic efficiency.

6.8 THE SHIPBUILDING INDUSTRIES

The shipbuilding industry is perhaps the industrial segment where more similarities exist across the three countries. All naval production is performed in state-owned arsenals, though with some private participation in the case of Argentina for producing submarines and Brazil for small corvettes. In these three countries, the navy is the organization in charge of running the shipyards, and significant importance has been given to technology transfer, mostly from the United Kingdom and Germany.

Chile is the country that has shown the lowest level of activity in the shipbuilding construction industry, relying more on the transfer of large secondhand ships than on the local construction of new ones.

This strategy seems to have been successful when considering the problems faced by neighboring Perú and Argentina when they embarked on the local construction of major warships. Brazil also had its own problems during the construction of the Niteroi frigates, and the country has been criticized because of the high costs incurred in the local production of warships when compared with the price of new units purchased abroad.

One of the aspects not considered by the respective shipyards when deciding to build large warships domestically is the low local demand for such units. In order to carry on such a significant project, there is need to establish a large capacity for handling heavy plates and all kinds of steel parts and to train professionals and technicians in engineering and constructing a particular design with imported blueprints. In all, a large effort needs to be devoted to creating a significant capacity, both human and technical, to construct such large naval vessels.

As it happens, once the first or second units are finished—with large investments and substantial technical difficulties—there is no more activity planned for the next five or so years, not even for constructing similar units. This makes the learning process useless and the installed capacity overrated for the expected demand of the next years. Also, most of the weapons systems and electronic equipment installed in those units are imported, with minimal participation of the local industry and with very scant technology transferred at high costs. In the end, shipbuilding companies must make an extremely large investment in order to provide employment to a reduced work force that will not be needed after a couple of years. This spending results in a minimal return on investment, if indeed there is any positive return.

In both Brazil and Argentina, there is ample installed capacity in the civilian shipyards for constructing large merchant vessels. It can be argued that if this capacity had been better utilized—for example, by assigning the construction of the naval vessels to the civilian shipyards—lower overall costs could have been achieved. These lower costs would then in turn have allowed for the transfer of the absorbed technology to produce civilian-use ships. In the case of Brazil, in the early 1990s some of the naval construction responsibility had been transferred to a private shipyard for constructing the Inahuma corvettes. This transfer indicates a move toward increased participation of civilian shipyards.

6.9   CHAPTER SUMMARY

The comparison of the defense industries of Argentina, Brazil, and Chile sheds light on the overall problems and circumstances faced by semi-industrialized countries in establishing an industrial policy aimed at fostering the emergence of a modern domestically based defense industry.

Private firms, and to a lesser extent universities, have played important roles in the emergence of the Brazilian defense industry. In Argentina, the defense industry is composed of state-owned factories that operate almost without regard for economic criteria. In Chile, even though there are a majority of state-owned defense firms, these firms operate as independent and self-financed economic units under a charter that forces these firms to have a strong commercial orientation. The lower profile of private firms in Chile when compared with Brazil and their almost absolute absence in the case of Argentina have been a consequence of the state-directed economies adopted by these countries during the 1950s and 1960s. The market-driven economy adopted in Chile after 1973 fostered the emergence of private defense firms. The privatization of the Argentinean defense industry was only at the planning stage at the end of the 1980s, with some efforts toward majority private participation when deciding how to establish new defense firms.

Even though they are influential players in industrialized countries, local universities have played a secondary role in the defense industries of Argentina and Chile. One of the reasons for their minimal participation has been the historically low technological capability that these institutions have had in Latin America in general. However, even this limited participation has helped reinforce the technological infrastructure and linkages of the local economies. Improving the technology-generating capacity vis-à-vis the science-generating capacity of universities may become a pressing need if these countries desire to achieve higher domestic technology content.

The emergence of a more sophisticated defense industry has increased the training and educational requirements of the members of the armed forces who participate in the management and production process of the state-owned defense firms. The armed forces have also needed to become more involved in operating the defense industry by defining the operational requirements of the locally produced defense equipment.

Naval construction is a capital-intensive endeavor that, in the case of semi-industrialized countries, has a low assured demand. Thus, in economic terms, this circumstance makes it hard to justify major naval construction programs that are discontinued after a few years.

Governments are one of the most important agents in this overall process, since, by establishing laws and policies, they create the environment in which defense firms operate. Therefore, the basis for a modern and productive defense industry depends on the following aspects:

- a free market economy,
- strong government support for R&D and technological innovation,
- heavy reliance on private firms over state–owned ones,
- open access to sources of technology from industrialized countries,
- a vision of the defense market as being global in nature with unrestricted access to all markets (after taking into consideration obvious strategic circumstances), and
- sustained political support by the government.

Legislation enacted to promote these conditions will foster the industrial innovation needed to produce advanced defense equipment.

As this chapter has shown, a sound industrial policy aimed at establishing a modern and productive defense industry in semi-industrialized countries has to deal with a large set of endogenous and exogenous variables, making it difficult to determine the best set of targeted policies to attain this goal. Some of the problems and possible solutions have been identified within this chapter.

7

The Relationship between Science and Technology and the Defense Industries in Latin America

This chapter analyzes the influence that the science and technology policies of Argentina, Brazil, and Chile have had on their respective defense industries. Both quantitative and qualitative analyses are performed on science and technology indicators collected from diverse sources. Also analyzed are the changes in degree of sophistication of the weapons produced over time by the defense industries of these countries.

One of the problems encountered during the research was the lack of consistent and reliable data on the science and technology indicators for Latin America. In part, this is due to the fact that the countries of Latin America do not have sound statistical collection capabilities and also to the emerging nature of the scientific and technological process in the region. Thus, the scientific and technological indicators of Latin America used in this chapter can be considered somewhat imprecise because (1) these indicators are collected with inadequate statistical accuracy and (2) very limited literature exists that reports truncated time series or only single-year figures. Unfortunately, no recent data are available about current defense R&D expenditures for Latin America.

Similarly, no defense production data are available. Therefore, total defense production for Argentina, Brazil, Chile, Colombia, Mexico, Perú, and Venezuela has been represented by a defense production rank based on estimated total defense production. We ranked Argentina, Brazil, and Chile based on the *approximate* calculations of total defense production of Chapter 8. Colombia, Mexico, Perú, and Venezuela were ranked on *assumed* total defense production. Therefore, taking into consideration the imprecision of the science and technology data and the approximate nature of total defense production, the conclusions that can be derived from the correlation of the defense production rank and the science and technology indicators should be considered only indicative of a tendency and not fully reliable.

7.1   SCIENCE AND TECHNOLOGY INDICATORS OF SOME SEMI-INDUSTRIALIZED LATIN AMERICAN COUNTRIES

Some of the indicators that can generally be used to assess the effectiveness of science and technology policies in developing countries are (adapted from Morita-Lou, 1985, p. 18):

- *Change in R&D expenditures over time.* An effective science and technology policy will tend to increase expenditures in science and technology over time. Bilich (1989, pp. 183–186) shows that there is a strong positive statistical correlation ($R^2 = 0.74$) between the percent of GNP that a nation devotes to R&D activities and the well-being of the society as measured by the GNP per capita. Because the development of military technology is resource intensive, it could be expected that a similar pattern of higher military production capability and military technological innovation will have a positive correlation with larger expenditures for research and development activities at the national level.
- *Number of scientists and engineers engaged in conducting research and development.* As in the case of R&D expenditures, effective science and technology policies will increase the total number of researchers working in R&D organizations.
- *R&D expenditures per researcher.* Increased R&D expenditures per researcher will improve the quality of research equipment and facilities, as well as the availability of better support personnel.
- *Number of patents granted to residents.* Improved science and technology policies will encourage the development of proprietary technology; thus, the number of patents awarded to residents will increase. The number of patents awarded to residents, however, is dependent on several factors besides the specific technical activity. Some of these factors include the

importance assigned to patents by industry;[1] government encouragement of the patent activity and enforcement of patents rights; and the relative importance of process technology vis-à-vis product development in the economy. In general, it can be argued that developing countries would be more inclined toward using process technology for exploiting primary resources where patents are scarce and difficult to enforce, as compared with industrialized countries where product development with the corresponding patents is given much more importance.

- *Patents per researcher, as a proxy for R&D productivity.* With improved research infrastructure and support personnel, it can be expected that the productivity of researchers will also increase. Since patents represent an indirect measure for assessing the productivity of researchers, the number of patents per researcher will increase with more effective science and technology policies.
- *Patents per dollar of R&D expenditures to assess the efficiency of the research system.* Considering funds as the input to the research and development process and patents as one of the outputs, more efficient research activities will be reflected in lower costs per patent.
- *Number of scientific publications per researcher.* This indicator indirectly helps to assess the productivity of scientists that cannot be appraised by using patents. Patents reflect to a greater extent the productivity of engineers.

Some of the science and technology indicators identified above for the countries that have the largest armed forces and the largest GNPs in Latin America are shown in Table 7.1. This table shows that Argentina, Brazil, and Chile have the largest number of scientists and engineers per million inhabitants, well above Mexico, Perú, and Venezuela. The number of scientists and engineers per million inhabitants for Colombia is extremely low, indicating that this country has a very low capacity to generate domestic technology. Therefore, it can be argued that Argentina, Brazil, and Chile have, in regional terms, the most qualified technical manpower to engage in developing indigenous technology.

---

1. Low importance for fast-changing technology like computer hardware and very high importance in the case of products that have long commercial lives and high development costs like pharmaceuticals.

Table 7.1

Science and Technology Indicators for Selected Latin American Countries

Country	Year	Sci& Eng/ Mill Habs[1]	R&D % GNP[1]	Total R&D Sci&Eng[1]	R&D Budget M US$[2]	Patents per Year[3]	M US$ / Sci&Eng	M US$ / Patent	Patents/ Sci&Eng
Argentina	1988	352	0.5	11,088	406.5[87]	1,590	0.0367	0.2557	0.1434
Brazil	1985	390	0.7[2]	52,863	2,218.4	1,308	0.0420	1.6960	0.0247
Chile	1988	363	0.5	5,323[2]	81.8[87]	71	0.0154	1.1521	0.0133
Colombia	1982	40	0.1	1,083	43	7	0.0397	6.1429	0.0065
Mexico	1984	215	0.6	16,679	1,698.1	138	0.1018	12.305	0.0083
Perú	1981	273	0.2	4,858	70	12	0.0144	5.8333	0.0025
Venezuela	1983	279	0.3	4,568	183.7	58[4]	0.0402	3.1672	0.0127

Sources: [1]UNESCO, 1990, for the year shown except where index indicates another year.
[2]CONICYT, Chile, 1990.
[3]Bilich, 1989, pp. 147–64.
[4]CONICIT, Venezuela, 1986.

Note: Patents per year are patents awarded to residents per year, circa 1980, according to Bilich, 1989.

In terms of the percent of the GNP devoted to research and development during the mid-1980s, Brazil stands out as the country that invested the most during the period, with 0.7 percent. Mexico is the second regional investor in R&D activities, with 0.6 percent GNP. Argentina and Chile follow in third place, with 0.5 percent of GNP devoted to R&D activities. Again, Colombia appears with the lowest relative investment in science and technology, with only 0.1 percent of GNP devoted.

In terms of total number of patents awarded to residents, Argentina stands out as the country with the most productive technological manpower of the region, even though it does not have the largest contingent of researchers nor the largest budget. As can be seen in Table 7.1, Argentinean researchers are the most efficient—measured in terms of dollars per patent—and productive—measured by patents per researcher—of the region. This would indicate that technology generation in Argentina has become an institutionalized process, with an important capability to develop domestic products and processes. In this area, Argentina is well above its closest regional followers, Brazil and Chile, when considering the efficiency and productivity of its research manpower.

The indicators of million dollars per patent and patents per researcher for Argentina appear to be outliers when compared with the same indicators obtained for the other Latin American countries, as shown in Table 7.1, as well as when compared with industrialized countries (Bilich, 1989, p. 115; CONICYT, Chile, 1990). However, the million-dollars-per-researcher indicator is well within the range of all these other countries. In the case of Argentina, this discrepancy would indicate either an overestimation of the number of patents granted to nationals or a patent-granting policy that has some bias against foreigners. Since patents are reported by an official organization of the Argentinean government, the only explanation would be a patent policy that favors granting patent rights to nationals over foreigners. Historically, the number of patents granted to nationals has been much higher in Argentina than in other Latin American countries (Evenson, 1984). Thus, the higher productivity of Argentinean researchers might be influenced by the patent policy of the country. The much higher figure of Argentinean patents per researcher and total patents when compared with industrialized and Latin American countries should be regarded with caution when deriving conclusions based on these two indicators for the Latin American region.

Table 7.2

Publications per Researcher for Selected Latin American Countries

Country	World Rank	Number of Publications	Publications per Researcher
Argentina	29	5,621	0.507
Brazil	28	7,494	0.142
Chile	38	2,951	0.554
Colombia			0.225*
Mexico	36	3,547	0.213
Perú			0.047*
Venezuela	43	1,555	0.340

*   For Colombia and Perú, from Bilich, 1989, p. 169, for
          period 1978 to 1980. Here multiplied by 5/3 to cover
          different time span with other countries' data.

Note: Publications per researcher derived from number of
          publications shown here and number of researchers shown
          in Table 7.1.

   Based on data published in 1988 by Glanzel and Shubert in
Scientometrics (CONICYT, 1990, p. 101) and by Bilich (1989, p. 169),
the number of scientific publications of the most productive Latin
American countries for the period between 1981 and 1985 are listed
in Table 7.2. According to the number of scientific publications per
researcher, Chile emerges as the country with the most productive
scientific work force in Latin America, followed by Argentina and far
behind by Brazil.
   Considering that publications are an index of scientific
productivity, and patents an index of technological productivity
(Bilich, 1989, p. 73), the fact that researchers in Brazil are much more

productive in terms of patents (ranked second in Table 7.1) than of publications would indicate that the research activities in Brazil are oriented mainly toward generating technological rather than scientific knowledge. Conversely, Chilean researchers are more oriented toward scientific rather than technological activities.

Another consideration is that in semi-industrialized countries scientists are almost exclusively employed in universities. Keeping this in mind, and also considering that patents are of prime importance to industry, it is possible to infer that most of Chile's scientific activity is centered at universities, whereas Brazil's technological activity takes place primarily in industry. This fact allows Brazil to have a more important industrial capacity, in spite of an apparently lower scientific productivity.

Since arms and weapons systems rely much more on technological than on scientific knowledge, and also on industrial more than on university research, it can be expected that arms production would be more predominant in Brazil than in Chile. This is in fact the case.

Table 7.1 shows that Argentinean researchers are the most productive in terms of patents (with the caveat already mentioned), and Table 7.2 ranks them second in terms of publications. This ranking indicates a balanced research work force able to support a broad spectrum of research and development projects, both science and technology based.

The case of Mexico is worth noting. In terms of number of researchers, the R&D work force of Mexico is the second largest of the region, with the largest budget in terms of total dollars and the second largest in terms of percentage of the GNP devoted to science and technology activities. This combination results in the largest R&D budget per researcher, more than double Brazil, its closest follower. However, in terms of dollars per patent, Mexican researchers spend almost 11 times the amount spent by Chilean researchers to obtain a patent and are 3 times less productive in terms of patents than Brazilian researchers. According to the indicator of publications per researcher, Mexico rates fifth following Colombia. The significance of all these science and technology indicators helps to conclude that the Mexican science and technology infrastructure, manpower, and related policies are somewhat inefficient, thus inhibiting the capacity of the Mexican scientific and technological community to develop domestic technology.

From the Latin American science and technology indicators presented above, it is apparent that the research and development infrastructure and work force of Argentina, Brazil, and Chile are the most productive and efficient of the region for generating domestic technology. These countries are followed by Venezuela, with Mexico, Perú, and Colombia in the less advanced group. Thus, the science and technology indicators shown allow us to infer that Argentina, Brazil, and Chile would possess a relatively higher capability to generate their own innovative technologies. According to this evidence, and taking into account that Argentina, Brazil, and Chile are also the countries with the most important domestic defense industries of Latin America, it can be argued that the generation of defense technology has a strong relationship to the technological capability of the country. This argument lends support to the postulate presented in Chapter 2—that the defense industry should be based on the overall industrial and technological infrastructure of the economy and cannot be created apart from it.

The relatively larger scientific and technological work force of Argentina, Brazil, and Chile, together with these countries' higher productivity and efficiency in the technology-generating field, could help overcome two of the many problems identified by Katz (1986) that may hinder the development of military technology in developing countries. These problems are (1) the low availability of scientific and technical personnel, which may become the bottleneck for technological advancement and (2) the requirement of unique talents for solving technical problems. These are the areas where less developed countries are notably weak (Katz, 1984).

In Perú, the lack of significant technological capacity as evidenced by its low standing in regional terms would help explain the failure of the Peruvian defense industry to produce modern arms and equipment, in spite of the demonstrated capacity to build two Italian frigates during the 1980s and the support provided by the large defense expenditures of the Peruvian government in the past decades (ACDA, 1990).

7.2   CORRELATION BETWEEN DEFENSE PRODUCTION AND SCIENTIFIC AND TECHNOLOGICAL INDICATORS

As will be shown in Chapter 8, Argentina is the Latin American country that produced the largest sales volume of defense products and weapons systems in the mid-1980s, followed closely by Brazil, with Chile occupying third place. Besides the three countries mentioned, Perú and Mexico also have some defense industry capacity, with the Peruvian being more significant than the Mexican (Brzoska and

Ohlson, 1987). Of the countries considered here, Venezuela and Colombia are the ones with the least important activity in the defense industry. These considerations allow ranking these countries according to their approximate and estimated defense production capacity as follows: Argentina, 5; Brazil, 4; Chile, 3; Perú, 2; Mexico, 1; and Venezuela and Colombia, 0. Table 7.3 shows the correlation coefficients between the science and technology indicators of Table 7.1, the publications per researcher of Table 7.2, and the defense production rank defined here.

As can be seen from Table 7.3, defense production rank is positively significantly correlated with three of these indicators: (1) the total number of patents granted to residents ($p = 0.009$), (2) total scientists and engineers per million habitants ($p = 0.022$), and (3) number of patents per researcher ($p = 0.038$). However, in order to test for the effect caused by the higher-than-expected number of patents in Argentina, when this country is removed from the sample, the correlation with patents decreases and becomes weaker. By removing Argentina, the other significant correlations also become weaker, indicating that Argentina has a strong statistical influence on the sample.

It can be argued that the defense technology utilized by the armed forces of semi-industrialized countries is more sophisticated and advanced than the technology utilized in the rest of the economy. Thus, the positive and significant correlation between defense production and patents granted to residents (with the caveat that it is based on scarce and somewhat inexact data) would suggest that the domestic production of arms and weapons systems is related to the domestic capacity for creating proprietary technology. This correlation between the level of defense production and the number of patents granted to residents provides further support to the proposition that the defense industry, and its capacity to produce more advanced weapons, is dependent on the overall technological infrastructure of the country.

Bilich (1989, p. 150) indicates that in Chile the ratio of patents granted to nonresidents over patents granted to residents—an index of technological dependency, according to Bilich—decreased from 15.46:1 in 1967 to 5.86:1 in 1987. Consequently, Bilich concludes, the technological dependency of Chile has been reduced significantly. Assuming that the number of patents granted to nonresidents in each country is almost constant over time—an exogenous variable dependent mainly on the patent activity of industrialized countries—it can be

Table 7.3

Correlation Between Science and Technology Indicators and Defense-Production Rank

Indicator	Correlation with Defense-Production Rank
Patents to Residents	0.8390 *** (0.7046)
Sci& Eng/Mill Habitants	0.7665 ** (0.7919)*
Patents per Sci&Eng	0.7051 * (0.6719)
R&D/GNP Percentage	0.6174 (0.6728)
M $ per Patent	-0.6145 (-0.4853)
Total Sci&Eng	0.4870 (0.6949)
Publ. per Sci&Eng	0.3312 (-0.0555)
R&D Budget M U.S. $	0.2766 (0.4760)
M $ per Sci&Eng	-0.2752 (-0.2999)

Note: Figures in parenthesis when Argentina is removed from the sample.

* $p < 0.05$
** $p < 0.025$
*** $p < 0.01$

concluded that local defense production goes hand-in-hand with reduced technological dependence. Bilich also shows that between 1974 and 1982 the number of patents granted to residents in Brazil increased more than 10-fold, from 119 to 1,308. Considering that this same period coincides with the emergence of a world-class Brazilian defense industry, it is possible to conclude that a significant reduction in the technological dependency of Brazil can be associated with, but not fully dependent on, the emergence of a prominent domestic defense industry.

The two other significant positive correlations—found between defense production with number of scientists and engineers per million inhabitants and with patents per researcher—provide further support to the hypothesis that the defense industry should be based on the overall industrial and technological infrastructure of the economy and cannot be created apart from it. Thus, a substantial availability of technically qualified and productive research personnel appears to be a prerequisite to the emergence of a significant domestic defense industry.

Neuman (1984) also found a strong positive correlation between the number of technical, professional, and industrial workers in each Latin American country and each country's military production capability. However, Neuman failed to realize the technological implications of this correlation by ascribing it to scale factors related to a country's population, GNP, number of personnel of its armed forces, and its land size. Because the variables employed here are relative (i.e., scientists and engineers per million inhabitants and patents per researcher), the scale effect has been taken care of, leaving only the technological explanation of the correlation. Thus, besides the scale effects found by Neuman as explanatory variables for military production capability, the availability of qualified and productive research professionals needs to be added. Steinberg (1985) argues that the emergence of the Israeli defense industry was possible only because of the large availability of qualified scientists and engineers at the inception of the state of Israel. This argument also gives support to the findings presented here.

As expected, the correlation between increased defense production and larger expenditures in research and development was found to be positive but small and nonsignificant. The same can be said about the correlation with total number of scientists and engineers, which was also small and nonsignificant. These nonsignificant correlations suggest that in Latin America increased defense production does not correlate with an increase in the R&D budget nor with the utilization of a larger contingent of researchers. However, it is not possible to assess what percentage of Latin American researchers work in defense-related activities.

The examples of Argentina, Brazil, and Chile illustrate that the emergence of modern defense industries in semi-industrialized countries creates mission-oriented research centers managed by the armed forces, and that this emergence also increases the interaction of defense firms with universities and other research centers. It can be concluded, then, that in semi-industrialized countries the emergence of modern defense industries strengthens the technology-generating infrastructure of these countries' economies, thus supporting one of the most important hypotheses of this book. This conclusion is based on the following facts:

- the creation of previously nonexistent defense research centers dedicated to developing advanced technology,
- the technical interaction they generate with the rest of the scientific and technological community, and
- the enhanced association they foster among defense firms, universities, and other local research centers.

Thus, it appears that there exists a positive reinforcing process between the defense industry and the scientific and technological capacity of semi-industrialized countries. However, it must be stressed that this enhanced capacity will be useful to the rest of the economy only if it is based on an open defense production system.

7.3   MEASUREMENT OF TECHNOLOGICAL ADVANCEMENT IN THE DEFENSE INDUSTRIES OF ARGENTINA, BRAZIL, AND CHILE

Technological change can be assessed either by measuring the changes in the relative utilization of the factors of production—technological change according to economic theory (Chambers, 1988, p. 203)—or by assessing the changes in the embodiment of technology in the goods produced as revealed by the characteristics of different products (Uzumeri, 1991, p. 75). The first of these two methods requires the availability of complete time series for prices and levels of production factors and of the inputs to, and outputs of, the production process—in this case, related to the defense industry. The scarce available data of the defense industries of Latin America do not allow the measurement of technical change according to economic practice; thus, the only other method available will be utilized here. This method is the assessment of the changes in technology embodiment as revealed by changes in the technical characteristics of the products.

It is customary to analyze defense production by focusing on only four broad groups of major arms and weapons systems: aircraft, armored vehicles, warships, and missiles. This convention is utilized in particular by SIPRI (1990) for analyzing the production, development, and transfer of arms. Since this classification is a clustering of weapons systems according to their use, it is also an implicit classification of the core technologies (Abetti, 1989) required for designing and producing the respective weapons types. Thus, this same classification will be adopted here for assessing technological change in the Latin American defense industries as measured by changes in the technical characteristics of defense products.

Even though defense production in Argentina, Brazil, and Chile can be traced back to the last century, as the previous chapters on each country have shown, the most significant events that are related to the emergence of a modern Latin American defense industry date only from the 1960s onward, in particular, the 1980s. According to this time frame, a data base of defense products was built for Argentina, Brazil, and Chile with the main weapons systems already identified, according to the information provided by the specialized *Jane's* set of defense publications. These publications describe aircraft (*Jane's All the World Aircraft*, 1960 to 1991), armored vehicles (*Jane's Armour and Artillery, 1991-92*, 1991), and warships (*Jane's Fighting Ships*, 1970, 1980, 1991). For the purposes of this book, the period from 1960 to 1991 was divided into three decades, a decade being a reasonable time for the development of new weapons systems.

To assign scores and measure technological change, weapons either assembled or produced in each of the three countries since the 1960s were first categorized by class: aircraft, armored vehicles, or warship[2] (subindex i). These "i" classes were further divided by type: fighters, bombers, transport, and trainers, in the case of aircraft; destroyers, frigates, corvettes, submarines, and transport, in the case of warships; main battle tanks, light tanks, howitzers, and armored personnel carriers, in the case of armored vehicles (subindex j). For each class

---

2. Missiles and rockets were excluded from the data base because the information available was incomplete for most of the different systems produced.

i and type j weapon system, a set of $k_{i,j}$ technology-related characteristics was identified (e.g., speed, altitude, power plant size, etc.). A particular score was assigned to each one of these characteristics according to their degree of technical sophistication. Finally, the sum of all the $k_{i,j}$ scores for each type of weapon system gives a consolidated technology merit index.[3] Thus, the technology merit index for each weapon system type j of class i is obtained as:

Tech. merit index weapon type j class i = Σ_k tech. scores $k_{i,j}$

where weapons type j = different weapons types of the same class i; and class i = warships, armored vehicles, and aircraft. The more sophisticated the weapon system type either produced or assembled in the country, the higher its technology merit index.

For each decade, the technology merit indices of the new weapons types produced in each class were added, resulting in an overall technological score for each class. Further adding these scores across classes yielded a consolidated technology merit index for the whole country during the decade:

Country tech. merit index = $\Sigma_i \; \Sigma_j$ tech. index$_{i,j}$

As such, when assessed during the three decades, this technology merit index reflects across several dimensions the evolution of the technological capabilities of the domestic defense industries. It reflects the production of several types j of the same kind of weapons systems class i (technological variety or "depth"), different classes of weapons systems i (scope or "breadth"), and the degree of technological sophistication of the various types of different classes of weapons systems produced (technology embodiment).

For comparative purposes across countries, technology embodiment in relative terms (relative degree of sophistication) is obtained for each decade and class as the *maximum* technology merit index for each type j of weapon system:

Tech. embodiment index class i = max$_j$ (tech. index type i,j)

This procedure made it possible to measure for each decade the degree

---

3. The full data base can be found in Maldifassi (1992), together with the explanation for the assignment of scores.

of technology embodiment in the new weapons systems produced in Argentina, Brazil, and Chile, as reflected by the constructed technology embodiment index. These measurements are presented and discussed in detail in the following sections.

7.3.1   Technological Development in the Argentinean Defense Industry

According to the evolution of the technological merit index of the Argentinean defense industry during the last three decades, as calculated according to the procedure described above and shown in Figure 7.1, it can be concluded that the development of defense technology in Argentina has been steadily increasing since the 1960s. This increase in the technology merit index has been achieved by means of only a slight increase in the case of aircraft, mostly because aircraft had been produced locally in Argentina before 1960; some noticeable increase in the production of armored vehicles, achieved with the family of the TAM series of armored vehicles; and a very important increase in the development and production of warships, which during the 1960s showed no activity.[4]

The fact that in Argentina the three types of major weapons systems experienced an increase in their respective technological merit indices in each of the three decades indicates a substantial and sustained effort in the development of all kinds of military technologies.   Even though this important effort is indeed a technological accomplishment, it also resulted in the overcapitalization of the Argentinean defense industry, as will be shown in Chapter 8. Hence, the Argentinean defense industry during the 1980s became the most inefficient among the three defense industries studied here.

As can be observed in Figure 7.1, the technology merit index in Argentina almost doubled (100 percent increase) every decade, and there is no evidence in the literature of a comparable level of technological change and degree of sophistication in the rest of the Argentinean economy.   The only possible exception is Argentina's nuclear program, which was also strongly linked to its armed forces.

---

4. Argentina built an indigenous family of corvettes in the late 1950s that was not covered by the time frame chosen here (Jane's Fighting Ships, 1970).

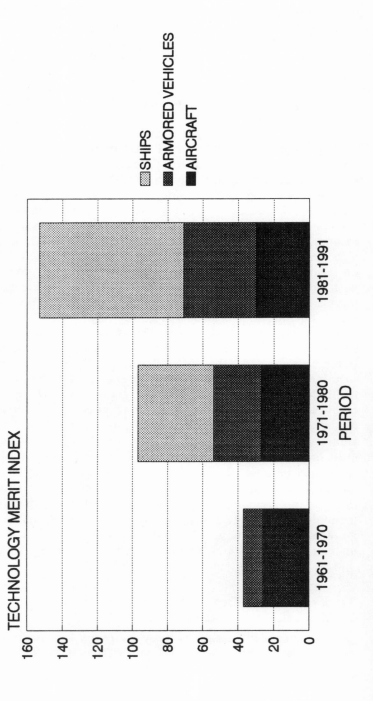

Figure 7.1

Argentina: Technological Development of Weapons Systems

According to the evolution of its technology merit index, it can be concluded that the development and embodiment of technology in the Argentinean defense industry have exceeded the advancement of technology in the rest of the nondefense industry. This finding indicates that the defense industry has clearly been in the forefront of the technological boundary of Argentinean industry, corroborating the relationship found between defense production and patents granted to residents.

7.3.2 Technological Development in the Brazilian Defense Industry

In Brazil during the 1960s, it was possible to find activity only in the aircraft industry, even though, as in Argentina, a family of domestic warships was produced during the late 1950s. As can be seen in Figure 7.2, defense production had a radical improvement in the three classes of systems considered, with an almost ninefold (900 percent) change in the technological merit index from the decade of the 1960s to the 1970s. This dramatic and almost explosive change in the capacity to generate indigenous defense technology in Brazil may explain the large amount of publicity with which this process was surrounded, not to mention its marketing effect, which was labeled as an "economic miracle" (Brigagao, 1986). As in the case of Argentina, no evidence exists of such a dramatic improvement in Brazil's level of technological sophistication of the nondefense industrial sector.

As indicated in Chapter 3, Brigagao (1986) explains that the Brazilian defense industry took up the excess capacity in other technological and industrial sectors that resulted from its economic recession during the 1960s. Thus, the emergence of a significant defense industry in Brazil required no additional investment in new manufacturing capacity, and the overcapitalization of the defense industry experienced by Argentina was avoided.

Even though there was an increase in the technological merit index of the Brazilian defense industry from the decade of the 1970s to the decade of the 1980s, this increase was small in comparison to the previous one. This increase was experienced mainly in armored vehicles and warships.

During the 1970s, the major export products of the Brazilian defense industry were civilian and military aircraft. Aircraft was also the class of weapons that experienced the most significant change in the technology merit index from the previous decade, if one takes

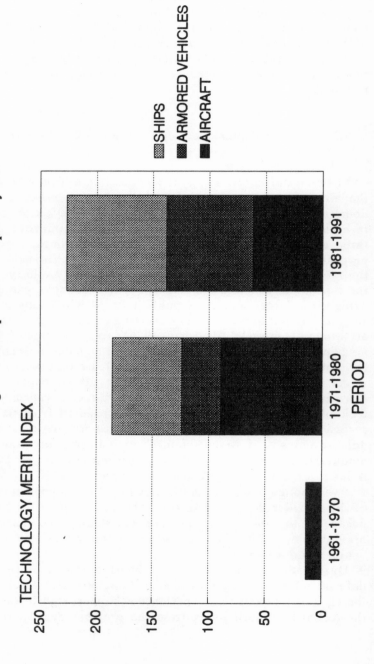

Figure 7.2

Brazil: Technological Development of Weapons Systems

into consideration that in the late 1950s the shipbuilding industry experienced some activity. During the 1980s armored vehicles were the main export items of the Brazilian defense industry—again, the class that experienced the largest increase in the technology merit index during the same decade. According to this analysis, it can be argued that the development of weapons in Brazil has been tied more to international market considerations than to the requirements of the Brazilian armed forces.

It appears that during the decade of the 1980s Brazil attained the maximum point in the development of conventional weapons, producing main battle tanks, frigates, subsonic fighters, and short-range missiles. According to this level of sophistication, it can be expected that during the 1990s there will occur still another increase in the technological merit index in the Brazilian defense industry. This increase will lean toward even more sophisticated technology. Some evidence of this shift is already shown by the nuclear submarine project and by missiles of higher precision and longer range.

Taking into consideration that the main market for Brazilian weapons during the 1980s was the Third World because of the ruggedness and convenient prices of the weapons exported, this shift toward weapons of higher sophistication will reduce the marketability of Brazilian weapons and will also increase development costs. The combination of both effects will contribute to the total costs of this production effort to the Brazilian government, which is already overburdened by the external debt problem. Thus, it can be expected that the variety of weapons produced in Brazil will decline substantially, at the same time that the degree of sophistication of the weapons will increase. Some evidence of this increased sophistication at the expense of reduced variety already exists in aircraft production. Even though experiencing an overall decline in the technology merit index during the decade of the 1980s, aircraft showed an increase in the degree of sophistication (see Figure 7.5).

7.3.3   Technological Development in the Chilean Defense Industry

As mentioned in Chapter 5, during the decades of the 1960s and 1970s, the most significant activity of the Chilean defense industry was carried out by ASMAR with the construction of small naval vessels. The lack of activity in the production of armored vehicles and aircraft during these two decades can be seen in the very low technology merit index up to 1980, as shown in Figure 7.3. Also, the low technology merit index of the 1960s and 1970s can be attributed to excessive reliance on imported weapons and to the general low level of industrialization of the Chilean economy.

With the enhanced capacity provided by the new slipway that ASMAR inaugurated in the mid-1970s, the establishment of ENAER for aircraft manufacturing, and the licenses obtained from Switzerland for the local production of the first armored vehicles ever produced in Chile, the technology merit index increased almost 13-fold (1,300 percent change) from the 1970s to the 1980s. The most important activity can be seen shifting from warships to armored vehicles, where the activities of the private firm Cardoen Industries can be considered of prime significance. However, several of the armored vehicles included in the Chilean data base during the decade never reached full production and were limited to prototypes.

Although the magnitude of the change in the Chilean technology merit index from the 1970s to the 1980s can be considered more prominent than in the cases of Brazil and Argentina, in absolute terms it was attained with heavy reliance on imported licenses and starting from a very depressed prior activity of the local defense industry, which made any improvement seem very significant. Also, existing manufacturing capability and infrastructure were utilized, and, with the exception of Cardoen Industries, production was located almost entirely within the existing state-owned companies. These facts would indicate that a great amount of existing industrial, human, and technological capability was underutilized during the decade of the 1970s. Evidence of the underutilized capacity of the Chilean defense industry is provided by General Boisset of the Chilean Air Force, who indicated that the technology transfer from Spain to produce the Halcón aircraft in Chile was much faster than what the Spanish engineers and managers had expected (Boisset, 1991). More evidence of this underutilization comes from the shipbuilding industry. The first naval craft fabricated in ASMAR's new slipway was an oil-drilling rig, a very complex structure and engineering system that demanded a great degree of diligence and expertise by ASMAR engineers and production work force. The manufacturing contract for this project was won in an open international competition.

Given that the industrial capacity existed, the most probable reasons for the Chilean defense industry's ability to create locally produced sophisticated weapons were the political decision to do so and the funds needed for the initial investments. Most probably, the political decision was prompted by the embargo imposed by the

Figure 7.3

Chile: Technological Development of Weapons Systems

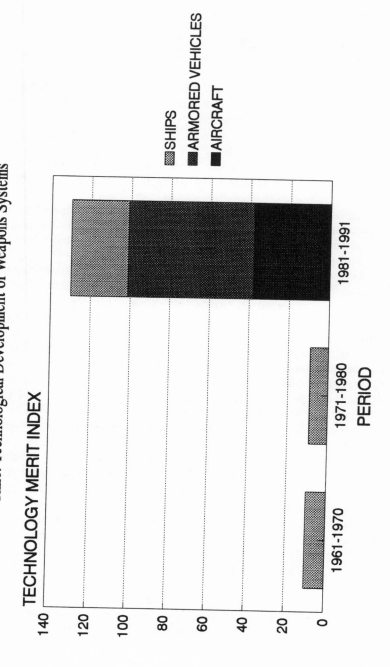

United States and some European countries during the late 1970s, whereas the funds probably came from the reduction in weapons imports caused by the same embargo.

The dramatic change in the technology merit index of the Chilean defense industry from the 1970s to the 1980s cannot be compared with any similar change in the overall Chilean economy. As in the previous cases of Argentina and Brazil, one can infer that the defense industry in Chile has also been in the forefront of the technological industrialization of its economy.

7.3.4   Comparison of the Technological Development in the Defense Industries of Argentina, Brazil, and Chile

The descriptions of the technological development in the three countries studied here show different patterns.   To help in the comparisons, Figure 7.4 shows the overall technology merit indexes for Argentina, Brazil, and Chile.

Argentina has been gradually increasing its domestic capability to produce military technology, based mostly on its institutionalized capacity to generate its own technological innovation via its highly productive and efficient science and technology work force.   This industrial and technological effort to produce more sophisticated defense equipment and arms in Argentina has been sustained for several decades, with a balanced distribution of resources among the different classes of major weapons systems, resulting in a very deep industrial capability.   As already mentioned, this increased industrial capacity led to the overcapitalization of the Argentinean defense industry because of the need for a large variety of highly specialized manufacturing equipment with low utilization factors.

Brazil, after a slow start during the 1960s, increased the number of weapons produced and their degree of sophistication by using idle manufacturing capacity in the rest of the economy.   Also, with the help of imported technology, particularly for components, Brazil surpassed the technological capability of Argentina in a single decade, then maintained its lead.   Thus, it seems highly improbable that Argentina will surpass Brazil in the future.

In the 1960s, Brazil and Chile showed very similar defense technological capabilities.   However, after the explosive growth of the Brazilian defense industry during the 1970s, Chile was relegated to a very distant third place.   According to the technological merit index of the 1980s, Chile can be considered to be more than 20 years

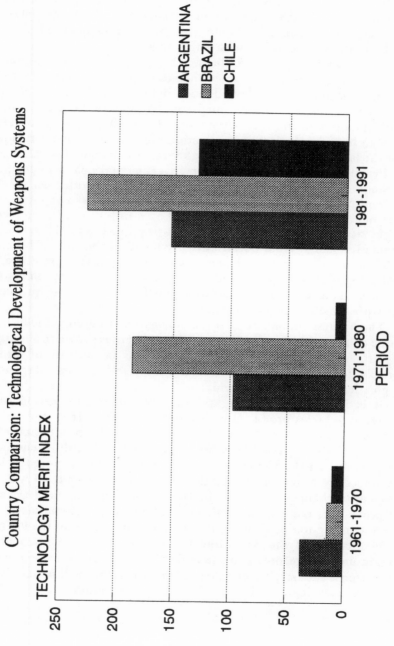

Figure 7.4

Country Comparison: Technological Development of Weapons Systems

behind the technological capability of the Brazilian defense industry, in spite of the significant improvement of the Chilean defense industry during the same decade. However, Chile has shown a dramatic increase in its technology merit index during the last decade and has almost caught up with Argentina.

As shown in Figure 7.5, during the 1960s and 1970s Argentina's aircraft were more sophisticated than those of Brazil, as evidenced by the highest technology embodiment index in this class of weapons systems. However, Brazil surpassed Argentina in the degree of sophistication of its aircraft during the 1980s, showing a rate of change in technological sophistication much higher than Argentina's for the last three decades. This higher rate of change of sophistication in Brazil was achieved by greater governmental commitment to the technological development of new weapons, as evidenced by large expenditures in research and development for military purposes. Chile lags behind both Argentina and Brazil by a full decade in the level of sophistication of aircraft produced during the 1980s. However, the dramatic change from no aircraft produced during the 1970s to the fabrication of aircraft with some degree of sophistication during the 1980s highlights the commitment of the Chilean defense industry to increase its level of technological sophistication and attempt to catch up with the other two countries.

The highest embodiment of technology on armored vehicles by the three countries during the time considered here is shown in Figure 7.6. Again, Argentina clearly leads, and, just as in the case of aircraft, Brazil took more than two decades to surpass Argentina's sophistication in armored vehicles.

It is interesting to note that the level of sophistication of the armored vehicles produced by Argentina declined from the 1970s to the 1980s. This decline can be attributed to the production of the TAM tank during the 1970s, an achievement difficult to emulate or surpass during the following decade. Most of the armored vehicles produced by Argentina during the 1980s derived from the TAM, with no major changes to the basic frame, thus making it difficult to improve over the original tank and its technology embodiment.

According to this finding, it is possible to assert that the degree of sophistication of the Argentinean armored vehicles has reached its maximum. Therefore, a substantial effort by the government and by the defense industry's technological infrastructure will be required to attain higher degrees of technological sophistication.

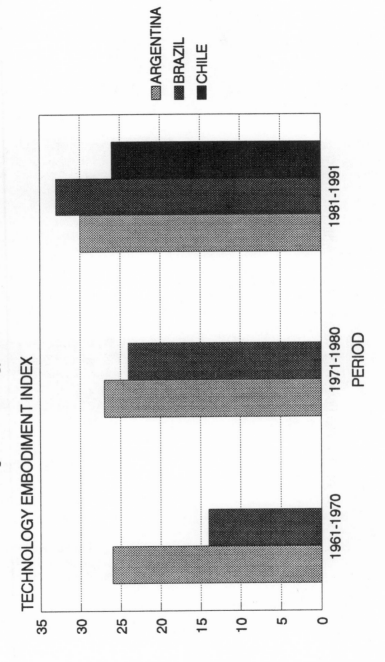

Figure 7.5

Highest Technology Embodiment Index: Aircraft

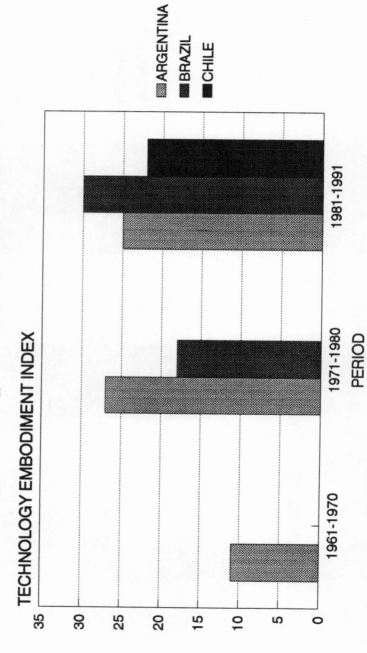

Figure 7.6

Highest Technology Embodiment Index: Armored Vehicles

The steady increase in the sophistication level of the Brazilian armored vehicles, as in the case of aircraft, is clear again. The degree of sophistication of the TAM was surpassed by Brazil only one decade later, by two domestically designed main battle tanks—the Tamoyo of Engesa and the tank by Bernardini. These two tanks have reached only the prototype stage, whereas the TAM reached full production and was even being exported. The effort required for designing and engineering the Tamoyo main battle tank drained the resources of Engesa, indicating the high degree of effort required for manufacturing such units in spite of the large number of components of European origin (Sohr, 1990).

Since main battle tanks are the most sophisticated armored vehicles to be produced, it can be expected that in the future Brazil will give more emphasis to the domestic development of currently imported components in order to increase the level of local technology and value added. However, the market for main battle tanks is very small, and the industrialized countries have control of that segment of the international arms market, thus making it difficult for Brazil to recover the investment made in developing and producing this kind of armored vehicle. Such recovery is even more difficult if one considers that there are two Brazilian firms with prototypes ready for production. Thus, it appears that Brazil has reached the maximum level of sophistication of its armored vehicle, almost reaching the same level of sophistication of industrialized countries. In no other industrial field has Brazil ever been able to achieve this high level of sophistication of its products, thus showing that defense technology is at the vanguard of the technological development of the Brazilian economy.

In armored vehicles, Chile stands almost 10 years behind the technological level of sophistication of Argentina and even farther behind Brazil. Chile lacks the capability to design the more advanced vehicles of this class. In fact, the most sophisticated armored vehicle fabricated by Chile was a self-propelled Howitzer licensed from South Africa, of which only a prototype had been built by the end of 1990. However, during the 1980s Chile did have technical expertise for producing armored vehicles similar to the ones produced by Brazil 10 years before.

As already mentioned, both Argentina and Brazil constructed some warships before 1961. These warships were not included in the time frame of the data base employed here. Thus, it appears that of the three countries studied, Chile was the only one to show some degree of activity in the construction of warships during the 1960s, as shown in Figure 7.7. However, the degree of sophistication of the Chilean naval craft fabricated during the 1960s was low and was thus very easy to surpass during the following decade.

The Niteroi class of frigates produced by Brazil during the 1970s was the most sophisticated warships ever produced in Latin America. Two of these units were built in Brazil (*Jane's Fighting Ships, 1991-92*, 1991, p. 57), along with a training ship that has the same basic characteristics of the Niteroi class. This Brazilian achievement lasted for the whole decade, until Argentina produced under license the British Type 42 destroyer during the 1980s. This destroyer has a slightly higher technology embodiment index. However, the large amount of human and capital resources required for the local production of the Type 42 destroyers in Argentina has not been well utilized. Only a single unit has been built, limiting the country's opportunity to reap the benefits of the learning curve and of higher capacity utilization. As already indicated, this process reduced the efficiency of the Argentinean defense industry.

The two other kinds of warships more sophisticated than those already produced by Argentina and Brazil are aircraft carriers and nuclear submarines. Currently, both Argentina and Brazil have the technological capability to produce conventional submarines, albeit under license. Some indications exist of Argentina's intent to locally produce a nuclear submarine (*Tecnología Militar*, no. 3, 1983, p. 97), and the Brazilian nuclear submarine project is already being executed (*Jane's Fighting Ships, 1991-92*, 1991, p. 53). From this buildup, one can infer that the production of warships in both countries has reached levels of technological sophistication similar to the levels existing in industrialized nations. Again, these levels surpass the technological level of the civilian industry.

The change in the level of technological sophistication of the Chilean warships, when compared with the changes experienced by the other two countries, is notably small. In fact, Chile lags behind Argentina and Brazil by more than 10 years with respect to the technology embodiment of its new naval constructions, in spite of the increased capacity provided by ASMAR's slipway and the existing human expertise to carry out significant engineering projects. Sohr (1990, p. 76) indicates that this reduced level of naval construction in Chile has not been a drawback but a correct decision in light of the problems experienced by both Perú and Argentina in their respective naval programs for producing foreign-designed warships locally. In this sense, Chile has been cautious to build up its capability for locally producing warships, avoiding unnecessary overinvestments that will

Figure 7.7

Highest Technology Embodiment Index: Warships

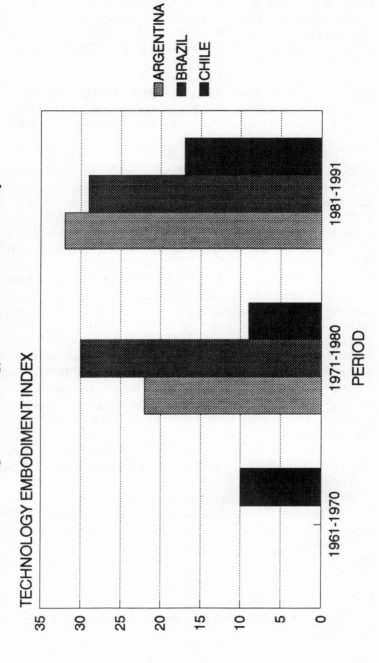

not be utilized in the short run. This prudent approach has been supported by the purchase of secondhand warships that have been repaired and modernized at costs well below those of producing new units, thus helping to explain the high efficiency of the Chilean defense industry. This subject will be explained in the next chapter.

7.4 COMPARATIVE ASSESSMENT OF THE SCIENCE AND TECHNOLOGY POLICIES WITH THE MILITARY TECHNOLOGY POLICIES OF ARGENTINA, BRAZIL, AND CHILE

Barke (1987, pp. 11–12) defines science and technology policy as "a governmental course of action intended to support, apply or regulate scientific knowledge or technological innovation." Stoneman (1987, p. 36) defines technology policy as "policies involving government intervention in the economy with the *intent* of affecting the process of technological innovation" (emphasis added). Both definitions point to government intervention through several actions as an element that affects the pace of technological innovation.

In the case of military technology, given the high levels of sophistication of modern arms and weapons systems, and the particular interest of the government in having effective and efficient armed forces, there is a clear need for governmental support of the technological innovation process in the development of military technology. This need for support is evidenced by the large budgets allocated for this purpose in industrialized countries.[5] Katz (1986) argues that there is a remarkable similarity between military technology policy and mainstream science and technology policy in the Third World; thus, important insights can be gained concerning the development of indigenous military technology by analyzing the science and technology policies of the Latin American countries of interest.

In order to be able to assess the impact of the national science and technology policies (S&TPs) on the respective defense industries, one must first assess the main characteristics that the local S&TPs have along several parameters and then compare these parameters across countries.

---

5. See Table 3.3 for defense R&D expenditures in industrialized countries for the mid-1980s.

7.4.1   Science and Technology Policies of Argentina, Brazil, and Chile

Bilich (1989, p. 62) presents a framework for analyzing and comparing the S&T strategies of nations taking, into consideration the following situational categories:

- *Science and technology commitment.* The amount spent for science and technology development as a percentage of the GNP will be used as the variable to measure the commitment with the S&T process. The percentage values for this variable were introduced in Table 7.1.
- *Timing.* Timing will be defined as the relatively earlier or later emergence of an institutionalized national science and technology capability, with an earlier capacity considered to be a positive indication of the S&TP characteristics. There are several organizations chartered to develop specific technologies that can be considered to determine historically the emergence of indigenous technological capabilities. However, some of these technologies are more significant than others in terms of their technical requirements and political commitment. Since nuclear energy is a very sophisticated technology based also on scientific activity, its emergence is marked by a purposeful government policy and important financing. Thus, the decade when an important capacity to absorb and develop nuclear technology was demonstrated will be used here as the time when the emergence of an indigenous technological capacity took place. In Latin America, the first country to develop an important indigenous capability in nuclear energy was Argentina in the 1950s, followed by Brazil in the 1960s, and of the countries of interest here, later by Chile in the 1970s (Maldifassi, 1988a, p. 64). Vessuri (1990) indicates that Argentina was the Latin American country that developed its scientific and technological base at an earlier stage, thus giving support to ranking Argentina first among the three countries. According to this criterion, the order mentioned indicates the timing considered for developing an indigenous capability in S&T.
- *S&T breadth.* Bilich (1989, p. 84) uses as a proxy for S&T breadth the number of scientists and engineers per million inhabitants. The figures for this variable were presented in Table 7.1.

- *S&T depth.* Again, the variable used by Bilich to assess this category is the dollars per researcher, as shown in Table 7.1.

Using the four indicators presented above, it is possible to infer that among the three countries studied here Argentina can be considered to have institutionalized the generation of domestic technology before Brazil and Chile.   However, Brazil's larger commitment to industrialization and technological self-sufficiency, when compared with Argentina during the 1960s and 1970s, allowed Brazil to increase the breadth and depth of its science and technology activities.   This increase allowed Brazil to cope with the advantage provided by Argentina's early start and thus surpass Argentina's S&T capability.   In any event, Argentina's balance of technological productivity (measured by patents per researcher) and of scientific productivity (measured by articles per researcher), when compared with the disparity of these two indicators for Brazil, would indicate that the Argentinean S&TP has been institutionalized to a higher extent than in Brazil.

The S&TP of Brazil appears to have outperformed in the four measures—commitment, timing, depth, and breadth—the S&TP of Chile.   This fact helps to explain the relatively higher technological and industrial capacity of Brazil.

Comparing the S&TPs of Argentina and Chile, it is possible to observe that Chile outperforms Argentina only in the case of breadth, with Argentina having a much earlier start in creating a science and technology capability and also a greater depth in implementing its S&TP.   Chilean scientists apparently outperform their Argentinean peers only in terms of publications per researcher. Since this indicator is not an important aspect for developing military technology, the capacity of the Argentinean S&TP to generate defense products can be expected to be higher than that of Chile, as is in fact the case.

Comparing the S&TPs of Argentina, Brazil, and Chile leads to the conclusion that the more comprehensive and supported the overall S&TP of a country, the stronger would be its technological capacity to generate domestic defense products.

7.4.2   Assessment of the Military Technology Policies of Argentina, Brazil, and Chile

Using the same framework discussed previously for assessing the overall science and technology policies of these countries, according to Bilich's methodology, the following can be stated about the military technology policies of Argentina, Brazil, and Chile:

- *Commitment.* As already indicated in the chapters on Argentina, Brazil, and Chile, the development of military technology has enjoyed different degrees of support by the respective governments' budgets for the development of science and technology. In broad terms, this support has been important in the case of Brazil, with approximately $245 million a year, or 13.7 percent of Brazil's science and technology budget during the late 1980s dedicated to military technology development. This support has been less important for Argentina, which in 1978 officially devoted 17.94 percent of national R&D expenditures for the Ministry of Defense, 0.2 percent to the Argentinean Navy, and 1.72 percent to the Argentinean Air Force. In 1983, this support was reduced to only 4 percent of the Argentinean R&D budget allocated for the Ministry of Defense (Roper and Silva, 1983, p. 6). Chile's government budget for science and technology development provided no direct support until 1990, even though defense research in Chile is conducted with funds allocated from the respective services' budgets and private and state-owned defense firms. Brazil's commitment to developing indigenous defense technology resulted in the highest rate of change in the technology merit index of the three countries studied here. This change helped Brazil—in a single decade—to improve from second to first place in the region in terms of technological sophistication and variety of its weapons systems.
- *Timing.* Argentina has been supporting R&D for military purposes since the 1950s, when it created the first organization for developing military technology. The evolution of the technology merit index shows that this timing allowed Argentina to have the most sophisticated defense industry of the Latin American region during the 1960s. However, this position was soon surpassed by Brazil with its higher commitment and overall investment in this area.
- *Depth.* The overall level of sophistication of Brazilian weapons during the 1980s was the most advanced of the three countries, followed by Argentina, with Chile in last place.
- *Breadth.* Again, during the 1980s Brazil was the country with the greatest military breadth, as measured by the number of

different arms and weapons systems produced, followed by Argentina and then Chile.

Except for timing, the Argentinean military technology policy is also surpassed by the Brazilian policy, just as in the case of the overall national S&TP described earlier.   This earlier start-up allowed Argentina to outperform Brazil only during the 1960s, since Argentina was not able to keep its advantage because of a relatively lower commitment to develop military technology and also, no doubt, because of a relatively lower availability of scientists and engineers. Another element to consider is Argentina's intent to pursue an independent—and thus expensive and time-consuming—military technology program based on state-owned and -operated research and production facilities and to rely on foreign technology and private firms only as a last resource. On the other hand, Brazil relied mostly on private firms and used foreign licenses and components to increase its military technological capability, reducing the time and costs required to produce similar equipment.   It is clear that Brazil's technological policies have been much more effective than Chile's at the military and overall national level.

By a relatively higher commitment to its military technology development than Chile, Argentina has been able to cope with the larger breadth that Chile has measured in terms of researchers per million inhabitants.   This ability to cope with this disadvantage indicates a more effective military technological activity by the Argentinean technological base, which together with its earlier start and institutionalization of its S&TP has helped Argentina to keep ahead of Chile in the variety and level of sophistication of its domestic arms and weapons systems.

In Brazil, there is a good correspondence between the overall national science and technology policy and military technology policy. In the case of Argentina, the military technology policy has been more effective than the national S&TP because of Argentina's higher funding commitment that, when compared with Chile's, helped to overcome the relatively lower availability of scientists and engineers. Apparently, there is not much agreement between the military technology policy and the national S&TP in Chile, because there is a decrease in the commitment to developing defense technology, which has reduced, in comparative terms with Argentina, the breadth of this military technological effort. Given this relatively lower commitment, and the late entry of Chile into the development of military technology, the weapons produced by its defense industry have been of lower sophistication and variety than the ones produced by Argentina and Brazil. Chile, therefore, lags behind these two countries by almost a decade (or more, in some cases) in terms of these two indicators. In Chile, the relatively more predominant capacity toward creating scientific rather than technological know-how (as shown by its relatively higher standing in terms of publications per researcher than in patents per researcher) would have also hampered the capability of the Chilean defense industry to produce more sophisticated weapons systems.

It can be inferred that national science and technology policy affects and limits the characteristics and effectiveness of military technology policy by creating a human and technical base on which the defense industry draws its expertise and capabilities. Because defense technology needs a broad spectrum of techniques and thus access to, and availability of, many experts in each of these areas, efforts for creating domestic defense industries that are isolated from the technological realities of the country will be doomed to failure. However, some countries will only reach this conclusion after years of unfruitful efforts and large expenditures.

7.5 CHAPTER SUMMARY

This chapter shows that a close relationship exists between the national science and technology policy and the military technology policy of the semi-industrialized countries. The S&TP shapes the military technology policy and provides the defense industry with the necessary resources, infrastructure, and know-how.

A statistically significant correlation was found between the level of military production rank and the following indicators: number of patents awarded to residents per year, number of scientists and engineers (researchers) per million inhabitants, and number of patents per researcher. These correlations—with the express caveat already discussed—may suggest that military production is influenced by the relative availability and productivity of scientists and engineers who perform R&D and that such production is also related to the local capacity to generate proprietary technology. To support military production, technical activity (measured by patents awarded to residents and patents per researcher) is apparently more important than scientific activity (measured by publications per researcher).

The statistically significant positive correlation between defense production rank and the number of scientists and engineers doing research per million inhabitants also indicates that university education and research training can influence military production.

The statistically significant correlation between defense production rank and patents per researcher suggests not only that there is a need for a higher relative availability of scientists and engineers but also that these professionals need to be technically productive (as measured by the number of patents per researcher). This finding helps enrich the characteristics of countries able to produce significant levels of military equipment as identified by Neuman (1984), which can then be listed as vast land size, large GNP, large military forces, large population base, and a relatively significant and technically qualified research work force.

The capability to generate technical rather than scientific know-how can be said to be of greater significance for the development of military technology. This finding implies that technological developments pursued in industry resulting in patents are more important than scientific activity carried out at universities leading to journal articles. However, if universities employ the greatest pool of researchers and generate the larger body of know-how, the defense industry will need to resort, with appropriate incentives, to academic researchers to increase the generation of military technological innovation.

Military production rank proved to have a significant positive correlation with the total number of patents granted to residents per year. This correlation, however, was obtained using an approximate defense production rank and patent statistics considered to be highly biased in favor of locals over foreigners. Thus, the development of military technology can only be said to enhance local capacity to generate proprietary technology.

The emergence of defense industries in semi-industrialized countries was found to have a positive impact on the technology-generating infrastructure of their economies. This finding, together with the positive influence that science and technology policies have on the defense industry, shows that there exists a positive reinforcing process between the defense industry and the scientific and technological capacity of semi-industrialized countries. Only if it were possible to transfer the increased levels of technological sophistication of the defense industry to the rest of the economy either in terms of generic technologies, production processes, or design methods would the effort devoted to generating military technology be useful to the economy at large. This transfer process could be much easier if the same firms that are engaged in producing arms and defense equipment are also engaged in the production of civilian goods, particularly at the plant level, a proposition supported by Gansler (1980, p. 266). This technology transfer process through integration of civilian and military production would be very difficult if the state-owned defense firms operated by the armed forces are chartered as arsenals or factories and not connected with the rest of the economy.

The fast pace of change in sophistication of Brazilian defense products can be attributed to the heavy commitment shown by the Brazilian government in terms of financial resources, which helped overcome a slow start when compared with Argentina. However, this significant rate of change was also possible because a strong technical work force and idle industrial capacity existed, thereby providing this larger availability of financial resources in order to generate indigenous defense technology.

The weapons produced in Brazil during the 1980s reached levels of sophistication similar to industrialized countries—well above the level of sophistication of products manufactured by the civilian industry. In both Argentina and Chile, it is also possible to assert that domestically produced military equipment and weapons systems are well ahead in the degree of sophistication (as measured by their technology embodiment) when compared with the products manufactured by the civilian sector in general.

8

Assessment of the Economic Impact of the Defense Industries in Argentina, Brazil, and Chile

In this chapter an assessment is presented of the economic impact of the defense industries of Argentina, Brazil, and Chile. This is done by focusing on the actual results of the respective import substitution policies and on relative production, export, employment, and factor efficiency of the defense industry as compared with the national manufacturing sector. The assessment is carried out for the period between the early 1970s and the late 1980s, when the most significant increases in defense production occurred.

8.1 DETERMINATION OF DOMESTIC DEFENSE PRODUCTION

In order to assess the economic impact of the defense industry in a given country, we first need to determine the total production that the defense industry has achieved over time. As it is almost impossible to obtain actual production levels because of the confidentiality of such information, an approximate method is used.

The calculations to determine the production levels are based on the figures of dollars per soldier (DPS). This indicator is calculated as follows:

$$\text{DPS} = \frac{\text{Defense budget - defense imports}}{\text{Number of military personnel}}$$

For the three countries studied, Argentina, Brazil, and Chile, the yearly DPS was calculated according to the data published by ACDA (1980, 1990) covering 1969 to 1988. For this 20-year period, the minimum value of DPS realized was selected. This minimum DPS was assumed to represent the minimum possible expenditures per soldier that would allow the armed forces to operate. Thus, it is assumed that in the year when the minimum DPS occurred the defense budget was devoted to arms imports, minimum operational expenses, military personnel salaries, and minimum infrastructure maintenance, with no purchases at all of domestic arms and equipment.

This minimal national expenditure can be associated with financial difficulties at the national level that mandated a reduced defense budget, or with stringent political restrictions imposed on the defense budget by the respective governments. For Argentina, Brazil, and Chile it was found that the year when the minimum DPS occurred, the defense budget was also the lowest of the period analyzed, giving support to the assumption of minimum defense expenditures for that particular year.

According to the data provided by ACDA (1990), the following are the minimum DPS obtained:

Argentina:	$ 6,339 in 1972
Brazil:	$ 3,929 in 1979
Chile:	$ 1,609 in 1976

According to this indicator, the minimum DPS for Chile is almost four times smaller than the minimum DPS for Argentina. Dividing the DPS by the per capita GNP, to correct for dissimilar income across countries, results in another indicator called the DPS index. After dividing the minimum DPS by the respective per capita GNP, the minimum DPS index of Chile becomes only 2.87 times smaller than that of Argentina. Thus, the somewhat large difference in the minimum DPS between Chile and Argentina can be said to be caused in part by differences in the per capita income.

Assuming then that the minimum DPS is the least that can be spent per soldier to operate the armed forces, the total expenditures in military personnel for the other years during the period 1969 to 1988 are obtained as:

Soldiers costs year i = DPS_{min} × no. of military personnel year i

According to this methodology, after paying for arms imports and for soldiers costs each year, all remaining funds are *assumed* to be devoted to national purchases of defense equipment (including services) in the local defense industry. Thus, national defense purchases are obtained as:

National purchases = defense budget - defense imports - soldiers costs

In this way, the minimum personnel and operational requirements are satisfied for each year. The results of these calculations for Argentina, Brazil, and Chile are shown in the Appendix.

It must be recognized that the approximate nature of these calculations do not consider real salary increases to the members of the armed forces. Nevertheless, these changes are accounted for by real increases in the defense budget, giving more credibility to the assumptions made. Also, it must be realized that not all national defense purchases correspond to manufacturing (SIC 3). Some are construction services (SIC 5), explosives (SIC 2), or food or other services. With the level of aggregation of the data available, it is not possible to correct for these nonmanufacturing-related purchases, resulting in a higher estimate of the actual national purchases of defense equipment.

On the other hand, it is also possible that in the year when the DPS are minimum, a certain amount of purchases of local defense equipment may have taken place. This means that the national purchase amounts as calculated here can be an underestimation of domestic arms production. Overall, with both effects taken into account, the national purchases figures can thus be considered a fair approximation of the actual total of national defense purchases.

The difference in the minimum DPS across countries may have also been caused by the intensity of the operations carried out by the respective armed forces in each country during the year when the minimum DPS occurred. A more intense level of operations will increase the minimum DPS because of larger amounts of fuel, supplies, spare parts, and food requirements.

If the minimum DPS for Argentina is considered too high when compared with Chile or even Brazil, then the national purchases of Argentina along time will tend to be higher than the figures obtained for the original calculations. In the case of Chile the inverse will tend to be true; that is, a higher minimum DPS will result in lower national purchases. The effects of these changes will be explored in the following sections.

8.1.1 Structure of the Argentinean Defense Budget

With the information provided by the above calculations it is possible to derive the approximate structure of the defense budgets of Argentina, Brazil, and Chile across time. The changes in emphasis between national purchases and imports and the share of the defense budget that they represent will allow us to determine the presence of import substitution policies.

Figure 8.1 shows the evolution of the Argentinean defense budget between the years 1969 and 1988. From 1969 to 1973 a very large share of the budget was devoted to cover what here has been termed "soldiers costs." In fact, in 1972 around 85 percent of the budget was devoted to cover soldiers expenditures.

In 1972 the Argentinean defense budget was the lowest of the 20-year period analyzed. After 1973 a gradual increase in the defense budget can be observed, which until 1977 was devoted mainly to national purchases. From 1978 onward, when the border disputes with Chile intensified, a sustained military buildup occurred. Imports increased from $72 million in 1977 to $621 million in 1978. This high level of arms imports was sustained until 1983, when—after the South Atlantic war—$1.1 billion was spent on imported weapons to replace arms and material lost during the war. Since 1983 the levels of military imports have steadily declined.

Figure 8.1 also shows that Argentina's national purchases increased dramatically from $88 million in 1973 to $4.4 billion in 1982, at an approximately compounded growth rate of 48 percent a year. This steady increase, together with a small increase or almost steady level of imports, indicates a strong military buildup effort supported by imported weapons and a strong component of local weapons. This military buildup culminated in the South Atlantic war of 1982.

As was shown in Chapter 7, the degree of technological sophistication of the weapons produced during this period can be considered moderate, well beyond the small arms and other simple weapons of low sophistication produced during the previous decade.

After the 1982 war the Argentinean defense budget decreased to a decade minimum in 1987, reducing imports almost to zero and at the same time reducing national purchases and soldiers expenses. In 1988 almost 80 percent of the Argentinean budget was invested in national purchases, the highest percentage during the overall 20-year period.

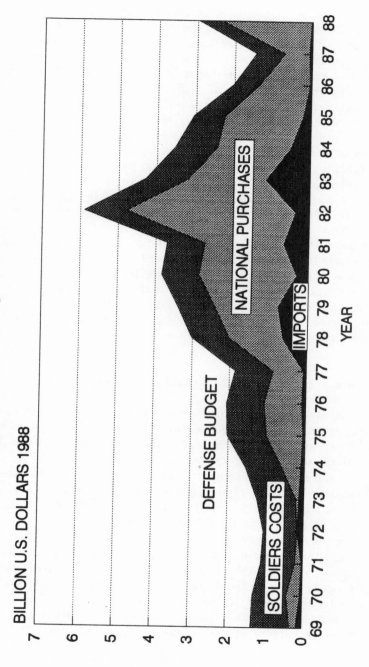

Figure 8.1

Argentina: Defense Budget Structure

Figure 8.2 shows that Argentina's ratio of national purchases to budget has been increasing steadily over time. While soldiers costs were the most significant in the defense budget in the late 1960s and early 1970s, national purchases have tended to dominate in the late 1980s, indicating a shift from personnel-intensive to technology-intensive (i.e., equipment-intensive) armed forces. This trend can also be seen in the number of military personnel that decreased from 175,000 in 1982–1983 to 95,000 in 1988, resulting in a nearly 50 percent reduction in personnel expenditures.

Figure 8.3 shows the ratio of national purchases to imports. An exponential regression curve has been fitted from 1979 to 1988. According to this curve, the national purchases to imports ratio has doubled every 2.3 years, indicating an import substitution policy under implementation, a process that can be traced back to 1945 (Porth, 1984). The substitution of defense imports and the reduction in the number of military personnel indicate that the shift from personnel- to technology-intensive operations of the armed forces is supported by the local production of defense equipment. It can be argued that this shift was possible only because of the domestic technological capacity developed by the Argentinean defense industry from the early 1970s to late 1980s, as was indicated in Chapter 4, supported by the transfer of European technology, mostly from West Germany.

8.1.2 Structure of the Brazilian Defense Budget

The structure and evolution of the Brazilian defense budget were obtained using the procedure described above, as shown in Figure 8.4. The period of analysis for Brazil ends at 1987 because the dollars-per-soldier figure for 1988 appears too low when compared with the other years and even when compared with other countries. Considering that 1988 is the last year of the figures reported by ACDA (1990), and that defense expenditures are sometimes hard to estimate accurately, in the case of Brazil the year 1988 has not been included.

Figure 8.4 shows that between 1969 and 1975 more than 50 percent of the Brazilian defense budget was devoted to national purchases.

From 1976 to 1987 personnel expenditures were more than 50 percent of the overall defense budget, reaching a maximum of around 85 percent in 1979, when the defense budget reached a minimum. Defense imports reached a maximum in 1979, when they composed around 15 percent of the defense budget, but in general, they have

Figure 8.2

Argentina: National Purchases and Budget

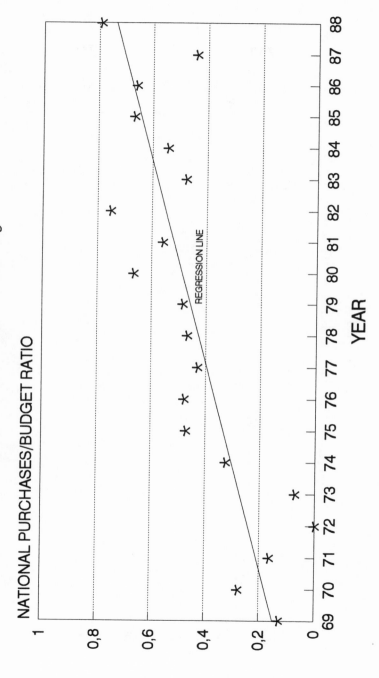

NATIONAL PURCHASES/BUDGET RATIO

REGRESSION LINE

YEAR

Figure 8.3

Argentina: National Purchases and Imports

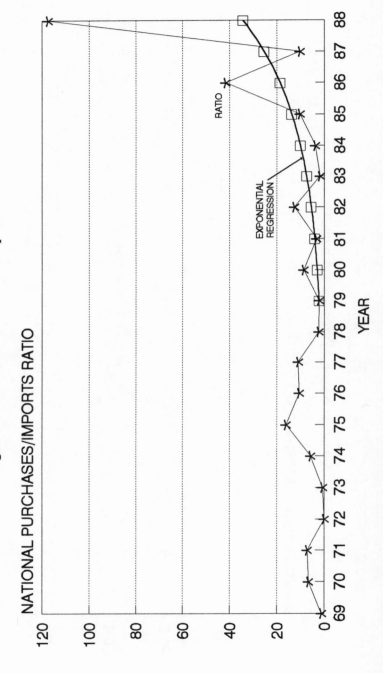

Figure 8.4

Brazil: Defense Budget Structure

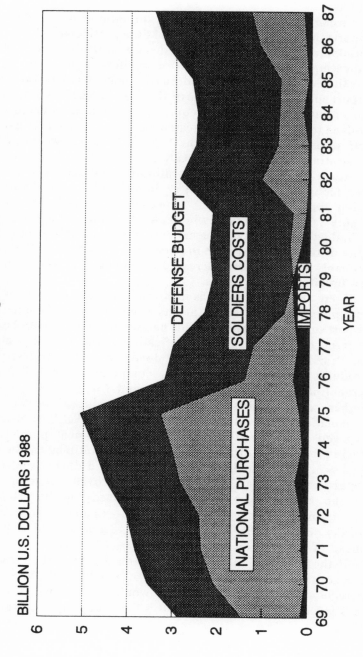

been of low monetary importance when compared with national purchases.

As can be seen from Figure 8.5, the ratio of national purchases to imports in Brazil does not seem to show a particular pattern over time. Paradoxically, this ratio decreased systematically from 1969 to 1979, indicating an import promotion policy instead of an import substitution one. This period can be considered as the technology import and consolidation stage of the Brazilian defense industry, when the structure of the defense equipment of the Brazilian armed forces evolved toward more sophisticated weapons. As another paradox, this period also coincides with the U.S. embargo of weapons to Brazil, illustrating the failure of the U.S. political effort in this case.

At the end of the 1980s the ratio of national purchases to imports was declining, indicating that an import substitution policy was not being applied at that time. However, from 1979 on, as shown in Figure 8.6, there is a steady increase in the ratio of national purchases to budget, principally at the expense of reducing the soldiers costs. In spite of the steady increase in personnel from 1984 to 1987, there was probably a shift toward increased technology-intensive operations of the Brazilian armed forces.

Even though Brazil has achieved notable exports of military equipment, the data show that its armed forces have not favored an import substitution policy. This paradoxical finding can be explained in terms of the degree of sophistication of the weapons employed by the Brazilian armed forces. The domestic defense industry of Brazil produces weapons of somewhat comparable sophistication to the Argentineans, but the Brazilian armed forces employ weapons of higher sophistication than the ones produced locally. Another explanation is the saturation of the local market. As Brazil has not engaged in any conflict, most of the equipment purchased locally during the decade of the 1970s was still operational by the end of the 1980s. Thus, what the Brazilians purchased during that period was sophisticated foreign equipment with improved technology, not more of the conventional equipment produced locally. Under these conditions, it did not matter that Brazil was able to produce weapons locally, because the Brazilian armed forces seemed to be keeping ahead of the local technology.

If the Brazilian defense expenditures and import figures for 1988 are accurate, as indicated by ACDA (1990), defense imports as a percentage of the defense budget would have grown from 2 percent in 1985 to 21.5 percent in 1988. This supports the argument that

Figure 8.5

Brazil: National Purchases and Imports

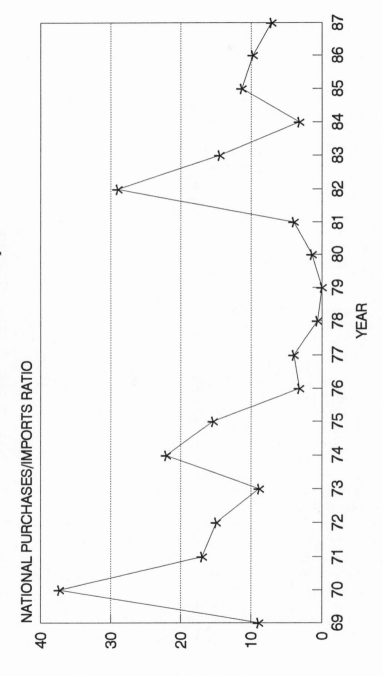

Figure 8.6

Brazil: National Purchases and Budget

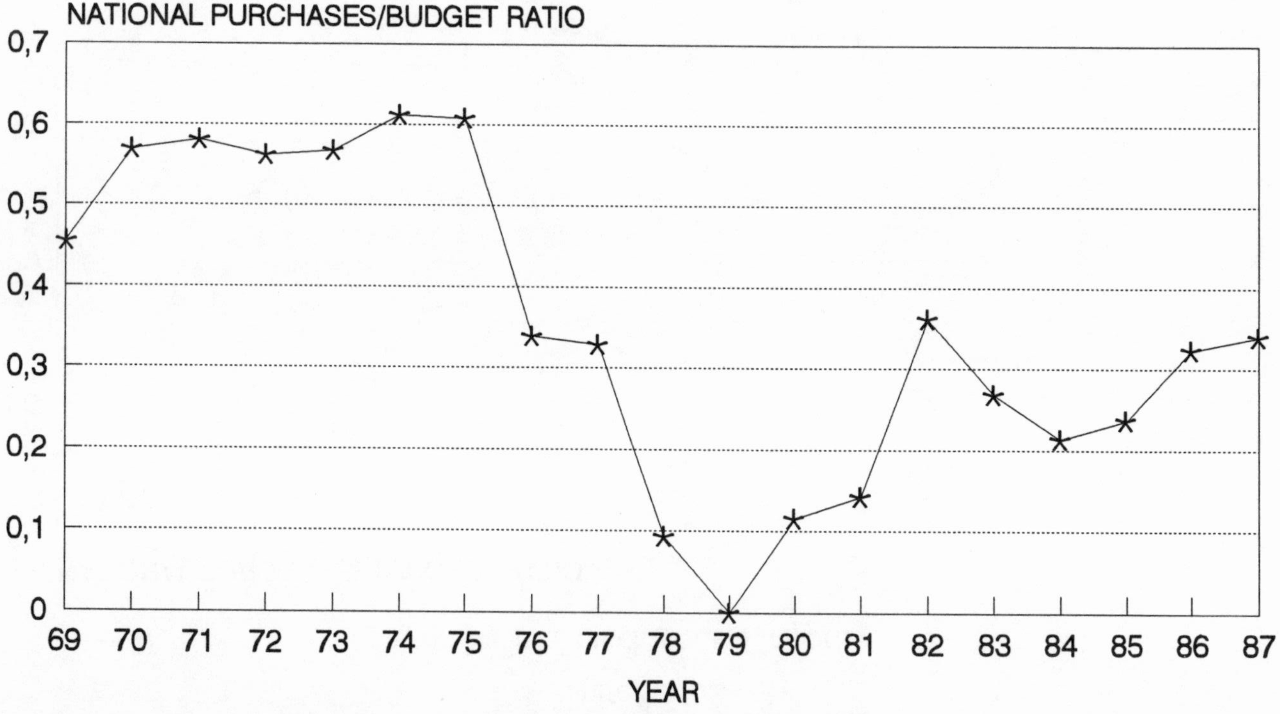

Brazil has increasingly relied upon foreign military technology, in spite of its recognized defense production capability.

According to these findings, the emergence of a world-class domestic defense industry in Brazil during the late 1960s and early 1970s did not result in the substitution of imports and the reduction of hard currency expenditures during the 1980s, as would have been expected. The main import substitution effect took place during the early phases of the emergence of the Brazilian defense industry (from 1969 to 1975, as can be observed in Figure 8.4), when high levels of national purchases of conventional local equipment were accompanied by increasing levels of imports of more sophisticated arms and weapons systems, indicating a massive militarization effort.

8.1.3 Structure of the Chilean Defense Budget

Figure 8.7 shows the evolution of Chile's defense budget from 1969 to 1988. The sharp increase in the defense budget for 1974 occurred after the Chilean armed forces assumed control of the government in 1973. Thus, national purchases for 1974 will be considered as an outlier for statistical purposes.

As can be seen in Figure 8.7, the main defense expenditures in Chile from 1969 to 1975 corresponded to national purchases. As the Chilean defense industry produced only unsophisticated arms at that time, the high levels of national purchases during that period can be assumed to represent import substitution of unsophisticated equipment that used to be purchased abroad.

The inability of the Chilean defense industry to produce more advanced arms and weapons systems can be seen by the steady increase in weapons imports from the beginning of the period analyzed up to 1981, when around 55 percent of the defense budget was devoted to the purchase of imported arms. Between 1978 and 1982, approximately 50 percent of the Chilean defense budget was spent on imported weapons. This period coincided with increased tensions with both Perú and Argentina.

With the demonstrated capacity to produce unsophisticated arms locally, these purchases were devoted to the acquisition of more advanced foreign military equipment. Paradoxically, as in the case of Brazil, an arms embargo by the United States and some European nations at that time forced Chile to purchase arms elsewhere, from Brazil, Spain, South Africa, or Israel, for example. In Chile, expenditures on imported weapons were reduced from $400 million

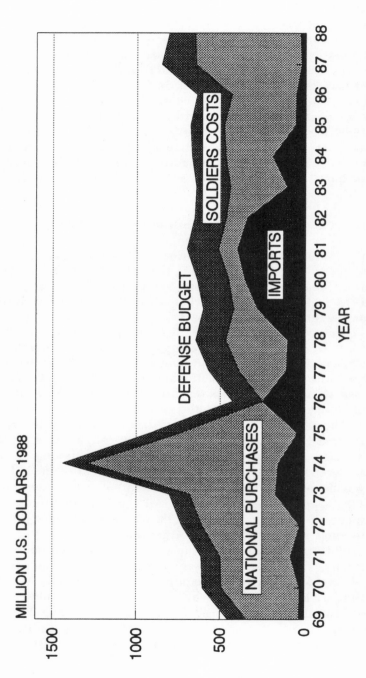

Figure 8.7

Chile: Defense Budget Structure

in 1981 to $30 million in 1988, at the same time that the defense budget increased and soldiers costs remained almost constant. After reaching a minimum of $98 million, a substantial increase in national purchases took place after 1980.

From Figure 8.8, we can see that Chile's ratio of national purchases to imports declined from 1969 to 1979. However, since 1979 a steady increase has taken place. The exponential regression curve of the national purchases to imports ratio shown in Figure 8.8 indicates that an import substitution policy has been in place since then. The doubling time of the exponential regression is 1.3 years. This would indicate that the Chilean import substitution policy is more drastic than the one implemented in Argentina.

In order for Chile to implement such a drastic import substitution policy, technology would have had to be either acquired or developed indigenously. As can be inferred from Chapter 5, where the defense industry of Chile is described in detail, there is no indication of a massive technology assistance program from any particular country. However, it is possible to find some specific cases of technology transfer by different countries such as Spain (aircraft), Israel (aircraft and electronics), South Africa (armored vehicles), and the United Kingdom (rockets and systems technology). It can be argued that the development of domestic technology has also taken place, as a result of increased cooperation with local universities and through research and development efforts carried out by the armed forces and the state-owned and private defense firms (Maldifassi, 1990).

For 1987 and 1988, as shown in Figure 8.9, the national purchases to budget ratio in Chile reached levels similar to the early 1970s, when an import substitution policy for unsophisticated weapons can be assumed to have been in place. All evidence indicates that during the 1980s Chile had an import substitution policy, with the aim of producing weapons of relatively more sophistication, and supported with foreign and indigenous technology. Sohr (1990, p. 97) indicates that increased defense production in Chile followed an explicit policy formulated by the Chilean government to overcome the embargo imposed by the United States and other European countries, in the presence of increased tensions with Perú and Argentina.

Figure 8.8

Chile: National Purchases and Imports

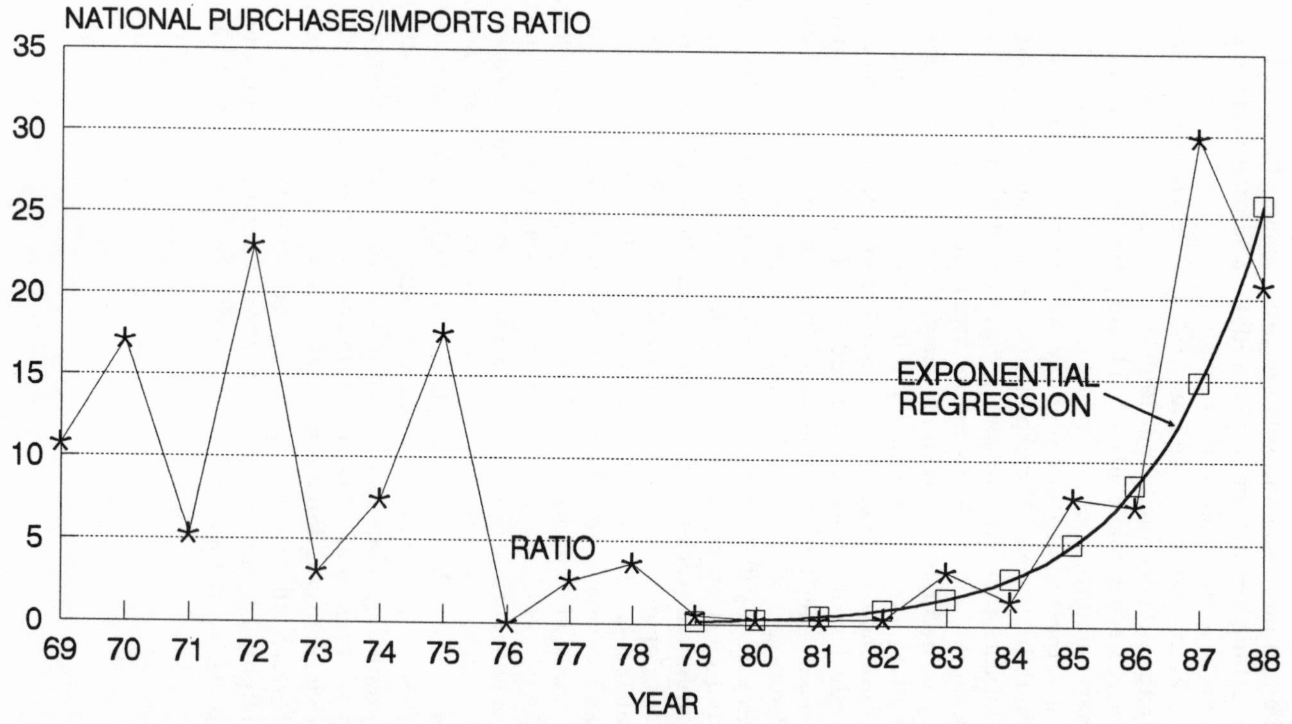

Figure 8.9

Chile: National Purchases and Budget

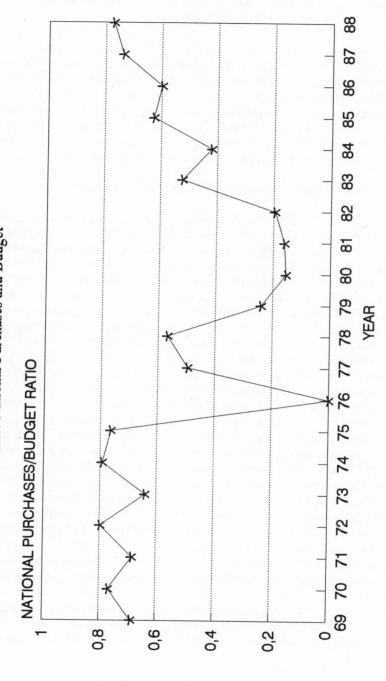

8.2   ASSESSMENT OF THE RESULTS OF IMPORT
SUBSTITUTION POLICIES

It has been stated that one of the main purposes of the establishment of domestic defense industries is import substitution. As import substitution is a trade-off between imports and local production, an effective import substitution policy should present a negative correlation between the indigenous production of goods and imports of the same goods. In this section, we will study the possible correlation that may exist between defense imports and national defense purchases as calculated above for Argentina, Brazil, and Chile.

8.2.1   Defense Import Substitution in Argentina

Using the figures of national purchases and defense imports for Argentina between 1969 and 1988, after removing 1982—an outlier with respect to national purchases because of the war—a *positive correlation* was found between defense imports and local defense purchases. The correlation proved to be significant at the $p = 0.012$ level, with a value of $R^2 = 0.26729$. Figure 8.10 shows the data points and the regression line for this correlation. This positive correlation, weak but nonetheless *not* negative, indicates that Argentina's defense imports and national defense production have increased simultaneously. Therefore, it can be argued that in Argentina the import substitution process was not effective, in spite of the large investments and sustained efforts made for that purpose.

Analyzing the historical data to determine the reason for this positive correlation between imports and local production, it was found that between 1978 and 1985 national purchases and imports were simultaneously maintained at high levels. The reasons for this can be considered to be (1) the heavy buildup of armaments during the crisis with Chile and the subsequent war with Great Britain in 1982 and (2) after that war (1983–1985), a large volume of imports and local production to replace the weapons lost during that conflict. Thus, it can be said that the import substitution policies adopted by Argentina in an attempt to reduce its political, technological, and economic dependency with respect to defense equipment have been ineffective and did not help to reduce imports, even during periods of crisis.

Increasing Argentinean national defense purchases for each year by 20 percent, to reflect a lower figure of minimum DPS, makes the correlation between national purchases and defense imports shift

Figure 8.10
Defense Import Substitution: Argentina, Brazil, and Chile

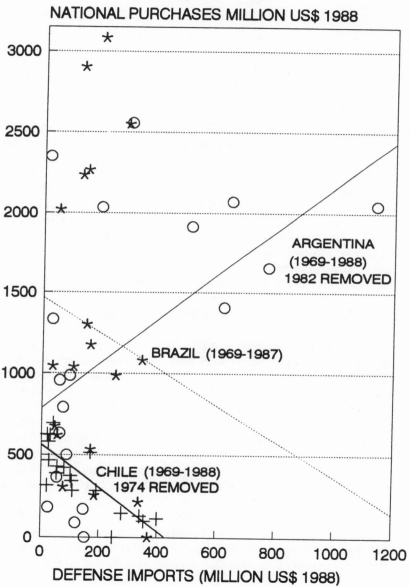

NATIONAL PURCHASES MILLION US$ 1988

ARGENTINA
(1969-1988)
1982 REMOVED

BRAZIL (1969-1987)

CHILE (1969-1988)
1974 REMOVED

DEFENSE IMPORTS (MILLION US$ 1988)

upward, with an even steeper slope. This would indicate even worse results of the import substitution policy when compared with the original calculations. According to this sensitivity analysis, the import substitution policy followed by Argentina can be considered to be ineffective even if higher volumes of defense production had occurred.

8.2.2 Defense Import Substitution in Brazil

In the case of Brazil, the data for the period from 1969 to 1987 indicate a negative correlation between defense imports and national defense purchases, as could be expected in an effective import substitution process.   However, this correlation appears to be extremely weak and nonsignificant, with a p-value of 0.312 and an R^2 of only 0.01453. Figure 8.10 shows the data points and the resulting regression line.   According to this finding, the Brazilian defense industry has not been able to generate an effective and significant import substitution effect. As such, the defense industry of Brazil can be considered almost neutral with respect to its ability to substitute local production for foreign equipment. Again, the reliance upon more sophisticated weapons systems by the Brazilian armed forces, as indicated previously, can be considered to be the cause of this lack of importance of the Brazilian defense industry with respect to its capacity to substitute foreign equipment.

8.2.3 Defense Import Substitution in Chile

The data for defense imports and national purchases for Chile between 1969 and 1988—excluding 1974, considered an outlier in national purchases because of the 1973 military takeover of the government—show that the import substitution process has worked effectively.   The correlation between defense imports and local production indicates a strong, negative significant correlation, with R^2 equal to 0.66582 and a p-value less than 0.001. Figure 8.10 shows the data points and the regression line. The slope of the regression line is -1.299. Therefore, between 1969 and 1988, an increase of $10 million in local defense production helped to reduce Chilean defense imports by $13 million.

The reasons for the effectiveness of the Chilean import substitution process, as will be shown later in this chapter, can be considered to be the higher efficiency of the Chilean defense industry when compared with Argentina and Brazil.   Also, the lower level of defense production compared both with Argentina and Brazil, in a regional defense industry characterized by decreasing returns to scale (as will be shown later), further reinforced the higher efficiency effect. The combination of both influences (i.e., higher efficiency of the production process and low volume production with decreasing returns to scale) can be assumed to have translated into lower prices of the locally produced Chilean defense equipment, effectively helping to substitute imported arms with those produced domestically.

If Chilean defense production is decreased by 20 percent to reflect higher soldiers costs, the slope of the regression line becomes less steep but still positive. This change in the magnitude of the slope of the regression line but not in the sign of the slope would indicate only a lower effectiveness of the import substitution process. Thus, sensitivity analysis indicates that the defense import substitution policy implemented in Chile has been effective even if lower national purchases had taken place.

An acid test of the effectiveness of an import substitution policy is the ability to export the items produced locally in the world market.[1] The high volumes of exports of the Brazilian—and in relative terms, also of the Chilean—defense industry help to corroborate the effectiveness of the import substitution policies adopted by these two countries. In contrast, the ineffectiveness of the import substitution policy of the Argentinean defense industry is further demonstrated by the low level of defense exports during the period analyzed here.

8.2.4 Cycles in Defense Import Substitution

The analysis of the import substitution processes followed by Argentina, Brazil, and Chile and the evolution in degree of sophistication of the weapons that they have produced (see Chapter 7) suggest the presence of technology-driven defense production cycles. Figure 8.11 illustrates these production cycles.

In the case of these three countries, local defense production with the aim of reducing defense imports while increasing the volume of indigenous weapons and their degree of sophistication has followed the following pattern:

---

1. This measure of effectiveness in the import substitution process has been recommended by Professor P. Hohenberg of Rensselaer Polytechnic Institute.

- *Simple technology*. Establishment of the capacity for producing small arms and ammunition. Production increases slowly while substituting simple imported weapons. The local production reaches a maximum but eventually decreases substantially due to saturation of the local market and obsolescence. The duration of this cycle is on the order of 10 to 15 years. All three countries have already completed this cycle: Argentina and Brazil in the mid-1960s; Chile in the early 1970s.

- *Intermediate technology*. With enhanced industrial and technological capacity, the defense industry invests in the infrastructure to produce locally armored vehicles, subsonic aircraft, and warships of low tonnage. Again, production reaches a maximum and decreases when the local market saturates. Only Brazil and Argentina can be considered to have completed this cycle by the mid- to late 1980s. Chile can be assumed to still be in this intermediate cycle, having passed over the maximum production volume and facing the declining production phase.

- *Advanced technology*. With the experience gained in the second cycle and further capital investment, the defense industry engages in the production of more sophisticated weapons systems such as main battle tanks, submarines, and supersonic aircraft. The data suggest Argentina has not yet entered this stage, apparently being stuck at its beginning because of economics. It can be assumed that Brazil has already entered this stage, as indicated by the capacity to design and produce main battle tanks, nuclear submarines, and missiles.

It can be argued that the transition from one cycle to the following one is achieved by mastering different kinds of technology of ever-increasing levels of sophistication. Thus, the science and technology policies adopted by the countries in one cycle will influence the capacity of the defense industry to enter the following cycle and may even accelerate or delay the transition. As experienced by Argentina, the economic condition of the country can also influence the capacity of the local defense industry to undergo the transition from one cycle to the next.

Figure 8.11
Production Cycles of the Defense Industry in Semi-Industrialized Countries

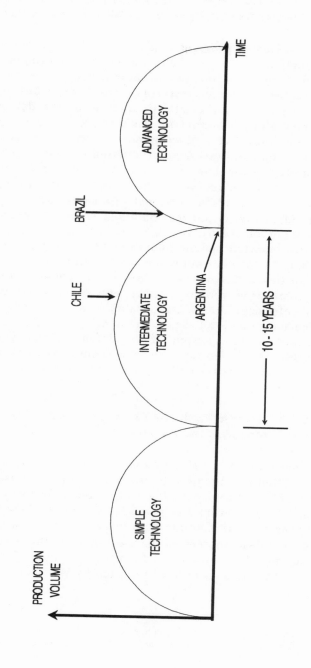

8.3　THE IMPACT OF DEFENSE PRODUCTION ON THE MANUFACTURING SECTOR OF THE ECONOMY

As indicated previously, given the high concentration of defense production in the manufacturing sector, the economic impact of the defense industry on the economy will be more important and noticeable at the manufacturing sector level. Thus, in this section we will analyze how the total production of the defense industry has affected the production of the manufacturing sector. In order to consider the effects of economic cycles, the effect of the defense industry on manufacturing production will be analyzed with changes in the GDP over time.

Total production of the defense industry for each year is determined by adding national purchases and arms exports. Total manufacturing output was obtained from UN publications (United Nations, 1986, 1990). It will be assumed that the total manufacturing figures reported include total defense production. It is possible that military factories do not report manufacturing figures to the economic authorities, a fact impossible to corroborate or correct for.[2] Also, if any correlation were to exist between total manufacturing output and total defense production, a causality relationship will be assumed from defense production to manufacturing. This takes into consideration the fact that the output of the defense industry is an exogenous variable controlled by external agents, namely, the government through the defense budget, the armed forces, and the Ministry of Defense.

8.3.1　Defense Production in Argentina and Its Impact on the Manufacturing Sector

The ratio of total defense production to total manufacturing production in Argentina between 1974 and 1988 is shown in Figure 8.12. This ratio increased steadily from 1974 to 1980–1981, when it reached values around 14 percent. This gradual increase is consistent with the previous findings with respect to the structure of the defense budget and the increasing share of national purchases. These figures of defense share of manufacturing output during the early 1980s are in accord with a 14 percent reported by Waisman (1986) for DGFM,

---

2. Kolodziej (1987b, p. 135) indicates that in France, up to the 1960s, the economic activity of the arms industry was not included in the national accounts.

Figure 8.12

Total Manufacturing Vs Defense Output: Argentina, Brazil, and Chile (Time)

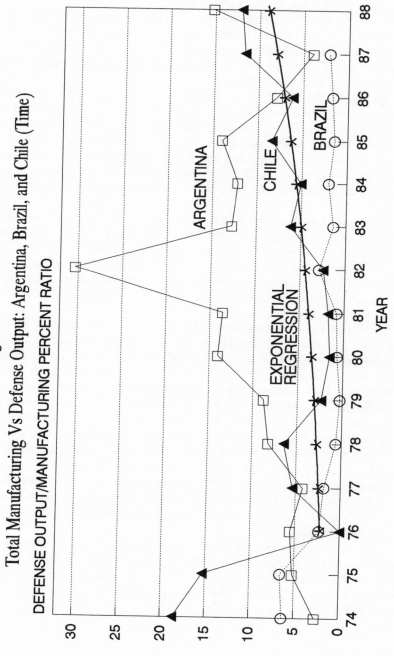

DEFENSE OUTPUT/MANUFACTURING PERCENT RATIO

considered Argentina's largest manufacturing company, which besides military goods also produces commodities.

The war in 1982 increased the defense to manufacturing ratio to 30.3 percent, returning to the prewar levels of around 13 percent between 1983 and 1985. After a decline to 3.9 percent in 1987, this ratio jumped back to what can be considered a historical level of around 15 percent in 1988.

Based on these values, it can be said that in Argentina military production is an important component of total manufacturing, reaching output share levels of around 15 percent during the mid-1980s. The surge capacity of the Argentinean industry for mobilization during the 1982 war is noteworthy, when approximately one third of total manufacturing was devoted to defense purposes, in particular if one recalls that the war effort itself lasted for only a couple of months.

Given the nonmarginal nature of defense production with respect to total manufacturing, it might be expected that the efficiency of the Argentinean defense industry and the resources it needs for production will affect the overall productivity of the manufacturing sector. Thus, statistical calculations were performed to determine the impact of defense production on the overall output of the manufacturing sector.

To take into consideration the impact of the overall economic activity on the manufacturing sector, first a lognorm regression calculation was performed with GDP as the dependent variable and time as the independent variable. The residuals of this regression were employed in a second regression calculation to determine if the changes in total output of the manufacturing sector could be attributed to changes in the economic activity, as represented by the lognorm regression residuals, or more properly to changes in the total output of the defense industry. Under these conditions, if total manufacturing output correlated higher with the residuals of the GDP lognorm regression as compared with the correlation with total defense production, then it could be concluded that any linear association between total manufacturing and defense outputs would be only a spurious correlation.

The following table shows the correlation matrix for the variables total defense output (DEFOUT), total manufacturing output (MANOUT), and the residuals of the lognorm regression of the economic activity (RESID) for Argentina, for the years between 1974 and 1988.

	Defout	Manout	Resid
Defout	1	-0.6699** (-0.5592*)	-0.3092 (0.0731)
Manout		1	0.5929* (0.4831)
Resid			1

* $p < 0.02$
** $p < 0.01$

As could be expected, total manufacturing correlates positively and significantly with the residuals of the economic activity. However, the significant correlation of the manufacturing output to total defense output was larger in absolute terms when compared with the economic activity, *and negative*. This would indicate that in Argentina increased defense output has had a negative and significant effect over total manufacturing output, more significant than what can be explained by changes in the economic activity alone. The negative but insignificant correlation between defense output and the residuals of the economic activity is something to be investigated further and probably relates to the very high levels of defense expenditures of Argentina during the period analyzed.

The figures in parenthesis in the table above are the correlation coefficients between the variables when the data for the year 1982 are removed from the sample. The removal of that year from the data set results in a substantial increase in the p-value of the DEFOUT-MANOUT correlation from 0.003 to 0.019, reducing its significance. However, because of the nonexperimental nature of the data, the p-value of 0.019 obtained in this case can still be considered significant.

Figure 8.13 shows the regression line of total manufacturing with respect to total defense output when 1982 is removed from the data set. The slope of the regression line turned out to be nonzero, as indicated by the value of the t-statistic of the slope:

$$\text{abs}(t) = 3.083 > 0.0104$$

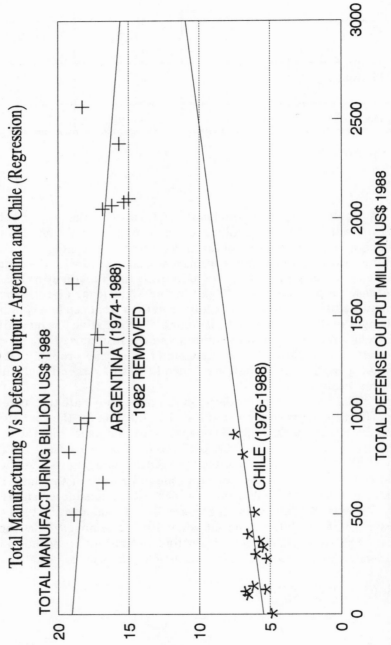

Figure 8.13

Total Manufacturing Vs Defense Output: Argentina and Chile (Regression)

TOTAL MANUFACTURING BILLION US$ 1988

ARGENTINA (1974-1988)
1982 REMOVED

CHILE (1976-1988)

TOTAL DEFENSE OUTPUT MILLION US$ 1988

After taking into consideration the effect of the economic activity residuals and the removal of the year 1982, the slope of the regression line for the variable DEFOUT came out as:

$b = -1.2238$

The magnitude and direction of this slope indicate that for every million dollars produced by the Argentinean defense industry, on average a reduction of $1.2 million can be expected in total output of the manufacturing sector.

Some explanations can be found for this significant negative effect. The first has to do with the use of specialized equipment and skilled personnel in the manufacturing sector, as argued by Waisman (1986). Whenever defense production increases, these scarce resources—in particular, scarce skilled labor and some commodities—need to be diverted from production of commercial products, reducing the total productive capacity of the manufacturing sector. This explanation would give support to the hypothesis of a high opportunity cost of the defense industry when compared with the production of civilian goods, as supported by Sivard (1987). This negative and strong influence of defense production on manufacturing output can also be a consequence of the closed nature of defense production in Argentina, performed by highly vertically integrated state-owned factories that are normally incurring "staggering losses" (Waisman, 1986).

The second explanation has to do with macroeconomic effects. Whenever the Argentinean armed forces need to purchase larger volumes of local defense goods, the government can increase the availability of money in the economy; that is, defense production is paid with inflation. In Argentina, inflation rates of 1,000 percent a year occurred during the 1980s, so it is possible that defense-induced inflation may have reduced the economic activity at the same time that defense production increased.

Finally, the issue of inclusion of defense production in total manufacturing output figures is an element of uncertainty that cannot be ignored nor corrected for with the level of aggregation of the available data. However, given the high share of defense output with respect to total manufacturing output, it would be surprising if defense production was not included in the reported figures of total manufacturing output.

The implications of this significant negative correlation between defense output and manufacturing output in Argentina become more important if one views the import substitution policy prevailing during the 1980s. If that policy persists, as may be presumed by the high indebtedness of Argentina that requires the maximum availability of hard currency to pay for its debt, and the entrance to the third production cycle is accomplished, decreasing levels of industrial production of the manufacturing sector should be observed, as induced by increased production levels of the defense industry.

If total defense production is increased, to reflect a lower minimum DPS, the slope of the regression line becomes less steep, indicating a less significant negative impact on total manufacturing output. However, the slope does not change its sign, still resulting in a negative impact.

8.3.2   Defense Production in Brazil and Its Impact on the Manufacturing Sector

The defense output to manufacturing ratio for Brazil between 1974 and 1987 is shown in Figure 8.12. As it is possible to observe from that figure, the Brazilian defense industry represents a very small part of the overall manufacturing output, with a maximum of only 6.5 percent in 1975. After a minimum of less than 0.5 percent in 1979, it increased to a level of around 2 percent at the end of the 1980s.

Given its relatively small importance, it might be expected that total manufacturing output would be more or less insensitive to the output levels of the defense industry.

The following table shows the correlation matrix for the variables total defense output (DEFOUT), total manufacturing output (MANOUT), and the residuals of the lognorm regression of the economic activity (RESID) for Brazil, for the years between 1974 and 1987.

	Defout	Manout	Resid
Defout	1	-0.3616	-0.5580*
Manout		1	0.2450
Resid			1

* $p < 0.02$

These correlation values show that even though manufacturing production is negatively correlated with defense industry output, the correlation is weak and nonsignificant. As expected, manufacturing output correlates positively with the economic activity, but again, this correlation is nonsignificant. As in Argentina's case, defense industry output correlates negatively and with some degree of significance with the economic activity, indicating a negative effect of total defense production on the economy, most probably caused by relatively high defense expenditures. The true meaning of this last negative correlation needs to be investigated further.

The conclusion that can be derived is that given the small fraction of the manufacturing sector corresponding to the defense industry in Brazil, the output of the latter can be considered not to affect the output of the overall manufacturing sector.

The fact that the Brazilian defense industry has world stature can be associated more with the overall size of the Brazilian economy and the sheer size of its armed forces—that in 1987 reached 512,000 soldiers in arms—than with a significant importance at the national level. The size of the Brazilian economy and the large number of soldiers of its armed forces have allowed for the emergence of such an industry. Thus, the relative importance that can be given to the Brazilian defense industry in economic terms is low. This finding corroborates what Neuman (1984) termed "economies of scale" for increased production of military equipment. This low economic impact, together with the relatively high levels of defense imports during the late 1980s, assumed to indicate the persistence of technological dependency, helped to demystify the notion that the emergence of the Brazilian defense industry has been an "economic miracle" (Brigagao, 1986).

Thus, from the results presented above, it appears that the Brazilian defense industry has not outpaced the rest of the Brazilian manufacturing sector but has been given much publicity, creating the feeling of an outstanding performer with important economic effects.

8.3.3 Defense Production in Chile and Its Impact on the Manufacturing Sector

Chile's defense output to manufacturing ratio is shown in Figure 8.12. For the years 1974 and 1975, the high values of this ratio can be considered to be influenced by the deteriorated condition of the Chilean economy, provoked by the economic policies of the leftist regime that was replaced by a military government in 1973.

Since 1976 up to the end of the 1980s, the trend has been of increasing levels of defense output over total manufacturing, illustrated in Figure 8.12 by the exponential regression shown. At the end of the 1980s the defense output to manufacturing ratio reached levels of around 12 percent, consistent with the import substitution policy present at that time. The increasing share of military production with respect to total manufacturing during the late 1970s and the 1980s would suggest that there might be some relationship between both output levels.

For Chile, the following table shows the correlation matrix obtained for the variables defense output (DEFOUT), manufacturing output (MANOUT), and the residuals of the lognorm regression for the economic activity (RESID), between the years 1976 and 1988.

	Defout	Manout	Resid
Defout	1	0.6419**	-0.0486
Manout		1	0.6321*
Resid			1

  $* p < 0.02$
$** p < 0.01$

It is noteworthy that in the case of Chile the correlation between defense output and manufacturing output turned out to be *positive and significant* and even slightly higher than the correlation between manufacturing output and the residuals that represent the economic activity, which came out as significant at a somewhat higher p-value. Thus, between 1976 and 1988, Chile's production of military equipment had a positive impact on the manufacturing sector, slightly stronger than the effect produced by the economic activity alone during that same period.

The negative correlation between defense production and economic activity is very close to zero, and much smaller than the same correlation found for Argentina and Brazil. This would indicate that defense production in Chile has not affected the economic activity at all, or at least not affected it in the same degree that the defense industries of Argentina and Brazil have negatively affected theirs.

For Chile, Figure 8.13 shows the regression line for total manufacturing as a function of defense output. The slope of the regression line turned out to be nonzero, as indicated by the value of the t-statistic:

$$t = 5.556 > 0.0002$$

The value of the slope coefficient for DEFOUT obtained by means of multiple regression that included the economic activity as represented by the residuals came out as:

$$b = 1.9171$$

This means that for every million dollars produced by the Chilean defense industry, it can be expected that the manufacturing sector would increase its total output by \$1.91 million on average. Two explanations can be considered possible for this greater-than-one efficiency. The first can be cast in terms of a monetary multiplier effect, suggesting the effects of a military Keynesianism phenomenon. The second, however, is that other political and economic circumstances existed in Chile during the decade of the 1980s that may have helped to increase manufacturing production at the same time that defense output increased, giving rise to a correlation, but not causality, condition. Nevertheless, the strong and positive correlation provides an indication that defense production in Chile has had a positive impact on the output of the manufacturing sector of the economy.

We have shown that Chile's defense production is presently declining. In view of the positive correlation found between defense production and total manufacturing output, decreasing levels of manufacturing output could be expected in Chile during the next years, caused by declining military production of the indigenous defense industry.

If Chilean national purchases are reduced to reflect a higher amount of soldiers costs, the slope of the regression line increases, becoming steeper. Under these conditions, the positive impact of defense production over total manufacturing output would be even higher, making it even more difficult to explain. Thus, in the case of Chile, this sensitivity analysis suggests that the minimum DPS and the approximate national purchases calculated are a good estimation of total defense output.

8.3.4   Economic Importance of Defense Exports

As indicated in Chapter 2, another way the domestic defense industry can influence the local economy is by defense exports. As the impact on the economy will depend on the relative amount of defense exports as compared with total exports, the percentage of defense export shares of total exports reported by ACDA (1990) has been utilized to assess this influence.

In the case of Argentina the defense exports share reached a maximum of 1.5 percent in 1984 and, for the period 1980–1988, had an average of only 0.4 percent of total exports. As such, when compared with total exports, it can be said that Argentina's defense exports have not had great importance during the last decade and also that they have not been used to increase production output in order to achieve economies of scale. Thus, Argentinean defense production has been primarily serving the domestic market.

The defense industry of Brazil has been more outward oriented than the Argentinean defense industry. The maximum share of Brazilian defense exports reached a value of 3.3 percent in 1982, with an average for the period between 1980 and 1988 of 1.53 percent. Given this low share of total exports, the internal economic impact of defense exports in Brazil has been small, even though at the international level the volume of Brazilian exports may have been significant.

In the case of Chile, the share of defense exports over total exports has been increasing almost steadily since 1983, reaching a maximum of 4 percent at the end of the period, and an average of 1.2 percent for the period analyzed. These increasing defense exports have occurred at the same time that the Chilean economy increased its overall exports at a rapid pace during the second half of the 1980s. Thus, it can be concluded that there has been a real and sustained effort to increase defense exports in Chile and that by the end of the 1980s defense exports were increasing to levels able to have a small impact on total exports.

Argentina, Brazil, and Chile have historically been exporters of raw materials and agricultural products. In fact, according to the figures published by the Comisión Económica para América Latina y el Caribe (CEPAL, 1989) for the period 1980–1987, only Brazil included among its ten most important export segments goods that can be considered to have a certain relation to arms and weapons: passenger motor cars and internal combustion engines. All the other export items for these three countries belong to the traditional exports of raw materials and agriculture. This implies that defense exports—considered to be manufactured goods—could compose a somewhat significant share of total manufactured exports.

Figure 8.14 shows the share of defense exports as a percentage of manufactured exports for Argentina, Brazil, and Chile between 1980 and 1988. For the period considered, the maximum share of defense exports as a percentage of manufactured exports for Argentina was found to be 8.7 percent in 1984, with a period average of only 1.9 percent. These figures are still not large enough to have economic significance even at the manufacturing level.

The share of defense exports as a percentage of manufactured exports for Brazil shows a somewhat constant value, with a maximum of 8.5 percent in 1982 and a period average of 3.6 percent. This average figure is larger than in the case of Argentina, but it is still not large enough to be of major economic significance. Even at the manufacturing level, Brazilian defense exports continue to be only marginal in economic terms. This justifies the "scales" effect mentioned earlier: Overall, Brazilian exports are so sizable that defense exports, though significant in world terms, are not important in national terms, even at the manufactured goods level.

The Chilean defense exports share as a percentage of total manufactured exports has been increasing almost constantly since 1983, reaching a maximum of 44 percent at the end of the period, with an average of 12.5 percent. This indicates that, taken as a separate segment, Chilean defense exports have had a significant and increasing importance with respect to manufactured exports. This

Figure 8.14

Defense Exports as Percentage of Manufactured Exports

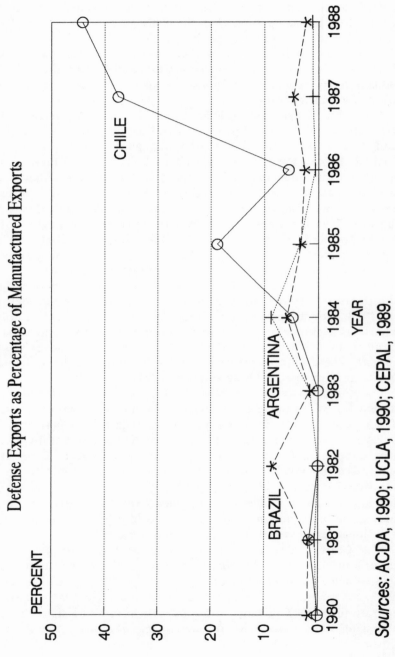

Sources: ACDA, 1990; UCLA, 1990; CEPAL, 1989.

situation arises mostly because of the low volume of manufactured goods traditionally exported by Chile. The sharp increase in Chilean defense exports can also be associated with the activity of the private firm Cardoen Industries that, as was mentioned in Chapter 5, between 1986 and 1989 exported $450 million in arms and other defense equipment, representing on average around 24 percent of Chile's annual manufactured exports for the years 1986 through 1988.

8.4 THE IMPACT OF THE DEFENSE INDUSTRIES ON MANUFACTURING EMPLOYMENT

The estimated number of people employed by the prime contractors of the defense industries of Brazil, Argentina, and Chile have been presented in Chapters 3, 4, and 5, respectively.

As the employment generated by defense production goes beyond the prime contractors alone, an estimated indirect employment multiplier needs to be used; in this case, the multiplier range between 1.5 and 2 suggested by Mosley (1985) will be adopted. For Brazil, given the extent of the defense industry and the many small subcontractors that support the prime ones, an estimated multiplier of 2 will be used. In Argentina, where most of the defense production is carried out by the state-owned factories, with very little private participation, a lower multiplier of 1.5 will be used. For Chile, where a mix between private and predominantly state-owned firms can be considered to exist, a multiplier of 1.6 is considered adequate. From the figures presented in the respective chapters mentioned, and the multipliers defined above, the number of people directly employed by the defense industry becomes as shown in Table 8.1.

These estimates are considered to be valid on average for the period between 1983 and 1986, so they need to be compared with the average employment in the manufacturing sector for that period. According to the International Labour Office (1991), the average employment in manufacturing between 1983 and 1986 for Brazil and Chile and between 1982 and 1985 for Argentina was:

Argentina:	1,503,000	workers
Brazil:	7,686,000	
Chile:	474,000	

Given these average employment levels, the percentage of manufacturing employment generated by the defense industry can be estimated as shown in Table 8.1.

Table 8.1

Total Employment in the Defense Industries of Argentina, Brazil, and Chile

Country	Defense Prime Contractors Employment	Employment Multiplier	Total Defense industry Employment	Defense as % of Total Manufact. Employment
Argentina	66,000	1.5	99,000	6.6
Brazil	36,400	2	72,800	0.95
Chile	9,800	1.6	15,680	3.3

These manufacturing employment shares are in agreement with the findings of percent share of defense output with respect to manufacturing output. The higher the production share, the higher the employment share.

As can be seen, the employment share generated by the Brazilian defense industry is very low, corroborating the marginal effect of the Brazilian defense industry on the overall manufacturing sector.

In Argentina, and to a lesser extent in Chile, the employment share of the defense industry with respect to manufacturing employment, even though relatively low, cannot be considered negligible. This is true also if one considers that in these countries high unemployment rates have occurred during the decade, especially in Chile between 1982 and 1985. However, as mentioned in the chapter about Argentina, the state-owned shipyards employ about 45 percent of the total work force of the shipbuilding manufacturing subsector. In the case of Chile, the employment of ASMAR may represent an even higher share of the shipbuilding industry—maybe as high as 80 percent. Thus, more than having a global employment impact, the defense industry is an important employer in particular industries of the manufacturing sector.

Even though defense employment is hardly significant even at the manufacturing sector level, it involves a much larger share in specific areas of particular interest for defense. Also, the skills and technical qualifications of the personnel employed in the defense industry can be considered to be well above the mean, so it can be expected that their productivity, on average, will be higher than the rest of the manufacturing sector. This assumption is corroborated by the analysis in the next section.

8.5 COMPARATIVE ASSESSMENT OF THE FACTOR EFFICIENCY OF THE LATIN AMERICAN DEFENSE INDUSTRIES

In this section the relative efficiency in the utilization of labor and capital of the defense industries of Argentina, Brazil, and Chile is compared with the local manufacturing sectors and with the defense industries of industrialized countries.

8.5.1 Labor Productivity of the Defense Industry Work Force

Given the total employment and production levels of the defense industries of the three countries of interest, and the similar indicators for the overall manufacturing sector found in the literature, it is possible to assess the relative employee productivity of the defense industry with respect to the manufacturing sector. These values are shown in Table 8.2.

The employee productivity values shown in Table 8.2 indicate that in Argentina, Brazil, and Chile defense employees are more productive than employees of the manufacturing sector on average. This is expected because, as previously indicated, defense employees tend to be more skilled and technically qualified than the rest of the manufacturing labor force, thus rendering them more productive. However, it is also possible that more efficient managerial practices boost even further the higher productivity achieved by the skills effect. Another explanation could be that higher utilization of capital can lead to higher labor productivity. In industrialized countries, in spite of the higher qualifications of the general labor force, this higher productivity of defense industry employees can also be expected as a result of the combination of both effects (skills and capital intensity). The relative productivity among the defense employees of the three countries maintains the pattern found for the overall manufacturing sector. Chilean employees are the most productive of the three, with Brazilian employees showing the lowest productivity and Argentineans in between.

Table 8.2

Employee Productivity for Argentina, Brazil, and Chile

Country	Defense Output M $ 1988	Defense Emp.	Defense Emp. Product. $/EMPL.	Mfg. Output M $ 1988	Mfg. Emp.	Mfg. Emp. Product. $/EMPL.	Defense Percent Higher Product.
Argentina	1,890	99,000	19,090	15,666	1,503,000	10,423	83 %
Brazil	1,110	72,800	15,250	68,145	7,686,000	8,866	72 %
Chile	389.4	15,680	24,834	6,043	474,000	12,750	95 %

Notes: Defense output is average output for the period 1983–1986 in million dollars of 1988; defense employees is estimate of total employment in defense production; manufacturing output is average output for the period 1983–1986 in million dollars of 1988, according to United Nations, 1986, 1990; manufacturing employees is average number for the period 1983–1986 according to International Labour Office, 1991; and productivity is 1988 dollars of output per employee.

The lower productivity increase showed by the Brazilian defense workers when compared with their civilian industry counterparts can be explained in terms of the integration between civilian and military production. As was already indicated, most defense production in Brazil is carried out by private firms that also manufacture civilian goods. Thus, the work force characteristics and managerial practices of the "defense industry" are not that different from the "civilian industry," reducing the possibility of large differentiation in productivity terms.

The range of the higher productivity of defense employees between 72 percent for Brazil and 95 percent for Chile provides a check for the results, adding more credibility to the assumptions made with respect to the employment multiplier factors adopted. In the case of Chile, it is not possible to explain the relatively higher productivity of defense employees as compared with local manufacturing employees without further detailed research.

The fact that defense industry employees are more productive than the average in the manufacturing sector can be used to help increase the efficiency in the production of civilian goods. It can be argued that these employee-based economies of scope will be realized only if the production of military goods is closely integrated with the production of civilian goods. In the case of the Argentinean defense industry, based mostly on state-owned factories, this integration seems to be very low, so not much of this effect can be expected to occur.

In Chile, there is still an important state ownership of defense-producing establishments. However, these organizations have been chartered as independent corporations, indicating a more commercial and efficiency-oriented production, where the provision of services and the production of civilian goods are an important part of their overall activities.

In Brazil, where most of the defense industry is in private hands, there is a high degree of integration between defense and civilian goods production. Therefore, important benefits can be expected to derive from the increased productivity of the employees that manufacture military equipment when they are engaged in the production of civilian goods.

The domestic defense industry of these three countries can serve as an example to other local manufacturing firms for increasing the productivity of their employees, the use of more productive manufacturing equipment, and the adoption of more efficient managerial practices. As already indicated, this effect can be assumed to occur only if there exists a high degree of integration of the defense industry with the rest of the manufacturing sector.

8.5.2 International Comparison of the Latin American Defense Industry

It was shown that the productivity of defense employees in the three Latin American countries of interest is higher than the local manufacturing sector. However, as domestic defense production has strong motivations for substituting imports, it will prove beneficial to assess how efficient the local defense industries are when compared with the defense industries of industrialized countries.

In order to assess the relative efficiency of the defense industry in international terms, again an approximate method will be used, based on the relative utilization of labor and capital in the production of defense goods and supported by the value-added share of total output in the manufacturing sector from where defense production derives.

The objective of the calculations that follow is to compare the efficient utilization of capital and labor across the different countries. Even though it is well known that industrialized countries are more efficient in the utilization of capital for productive purposes, it has also been found (Dosi, Pavitt, and Soette, 1990, p. 136) that they are also more efficient in the utilization of labor. Thus, it can be expected that the defense industries of the semi-industrialized countries of Latin America will be less efficient than their counterparts in industrialized countries. However, for policy purposes it becomes necessary to assess the degree of relative inefficiency that they have.

The estimated numbers of defense employees during the mid-1980s for the United States (Mosley, 1985, pp. 48–50), Germany (Wulf, 1988), Italy (Albrecht, 1986), France (Kolodziej, 1987a), and the United Kingdom (Rallo, 1986) were:

United States:	1,860,000	workers
Germany:	290,000	
France:	310,000	
Italy:	160,000	
United Kingdom:	400,000	

The next step requires the estimation of total defense production and the computation of capital utilization. As defined above, total defense production is calculated as:

Defense output = national purchases + defense exports

According to the *Statistical Abstract of the United States* (U.S. Department of Commerce, 1990, pp. 331–332), between 1983 and 1986, an average 54.4 percent of the U.S. defense budget was spent on national purchases, which in terms of constant dollars of 1988 represents $151.1 billion according to the figures reported by ACDA (1990). Average defense exports for the United States during that same period amounted to $11.9 billion (ACDA, 1990). In total, the average output of the defense industry in the United States between 1983 and 1986 was $163 billion. As no similar statistics have been found for the other industrialized countries, it will be assumed that 50 percent of the defense budget of France, Germany, Italy, and the United Kingdom is spent on national purchases. Based on this assumption, and the defense statistics published by ACDA (1990), Table 8.3 shows the average defense industry output for these countries.

The average productivity of employees in the defense industry measured as constant 1988 dollars per employee then can be calculated as:

United States	= $87,634 per employee ($46,133)	
France	= $71,580	
Germany	= $67,931 ($37,560)	
Italy	= $58,394	
United Kingdom	= $49,582 ($19,381)	

The figures in parentheses are productivity levels of manufacturing employees according to Sadler (1986) for 1984, in 1988 constant dollars. From these figures, it is possible to say that in the United States and Germany defense employees are 89 percent and 81 percent more productive than the rest of employees in the manufacturing sector, respectively. These figures compare reasonably well with the increased productivity found in the Latin American defense industry. However, in the United Kingdom, the extremely high productivity of defense employees as compared with the rest of the manufacturing sector (155 percent) cannot be reasonably explained and may be

Table 8.3

Defense Output of Selected Industrialized Countries

Country	Avg. Nat'l Purchases M $ 1988	Avg. Defense Exports M $ 1988	Avg. Defense Output M $ 1988
France	17,358	4,832	22,190
Germany	17,865	1,835	19,700
Italy	8,276	1,067	9,343
United Kingdom	18,133	1,700	19,833
United States	151,100	11,900	163,000

caused by the assumptions made with respect to national purchases as percent of defense budget, to underestimation of the number of defense employees, or to underestimation of the productivity of manufacturing employees in the United Kingdom as reported by Sadler (1986), or a combination of all these factors.

The higher productivity of defense employees in industrialized countries found here allows one to refute the unproven argument of the lower efficiency of the defense industry as supported by Vayrynen (1992, p. 28). If such industrial inefficiency really exists, it must be due to high overheads and financial costs associated with the industry but certainly not because of the low productivity of its employees.

For the calculation of the capital costs, the equation to be used here is:

Value added = w × labor + r × capital

where w is the cost of labor, and r is the cost of capital.

Table 8.4 shows the relative share of purchases, labor, and capital costs over total output for the two-digit SIC code industries for which the U.S. Department of Defense accounts for more than 25 percent of industry sales. In order to obtain average values of these factor expenditures for the overall "defense industry," a weighted average

Table 8.4

**Relative Share of Factors Costs in the U.S. Manufacturing
Sector and in the Defense Industry**

SIC Code	Purchases	Labor	Capital	Weight
28	63.6	18.71	17.69	0.37
33	69.84	26	4.16	0.71
34	57.04	29.77	13.19	6.21
35	55.11	31.98	12.91	0.98
36	55.9	32.84	11.26	35.06
37	64.27	25.47	10.26	49.37
38	43.64	34.6	21.76	7.3
Weighted Average	59.33	29.03	11.64	

Sources: Weight is percent of U.S. DoD purchases in SIC industries for
1987 according to OTA (1991c, p. 48); purchases, labor, and capital
shares over total output for 1984 are from "Klems Data for 2-Digit
Manufacturing Industries" as provided by Professor R. Norsworthy,
Rensselaer Polytechnic Institute, 1992.

was calculated. As each industrial sector accounts for a different
amount of expenditures, the weights assigned in Table 8.4 are the U.S.
percent share of defense expenditures in the respective industries.
The result of this weighted average indicates that approximately 41
percent of total output in the production of defense goods in the
United States is value added.

According to figures published by the United Nations (1986), the
value-added share in total manufacturing output for Chile is 35.82
percent; for Argentina, 40.53 percent; and for Germany, 37.06
percent. For Brazil, France, Italy, and the United Kingdom, given
that no similar statistics are available, the 41 percent calculated for
the U.S. defense industry will be used.

In order to determine the capital costs, either the wage rate or the share of labor costs of the value added is needed. The share of labor costs as a percentage of the value added for the industrialized countries will be approximated according to the figures shown in Table 8.5. For France, Germany, Italy, and the United Kingdom, approximately 26 percent of value added are capital costs, whereas in the United States this figure becomes only 21 percent.

In Table 8.6, for Argentina, Brazil, and Chile the average wage bill was calculated according to the wage rates reported by the International Labour Office (1991) for the years between 1983 and 1985. This second method was preferred for the semi-industrialized countries because of the sharp variations in employment levels from year to year, which render average share of salaries in value added for these countries more imprecise.

Table 8.5

Labor Share of Manufacturing Value Added

Country	Labor Costs Share in Manafacturing Value Added	Labor Costs Share in Metal Products, Machinery, and Equipment	Labor Share of Value Added Adopted for Calculations
United Kingdom	71.75	-	74
Italy	60.88	73.81	74
France	-	-	74
Germany	65.63	74.52	74
United States	71	79.17	79

Source: United Nations, 1986, *passim.*

Table 8.6

Average Wages and Wage Costs for Argentina, Brazil, and Chile

	Argentina	Brazil	Chile
Av Wage/Yr	1,835	3,261	4,691
Defense Employees	99,000	72,800	15,680
Value Added	766	455	140
Wage Bill	182	237	73.5
Capital Bill	584	218	66.5

Sources: Wage rates in national currencies and current values from International Labour Office, 1991; exchange rates from UNESCO, 1990; deflators from ACDA, 1990.

Note: Average wage rates between 1983 and 1986 for the three countries in constant 1988 dollars per worker per year; value added, wage bill, and capital bill in 1988 constant million dollars.

Finally, the cost of capital "r" is needed to determine capital input. For the industrialized countries a value of r equal to 7 percent will be used. For the semi-industrialized countries a value of 12 percent has been recommended.[3]

According to these figures and calculations, the capital input to the respective defense industries during the mid-1980s results as shown in Table 8.7. These capital inputs need to be compared in relative terms according to the productivity of the respective defense industries.

In order to assess the relative efficiency in the utilization of labor and capital in the respective defense industries, the reciprocal of employee productivity will be used, together with the ratio of capital input over total output (Scherer and Ross, 1990, pp. 670–671). Figure 8.15 shows the relative position of these countries in a two-coordinate graph, where the X-axis measures labor input per unit of ooutput, and

---

3. These values have been suggested by Professor Paul Hohenberg of Rensselaer Polytechnic Institute.

Table 8.7

Capital Input to the Defense Industries

Country	Value Added M $ 1988	Capital Costs M $ 1988	Capital Input M $ 1988
Argentina	766	584	4,867
Brazil	455	218	1,817
Chile	140	66.5	554.2
France	9,100	2,366	33,800
Germany	7,300	1,900	27,143
Italy	3,830	996	14,229
United Kingdom	8,130	2,114	30,200
United States	66,830	14,034	200,500

the Y-axis measures capital input per unit of output. According to this diagram, the countries closer to the origin are more efficient in the use of labor and capital than the countries located on a diagonal far from the origin.

As can be seen from Figure 8.15, the results of the above calculations indicate that the United States has the most efficient defense industry, followed closely by Germany. Of the industrialized countries, the United Kingdom appears as the most inefficient. As was explained, the low efficiency of the British defense industry is due mostly to the low productivity of its workers.

Of the Latin American countries, Chile appears with the most efficient defense industry. This relatively higher efficiency of the Chilean defense industry can be explained in terms of the findings of Tybout, de Melo, and Corbo (1991). These researchers, using the data from the Chilean industrial census of 1967 and 1979, found that during the intracensus period there was an increase in the efficiency of the Chilean manufacturing firms that underwent relatively large reductions in tariffs protection. During that same period, the

Figure 8.15

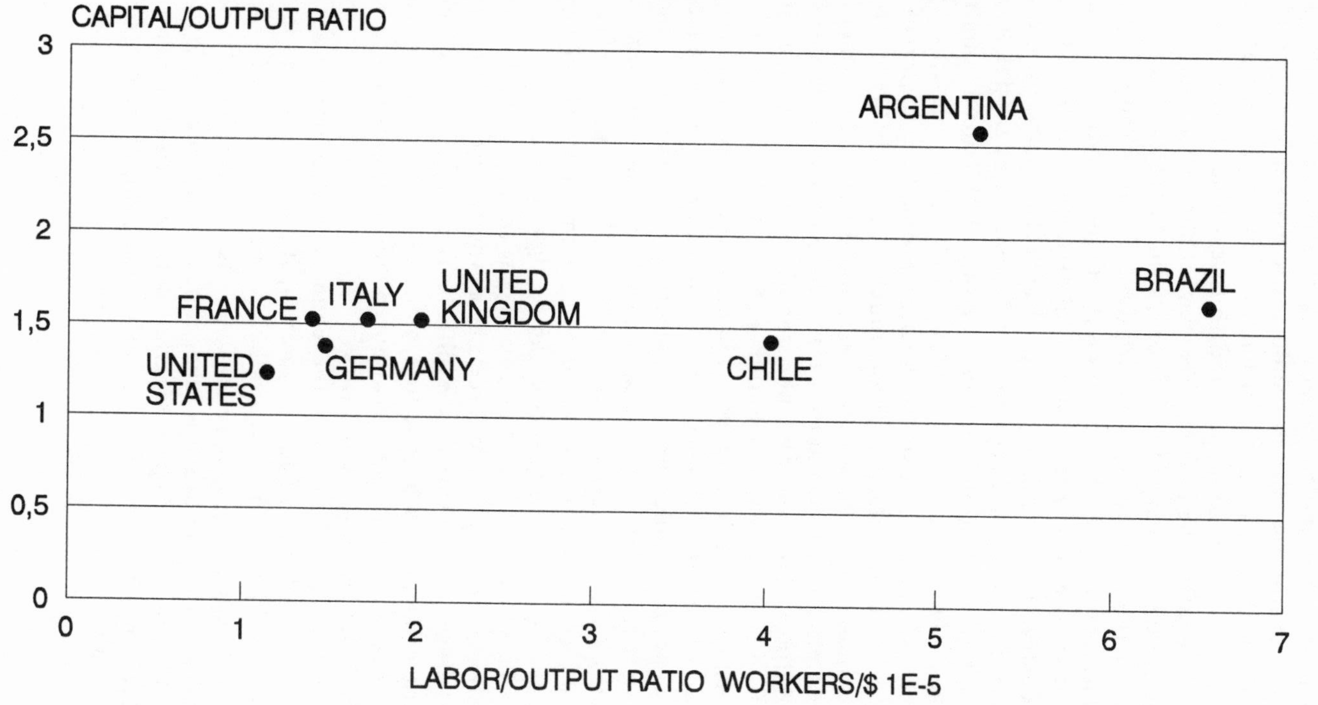

Efficiency Comparison Among International Defense Industries

domestic labor and financial markets had also been deregulated, and price controls on sales in the domestic market had been removed.

Even though defense output in Chile is the lowest of the three Latin American countries, and thus less able to reap economies-of-scale benefits, the internal free market conditions and the low market protection by means of tariffs prevailing after 1974 helped to increase the efficiency in the utilization of labor and capital in the manufacturing sector, of which the defense industry is part.

It is noteworthy that the capital efficiency of the Chilean defense industry is comparable with the efficiencies of industrialized countries. This similarity in the efficient use of capital, however, may result from existing overcapacity in industrialized countries—which takes the form of redundant and idling defense production plants—intended to cope with surge production in case of hostilities, whereas the Chilean defense industry is probably operating at its maximum capacity. Another source of increased capital efficiency in the Chilean defense industry is the utilization of unused spaces and old buildings. For example, the assembly line of the Pillan airplanes was set up in a 40-year-old building (Boisset, 1991), and ASMAR's new slipway was built in space available at the Talcahuano shipyard. The workers of the Chilean defense industry show productivity levels similar to nondefense manufacturing workers of industrialized countries, indicating high skill levels and the adoption of improved managerial practices. Under these conditions the benefits that can be obtained by integrating the defense firms more closely with the rest of the manufacturing sector can be significant.

Brazil emerged as the country with the second-most efficient defense industry of the three Latin American countries studied. The relatively high Brazilian capital efficiency as compared with the Argentinean may be due to economies of scale, in particular for the production of aircraft and armored vehicles, the main export items of the Brazilian defense industry.

Even though Brazil is the country that has the most publicized defense industry of Latin America, it came out as the least efficient user of labor: The overall low productivity of the Brazilian manufacturing employees affects the defense industry as well. In order to validate this low labor productivity, the employment figures of Embraer and Engesa, together with their sales as reported by Ross (1984, pp. 214, 282) for the early 1980s, can be used for comparison, as shown below:

Firm	Sales M $ 1988 Circa 1980	Direct Emp.	Total Emp. (* 2)	Employees per Million Dollars
Embraer	233.44	5,785	11,570	49.56
Engesa	158.46 (exports)	4,000	8,000	50.48
Average				50.02

Some of the differences in the average number of employees per million dollars of output shown in the table (50)—compared with the figure found before using national purchases and the estimated number of employees of the overall defense industry (65.6)—may be due to the fact that these two firms were the most successful private defense firms in Brazil at that time, expected to have the most skilled personnel and productive capital. They also represent only 28 percent of total defense industry employment, with the two largest state-owned firms IMBEL and Naval Shipyards not included—supposedly with much lower productivities.

It is also very possible that the approximate number of employees of the defense industry utilized here and the procedure used to determine total defense output may contain errors. However, the 23.6 percent higher efficiency of the work force of these two firms for the year 1980, as compared with the calculations carried out for the overall defense industry for the year 1985 (on average), may include time-induced errors. Overall, it can be assumed that the figure of 65.6 employees per million dollars of output is a numerical high—and efficiencywise low—estimate of the real (and unknown) employee efficiency of the Brazilian defense industry work force during the mid-1980s.

Argentina emerged as the country with the least efficient defense industry of the three Latin American countries studied. The relatively moderate efficiency of the Argentinean labor force is hurt by the extremely low efficiency in the use of capital. This can be explained by the historically high protectionism of the local industry, which tends to reduce efficiency, and the almost complete state-ownership of the productive infrastructure that tends to ignore economic considerations when deciding investments. As an example of the latter case, in Chapter 4 was mentioned the purchase of a bearings factory at a price of $500 million.

Diseconomies of scale can be another explanation for the low capital efficiency of the Argentinean defense industry, which historically has exported very little of the large variety of locally produced arms and defense equipment. As already indicated in Chapter 6, Dodaro (1991) argues that the export capability of a country rests in its ability to produce products that are competitive in world markets, entailing both price and quality considerations. The low efficiency of the Argentinean defense industry will entail high production costs, resulting in high sales prices for its products, reducing competitiveness and hampering export efforts. As an example, Porth (1984) reports that in order to export Pucará aircraft to neighboring Uruguay, Argentina priced them at only $1.8 million, whereas the manufacturing cost is considered to range near the $3 million figure, thus requiring a substantial 40 percent subsidy to make it attractive.

8.5.3 Statistical Validation of the Assumptions

In order to assess the validity of the assumptions made, in particular with respect to the approximate method adopted for calculating national defense purchases, and the degree of fit between total defense output, capital input, and labor input for the eight countries discussed above, correlation analysis was used. The following table displays the correlation coefficients among the logarithms of the variables total defense output (LOGOUTPUT), capital (LOGCAPITAL), and labor input (LOGLABOR) for the three semi-industrialized and five industrialized countries analyzed in this section.

	Logoutput	Logcapital	Loglabor
Logoutput	1	0.9946**	0.9756**
Logcapital		1	0.9827**
Loglabor			1

** $p < 0.001$

The correlation coefficients shown indicate that all the variables are significantly positively highly correlated, indicating that in spite of the approximations and constructed variables used for all of the above calculations, the assumptions made, and thus the results obtained, can be considered highly credible. The sensitivity calculations performed at various points in this chapter to check the validity of the dollars-per-soldier figures for Chile and Argentina also lend support to the credibility of the results obtained.

8.6 DERIVATION OF PRODUCTION FUNCTIONS

8.6.1 Returns to Scale

With the figures of value added, capital, and labor for each of the defense industries of the five industrialized and three semi-industrialized countries analyzed here, an attempt was made to determine statistically a value-added production function having a Cobb-Douglas form:

$$VA = a \times K^{\alpha} \times L^{\beta}$$

where K = capital in million U.S. 1988 dollars; L = labor in average number of employees for the year; and VA = value added in million U.S. 1988 dollars. When using a log-log regression equation for the full set of countries, the exponent of the capital input came out greater than one, with the exponent of labor input not different from zero. These results are clearly wrong. The problem is that while attempting to find a common production function for industrialized and semi-industrialized countries combined, it is assumed that they have the same production technology, something far from being true.

As the Cobb-Douglas production function has three unknowns, the defense industry data of the three semi-industrialized countries were used to construct a set of three simultaneous equations of the form:

$$LOG\ (VA) = LOG\ (a) + \alpha \times LOG\ (K) + \beta \times LOG\ (L)$$

From the solution of the system of equations, it was found that the value-added Cobb-Douglas function for the semi-industrialized countries is of the form:

$$VA = 0.193 \times K^{0.381} \times L^{0.472}$$
$$\alpha + \text{ß} = 0.854 \text{ (decreasing returns to scale)}$$

This function indicates that the Latin American defense industries have decreasing returns to scale, with labor output elasticity (0.472) being higher than capital output elasticity (0.381). According to this finding, it is not convenient in economic terms to increase production of domestic defense equipment in Latin America, but if it is the political intention to do so anyhow, increased production should be done by increasing labor and not by increasing capital. An additional benefit would be the employment and training of more skilled workers.

One reason for the decreasing returns to scale of the defense industry in these semi-industrialized countries is the production of several different kinds of weapons systems and other defense equipment of increasing sophistication, as shown in Chapter 7, that requires investment in several different areas simultaneously. The continuous change in the product's characteristics also requires the continuous upgrading of production processes and retraining of workers, with many new starts and short production runs. Thus, in Argentina, Brazil, and Chile it has not been possible to attain returns to scale because there is a discontinuous process of learning by doing, lack of effective specialization, and small-scale production. Thus, more than just true diseconomies of scale, these can also be considered to include diseconomies of scope.

Even though this is a deterministic and not a statistical empirical finding, the assumption in this case is that the defense industries of Argentina, Brazil, and Chile have the same production technology. This is much closer to reality than the assumption that all countries—industrialized or not—share the same production technology.

To illustrate the different natures of the production functions between the two groups of countries, using the same procedure described above and using the defense industry data for the three most efficient industrialized countries of the sample (France, Germany, and the United States), the following results were obtained:

$$VA = 0.0266 \times K^{0.622} \times L^{0.494}$$
$$\alpha + \text{ß} = 1.11 \text{ (increasing returns to scale)}$$

Thus, the defense industries of these industrialized countries possess increasing returns to scale, with the output elasticity of capital being higher than labor. These countries are able to produce defense equipment in large quantities much more cheaply than developing countries, with increased investment.

From the comparison of the two groups of countries, it can be argued that there must be a production volume of arms and weapons systems for which returns to scale become constant, above which they start increasing. Apparently, the Latin American countries are far from reaching that critical production volume of defense equipment. Thus, in the future they will continue producing domestically military goods more expensive than what they can buy in the international arms market. This empirical finding of decreasing returns to scale, combined with the above described lower efficiencies in the utilization of capital and, in particular, labor, supports the beliefs of political scientists like Ross (1984), for example, who explain the emergence of local defense industries of developing countries only in terms of reducing the political, economic, and technological dependency from industrialized countries in spite of increasing costs.

8.6.2 Optimal Capital/Labor Ratio

Given that Argentina, Brazil, and Chile had different wage rates during the mid-1980s, and having considered a uniform cost of capital of 12 percent, the optimal capital over labor ratio (K/L) will vary across the defense industries of these countries. According to Mansfield (1990, p. 198), the optimum combination of factor inputs occurs when:

$$MP_L \ / \ MP_K = P_L \ / \ P_K$$

where MP_i = marginal productivity of input i = $\delta Q \ / \ \delta i$; Q = output volume, measured here in dollars; P_i = price of input i; and i = production factors capital (K); labor (L).

For the case of a Cobb-Douglas function:

$$\delta Q \ / \ \delta K = \alpha Q \ / \ K$$
$$\delta Q \ / \ \delta L = \beta Q \ / \ L$$

Then, for a Cobb-Douglas production function the optimum capital over labor ratio becomes:

$$(K \ / \ L)_{optimum} = (\alpha \ P_L \ ) \ / \ (\beta \ P_K \ )$$

Table 8.8 shows the calculations of actual and optimal K/L ratios for Argentina, Brazil, and Chile according to the values presented previously.

The defense industry of Brazil came out to be operating very close to the optimal ratio, with a deviation in the ratio of 13.6 percent from the optimum. This close-to-optimal operating condition can be considered to be a consequence of the significant participation of the private industry in defense production in Brazil.

In the case of Chile, the deviation in the K/L ratio is only 12.0 percent, meaning that the combination of factor inputs is also very close to optimal in spite of the significant state ownership of defense production infrastructure. A sufficient explanation for this close-to-optimal operating condition was Chile's improved efficiency of firms and the market economy policy adopted after 1974.

Table 8.8

Optimal Capital over Labor Ratio for Latin American Defense Industries

Country	Capital	Labor	K/L	w	r	$(\alpha$ w)/ $(\beta$ r)
Argentina	4,869.769	99,000	0.04919	1,834.624	120,000	0.012340
Brazil	1,813.489	72,800	0.024911	3,260.732	120,000	0.021934
Chile	554.2	15,680	0.035344	4,690.854	120,000	0.031553

Notes: Capital in million U.S. dollars of 1988; labor average for the year; wage rate w annual per employee in U.S. dollars 1988; cost of capital r in dollars per million dollars of 1988.

For Argentina the actual K/L ratio found is far from optimal, with a deviation of 300 percent. The very high K/L ratio found is due to an excessive use of capital—four times what would be considered optimal for the number of employees in the industry—and to the cost of capital and labor prevailing at that time. As mentioned before, the predominant state ownership of defense production facilities in Argentina could have contributed to the overcapitalization of the industry.

8.7 CHAPTER SUMMARY

In this chapter an assessment was made of the economic impact of the most important defense industries of the Latin American region. As expected, the defense industries of Argentina, Brazil, and Chile proved to be less efficient than the defense industries of industrialized countries, in particular with respect to the utilization of labor.

It was found that in the mid-1980s the Brazilian defense industry was not the most productive in absolute terms, occupying second place after the defense industry of Argentina. The economic impact of the Brazilian defense industry as measured by the share in total manufacturing production is marginal, with an even smaller importance in terms of employment, not having been able to achieve an effective import substitution process. The armed forces of Brazil have apparently continued to rely upon sophisticated imported defense equipment, in spite of the world position of the Brazilian indigenous defense industry. This indicates that even though technological self-reliance has been achieved in certain areas, the Brazilian armed forces have remained technologically ahead of local developments. This technological lead of the Brazilian armed forces can be considered the driving mechanism for the indigenous production of weapons of higher sophistication over time.

Of the three countries studied here, the Brazilian defense industry was found to be the least efficient in the use of labor, resulting in an average overall performance in between Chile and Argentina. However, considering the different wage rates across the three countries, and assuming a uniform cost of capital, the Brazilian defense industry was found to be operating close to the optimal capital/labor ratio.

The Argentinean defense industry was found to be the one that in the mid-1980s showed the largest productive capacity of the region, and to have the greatest importance in terms of share of output and employment of the manufacturing sector. However, it was found to be the least efficient user of capital in the region. It was also found to have a statistically significant negative impact on total manufacturing output, not achieving the autarky sought through import substitution. This negative impact, together with the finding that during the 1980s there was in place a strong import substitution policy—ineffective but supposedly still persisting—will result in a sustained decline in the Argentinean manufacturing production.

The Chilean defense industry was found to have some interesting characteristics. Its importance in the manufacturing sector has been increasing since the early 1980s, with a strong import substitution policy in place that has allowed an effective reduction in imports by increasing local production. The efficiency in the utilization of capital by the Chilean defense industry was found to be similar to the efficiency levels of industrialized countries. The reasons for the high efficiency of the Chilean defense industry have been explained in terms of improved market conditions in the country's economy and a reduction in protectionist tariffs after 1974, as well as the very high productivity of its work force that has reached productivity levels comparable to nondefense manufacturing employees of industrialized countries.

Even though the Chilean defense industry is still far less efficient than the defense industries of industrialized countries in the utilization of labor, it was found to be the most efficient of the region, operating closer to the optimal capital to labor ratio, and with a positive and statistically significant impact on overall manufacturing output. This positive correlation, together with the assumption of production cycles, would indicate that in the future manufacturing output will decline as a consequence of declining defense production.

Even though Latin American defense workers proved to be more efficient than nondefense manufacturing workers at the national level, the clustering of the Latin American defense industries in a region of relatively low labor efficiency and the higher output elasticity of labor when compared with capital may indicate that improved and enhanced technical skills and managerial practices can be the best method of increasing total factor productivity in the short run.

The decreasing returns to scale of the Latin American defense industries found by using a deterministic Cobb-Douglas value-added function may recommend the reduction in the production levels of arms and weapons systems in the region, particularly in the case of Argentina.

Given the relatively low efficiency levels of the Latin American defense industries when compared with those of industrialized countries, in particular with respect to the use of labor, the respective governments of Argentina, Brazil, and Chile need to assess in detail which defense goods can be produced more efficiently locally and to purchase abroad the weapons with the highest local production inefficiencies. In the political short run, it may be more economic and efficient to purchase defense equipment abroad, but there is a need to reduce supply uncertainty by having a domestic defense industry. The balance is determined by a combination of economics and international politics.

The local production of arms and weapons was found to follow approximately a 10- to 15-year cycle, where the degree of sophistication of the indigenous weapons produced increases on each successive cycle. A cycle begins when the indigenous defense industry engages in the local production of weapons, all of them with comparable degrees of sophistication, with the intent of substituting for equivalent imported weapons. After the local market for the weapons produced locally saturates, a decline in the production volume of indigenous weapons occurs, bringing a cycle to an end.

Sensitivity and statistical analysis of the results presented here indicate that the assumptions made and the approximate method derived to calculate national defense purchases can be considered reasonably adequate.

9

Conclusions

The main conclusions of our research are presented in this chapter. Specific conclusions related to the defense industries of Argentina, Brazil, and Chile are introduced first. Conclusions pertaining to the overall Latin American region are presented following the country-specific conclusions. Finally, the findings and conclusions obtained from the study of the defense industries will be used to derive implications for the design of industrial policies for semi-industrialized countries.

9.1 COUNTRY-SPECIFIC CONCLUSIONS

The defense industries of the three countries studied—Argentina, Brazil, and Chile—appear to be a representative sample of the types of defense industries to be found in other semi-industrialized countries. The representability of these defense industries derives from the different size, different industry structure, varying degrees of government participation, and different characteristics and capabilities of the respective national industrial and technological infrastructures.

From the description and analysis of the main characteristics and economy-related indicators of the defense industries of Argentina, Brazil, and Chile, it is possible to infer that these industries have multiple impacts on the respective economies. These impacts can have varying degrees of positive or negative significance, depending on several conditions. The most important conditions are (1) the degree of private participation and ownership of defense firms and (2) the importance assigned to economic criteria in decision making by the state-owned defense firms. In fact, private firms utilize economic criteria for their decisions, improving the allocation of human, financial, and technical resources, thus increasing the efficiency of the overall defense industry. In some countries, however, state-owned factories have operated without economic considerations. These state-owned factories, with easier access to large amounts of capital, often engage in the manufacture of uneconomic products, reducing the efficiency of the allocated resources.

9.1.1 Argentina

Argentina's closed defense industry, heavily guided by autarkic objectives, entails minimal participation of private firms and a large share of total manufacturing production carried out by state-owned factories. Thus, the Argentinean defense industry has significantly restricted the output of the manufacturing sector. Vayrynen (1992, p. 105) argues that "one of the main reasons for the transformation of the positive contribution of military industrialization into a negative one is the isolation of the military R&D and production from the competitive pressures of the market." The negative impact of military production on total manufacturing found in the case of Argentina and the low efficiency of its defense industry lend support to Vayrynen's argument.

The absence of private firms in the Argentinean defense industry was also considered to be the main cause for the very low volume of defense exports. In fact, during the mid-1980s Argentina reached the largest sales volume of defense equipment of the Latin American region. However, during the 1980s its defense industry showed the lowest level of defense exports of the three defense industries studied. This was probably a consequence of a government policy not to export or an inability to do so because of high prices due to high production costs.

In spite of the moderate efficiency of Argentina's defense workers, the large overcapitalization of its defense industry resulted in the most inefficient of the three industries studied. This overcapitalization can be assumed to be a consequence of a nationwide long-standing application of an import substitution policy that demanded the establishment of a significant production infrastructure, regardless of cost.

Even though it was found that an import substitution process was in place during the last 20 years, the Argentinean defense industry was not able to effectively replace imports with national production. High levels of imports and large national purchases of defense equipment occurred simultaneously. In spite of having the longest history of defense manufacturing and producing the largest sales volume of defense equipment in Latin America, the Argentinean defense industry was not able to reduce its technological—and thus political—dependency on industrialized countries, a goal of the military industrialization process since its beginning.

The most salient and positive contribution of the Argentinean defense industry to the local economy can be assumed to be the institutionalization of the process to generate domestic technology. The capacity of the Argentinean defense industry to generate its own technology, coupled with the high degree of vertical integration of its defense industry, resulted in an appreciable logistical depth for the manufacture of some local defense products. However, this logistical depth was attained at significant costs, providing the capacity to embody in its products only outdated technology when compared with defense products of industrialized nations, more or less easily available in the international arms market.

9.1.2 Brazil

The defense industry of Brazil proved to be the most important exporter of defense equipment in Latin America, producing the second largest total sales volume of weapons and other defense equipment of the region in the mid-1980s. However, given the large size of the Brazilian economy, its defense exports constituted only a small proportion of total manufactured exports.

At the manufacturing level, the total production of Brazilian defense equipment is a small percentage of total manufacturing production, and no statistically significant correlation was found between defense production and manufacturing output. It was shown that the Brazilian defense industry employs less than 1 percent of total manufacturing employees. Because of this, it is possible to infer that the defense industry of Brazil is a consequence of economic "scale effects" at the national level (large armed forces, large population, large GNP), with a marginal contribution to total national output, showing a very small economic impact. In support of this conclusion, Vayrynen (1992, p. 104) indicates that "if measured in terms of macro-economic variables, the Brazilian defense industry would have probably performed better in an expanding world economy."

The preponderant participation of private firms in the Brazilian defense industry has allowed the effective transfer of product, process, and managerial technological innovations resulting from defense production to the rest of the civilian economy. At the firm level, this total integration of civilian and military production eliminates the need to resort to isolated spin-off events of minimal importance in order to benefit from military industrialization. The strong presence of these private defense firms can also be considered one of the main reasons for the sustained high levels of Brazilian defense exports during the last 15 years of the period analyzed.

In spite of the lower productivity of Brazilian defense workers when compared with their Argentinean peers, the efficiency of the Brazilian defense industry proved to be higher than the Argentinean. This higher efficiency can again be attributed to the private firms that account for almost the entire Brazilian defense industry and to a more efficient utilization of capital equipment.

In Brazil, as in the case of Argentina, one of the most important contributions the emergence of an important defense industry has made to the local economy is the capacity to generate domestic defense technology. This can be observed in the weapons produced by the Brazilian defense firms. These products have experienced rapid change in the embodied technology. It was shown that the technological sophistication of the weapons manufactured in Brazil has reached levels similar to the levels of industrialized countries. Thus, it appears that the defense industry of Brazil has been the first industry of the Brazilian economy to achieve such a degree of technological sophistication.

9.1.3 Chile

In Chile, the local defense industry acquired importance only in the late 1970s and early 1980s. This importance is reflected in the increasing volume of national purchases and a significant amount of exports attained since then. In Chile, a significant import substitution policy was found to be in place. According to statistical analysis, this import substitution policy has effectively allowed the reduction of imported weapons by expanding local production. Based on the Brazilian experience, Vayrynen (1992, p. 100) concluded that in an upwardly moving peripheral country the military industry can also stimulate civilian industrial development. Assuming Vayrynen's hypothesis is valid, and taking into consideration the positive impact that the Chilean defense industry was shown to have on the national economy, it is possible to conclude that Chile can be considered an upwardly moving nation among the peripheral countries.

It was also found that in Chile there exists a significant and positive correlation between defense production and manufacturing output. In addition to the net increase in manufacturing output caused by increased defense production, two alternative explanations for this correlation were formulated. The first of these explanations was in terms of a monetary multiplier effect, and the second, a correlation but not causality phenomenon assumed to be influenced by other economic policies.

Even though the Chilean defense industry is the one that has produced the lowest sales volume of the three industries studied here, it has been able to effectively export a substantial volume of weapons. These exports reached a significant share of manufactured exports, apparently promoted by private firms. The export capacity of the Chilean defense industry would indicate that the import substitution policy adopted has been successful in helping the development of the local industry.

The Chilean defense industry proved to be the most efficient of the three industries studied, even though there is still an important presence of state-owned firms in the industry. This high efficiency was attributed in part to the charter of the state-owned corporations as independent economic units, forced by this charter to become self-sufficient. In addition, the free market economic system adopted in Chile after 1973 increased the overall efficiency of local firms, a phenomenon that also affected the defense industry.

In the past, the capacity of Chile's defense industry to generate its own indigenous technology was hampered by a low utilization of the technological capabilities of the local universities. At present, however, the impetus of defense exports and the present import substitution policy has increased the technological demand and, as a consequence, has improved the ability to generate domestic technology. Nevertheless, the degree of sophistication of the Chilean weapons remains the least advanced of the three countries studied here, lagging more than 10 years behind Argentina and Brazil.

9.2   REGION-SPECIFIC CONCLUSIONS

It was found that the emergence of defense industries strengthens the technological infrastructure of semi-industrialized nations. This conclusion is based on the following facts:

- an enhanced capacity to produce advanced weapons is supported by previously nonexistent R&D laboratories, and
- the required interaction of defense firms, universities, and all types of R&D units.

However, the economic benefits to be obtained from this strengthened technological infrastructure are determined by the openness of the defense industry: The more open and integrated with civilian production, the better.

Defense production was found to be also positively correlated with the number of scientists and engineers doing research and development per million inhabitants, and their productivity in terms of patents per researcher. In this case, the positive correlation was explained in terms of an existing national technological capability to develop and produce more sophisticated products. This last finding was able to enrich the pool of characteristics—pure "scale effects" according to Neuman (1984)—that would enable a country to establish the capacity to produce more advanced weapons. At the regional level, larger defense production volume also proved to be positively correlated with the number of patents granted to nationals. These three positive correlations support the proposition that the defense industry should be based on the existing capacity of the economy to generate technology and that it cannot be created apart from it.

The technological capability of the local defense industries to produce more sophisticated weapons and other defense equipment was found to be dependent on the respective national science and technology policies. The capabilities created by the science and technology policy adopted in each country shape the technological infrastructure of the economy. Thus, the science and technology policy, possibly adopted decades before, predetermines the technological capacity of the research infrastructure. It also determines the technical characteristics and number of scientists and engineers that work in industry, universities, and national laboratories. Then, according to the technological capability and infrastructure that is institutionalized by the science and technology policy, the defense industry is either favored or restricted in its capacity to develop and produce weapons of varying degrees of sophistication.

Assuming a Cobb-Douglas value-added production function for the defense industry, it was found that the defense industries of industrialized and semi-industrialized countries have different characteristics. The production function of industrialized countries showed increasing returns to scale, with a higher output elasticity of capital than labor. For semi-industrialized countries, the production function showed decreasing returns to scale, with an output elasticity of labor higher than that of capital. These differences were found using deterministic rather than statistical results. However, the findings are supported by the realistic assumption that the defense industries of semi-industrialized countries employ a different production technology than industrialized countries.

In semi-industrialized countries, the decreasing returns to scale of the defense industry were assumed to be caused by heavy investments needed to produce only a few units of certain weapons classes; by the absence of learning effects due to short production runs; and by large expenditures in research and development that are not amortized, given the production of only a few units of each type of weapon. This finding supports the argument by some researchers that semi-industrialized countries are less able to produce advanced weapons at lower costs than industrialized countries in spite of lower labor rates.

The fact that the output elasticity of labor was higher than the output elasticity of capital for semi-industrialized countries indicates that skills and innovative managerial practices should be enhanced before embarking in large capital investments. This conclusion is supported by the work of Suri et al. (1992) in the case of some civilian firms.

The production of defense equipment in Argentina, Brazil, and Chile was shown to follow a cyclic pattern. The length of the cycle was estimated to be around 10 to 15 years. It was assumed that the defense production cycle is driven by the technological characteristics of the weapons and determined by the saturation of the local defense market. The importance of this production cycle depends upon the impact on the infrastructure created for the production of weapons. As weapons become more sophisticated, a smaller quantity is needed to satisfy the requirements of the local armed forces. Therefore, shorter production runs result. However, the production of more sophisticated weapons demands the investment of larger amounts of capital and renders previous capital investments obsolete. This would indicate that the evaluation of capital investments for the production of domestic defense equipment is a critical aspect of the military industrialization of semi-industrialized countries. The negative returns to scale found in the Latin American defense industry, with a lower output elasticity of capital than of labor, lend further support to this argument.

9.3   INDUSTRIAL POLICY IMPLICATIONS

In Chapter 1, it was mentioned that the industrial policies adopted by the government for the establishment of a modern defense industry, and their outcomes, could be used as examples to derive industrial policies of wide applicability to the rest of the economy. The conclusions to be derived here pertain to the design of effective industrial policies for semi-industrialized countries based on the results of the cross comparison of the defense industries of Argentina, Brazil, and Chile.

9.3.1   The Role of the Government

As was mentioned in Chapter 6, from an industrial policy perspective, the efficiency and productivity of the industry and the role played by private firms are contingent upon the adoption of a predominantly free market economy by the government. The search for autarky at any cost and by all means, coupled with a closed economy, hinders the efficient allocation of resources in any industry, reducing its efficiency. Autarky is an illusive and elusive goal. It can never be achieved, and in the attempt, increasing levels of resources are required. The isolation of the local industry from the world markets results in higher production costs and outdated embodied technology. The local industry is favored when international relations are open, the sources of technology are many, and the targeted market is the world market.

Repeating some of the findings of Chapter 6, the basis for the emergence of a modern and productive industry and some of the actions to be undertaken by the government can be:

- the establishment of a free market economy,
- no subsidies to local industries,
- total reliance on private rather than state-owned firms,
- promotion of intense competition among firms,

- strong government support for R&D and technological innovation by means of a properly orchestrated[1] science and technology policy,
- open access to all sources of technology from industrialized countries,
- a vision of a global market with unrestricted access to all buyers and a strong level of exports, and
- sustained political support by the government, mostly in the form of soft credits.

The government is responsible for ensuring that all these conditions are met in order for the defense industry, as with any other industry, to become an efficient and fruitful sector of the economy.

Obviously, the transition from a closed or restricted economy to an open economy will require some temporary measures, such as retraining of workers and gradual reduction of tariffs. However, a plan should be established and implemented to gradually phase out these transitional measures.

9.3.2 Science and Technology Policies

As mentioned, a positive and significant correlation was found between total defense production and the number of scientists and engineers per million inhabitants engaged in research and development, and the productivity of these researchers as measured by patents per researcher. Similar correlations can be expected to be found in other technology-intensive industries. This finding indicates that to increase the production levels of technology-intensive industries, as well as the level of sophistication of the products manufactured by such industries, the science and technology policies of semi-industrialized countries should be aimed at increasing both indicators: the degree of technologization of society and researchers' productivity.

As already mentioned in this chapter, the science and technology policy instituted by the government shapes the technological resources and infrastructure of the industry. The higher technology content of

---

1. By "properly orchestrated" is meant a policy based on technical grounds, with clear objectives and adequate funding.

Brazilian—and, to a lesser degree, of Argentinean—weapons, was associated with a higher commitment by the respective governments for the establishment of science and technology policies of higher impact. This higher commitment was associated with larger amounts of money spent in research and development activities by the government. In order to increase the level of sophistication of all kinds of products manufactured locally, there is a need to increase the number of scientists and engineers working in industry, in universities, and in research organizations. This can be achieved by increasing the state budget devoted to the scientific and technological effort of the country, by providing incentives to increase research and development expenditures in industry, and by facilitating technology transfer from government laboratories and universities to industry.

In Argentina and Brazil, advanced defense technology was developed in research centers dedicated to the study of particular problems related to weapons and defense equipment (mission-oriented R&D organizations), with a high degree of specialization. According to this finding, special attention should be given to the establishment of specialized centers devoted to education, training, research, and development of particular technologies for specific industries. This conclusion is supported by the findings of Porter (1990).

9.3.3 Universities

Brazil, with the highest technology content in its defense products, also showed the most significant participation of universities in the development of defense technology. Conversely, Chile experienced low university participation and low technology embodiment in its defense products.

Universities sometimes possess the most important pool of technological expertise and research capability in semi-industrialized countries. This fact indicates that these institutions need to be better utilized by industry. However, in semi-industrialized countries the link of industry with universities has historically been weak. This situation mandates the establishment of improved two-way communication mechanisms and technology transfer between universities and industry.

In this study, it was found that the generation of basic scientific knowledge in universities does not favor the development of more advanced products by industry. What is needed is more technology generated by university research units with important direct application to the needs of local industry. University researchers should understand that they have a social role that goes beyond teaching and the creation of new knowledge in the benefit of pure science. In semi-industrialized countries the professors and researchers who work in universities, being the nation's most important scientific and technological assets, should devote some of their time and talent to the development of applied technology that would benefit the local industries. Appropriate public and private incentives can stimulate activities to this end.

State-owned laboratories and research centers should make their technological capabilities available to industry. The vicious circle of technological dependence must be broken at some point. Increasing the offer of technological services may be one of the alternatives.

9.3.4 Imported Technology

Of the three defense industries studied, Brazil's proved to be the most successful in terms of total exports. This achievement was possible only by the use of imported technology in the form of advanced components. Furthermore, the most advanced products manufactured by the three defense industries were based on substantial—if not total—imported technology. This finding indicates that in semi-industrialized countries advanced foreign technology is essential for the manufacture of sophisticated products.

According to this finding, foreign technology must be made easily accessible to the firms of semi-industrialized countries whenever possible. As the only way a foreign firm might be willing to provide technology is by economic rewards, recipient firms must also be willing to pay for it. In order to render this technology transfer process effective, local firms must determine clearly what kind of technology they need, where it can be found, how much they are willing to pay for it, and how they can obtain government approvals from their home country and the exporting countries.

Some of the examples in this book indicate that there are substantial technology and know-how available in the economies of semi-industrialized countries that have historically been underutilized. Firms in semi-industrialized countries should engage in intense technology search processes in the local economy before deciding to import technology. This will reduce the costs of importing technology that is readily available and will also increase the probability of successful application of the available technology. An increased demand for local technology will also increase the capacity to generate indigenous solutions, another alternative for breaking the vicious circle of technology dependence.

9.3.5 Export Marketing Strategy

When Argentina, and especially Brazil, attempted to market their most sophisticated defense products in the world's arms markets, they found themselves competing against the most important defense companies in the world. Behind most of these companies were also their respective governments, providing financial and political support to their exports.

Semi-industrialized countries must recognize that the sophisticated world markets are dominated by multinational corporations. On the other hand, developing countries possess the capacity to produce goods of low sophistication for their own consumption.   Thus, semi-industrialized countries should concentrate on the development and production of goods of intermediate sophistication and intermediate price but of the best quality possible. This niche strategy will allow access to the markets of relatively less industrialized countries, as well as industrialized countries, without entering into head-to-head competition with multinational corporations.

9.3.6 Manufacturing Technology

The Argentinean defense industry—the most inefficient of the three studied here—reached that condition by substantial overinvestment in productive infrastructure. This overinvestment was needed to produce many different types of weapons in very small quantities, resulting in a very low utilization of capital. On the other hand, the Chilean defense industry—the most efficient of the three industries studied here—can be said to have followed a very cautious capital investment policy, yielding a high capital efficiency.

According to this finding, existing manufacturing equipment should be utilized at its maximum available capacity. The investment of large amounts of money to establish new production facilities should be avoided whenever possible, because it may result in lower efficiencies in the utilization of capital. On the other hand, export market development will increase the utilization of existing plants and equipment, thereby improving the return on investment.

Appendix: Calculations of National Purchases and Total Defense Production

Table A.1
Calculations of National Purchases and Total Defense Production: Argentina

Year	Def. Budget	Arms Imports	Nat'l Expend	Soldiers (000)	Dollars / Soldier	Soldiers Cost	Nat'l Purch.	Def. Exports	Total Def. Product
1969	1331	146	1185	160	7407	1014	171	0	171
1970	1302	54	1248	140	8916	887	361	0	361
1971	1093	25	1068	140	7627	887	180	0	180
1972	1039	152	887	140	*6339	887	0	44.6	44.6
1973	1221	119	1102	160	6888	1014	88	41.4	129.3
1974	1537	87	1450	150	9668	951	499	0	499.4
1975	2033	60	1973	160	12333	1014	959	0	959
1976	2064	94	1970	155	12708	983	987	0	987
1977	1851	72	1778	155	11474	983	796	15.9	812
1978	3011	621	2390	155	15419	983	1408	0	1408
1979	3407	772	2635	155	17000	983	1653	15	1668
1980	3837	297	3540	155	22839	983	2558	7	2565
1981	3699	645	3054	155	19703	983	2072	13	2085
1982	5893	352	5541	175	31663	1109	4432	0	4432
1983	4291	1138	3153	175	18017	1109	2044	23	2067
1984	3525	507	3018	174	17345	1103	1915	135	2050
1985	3049	197	2852	129	22109	818	2034	66	2100
1986	2025	32	1993	104	19163	659	1334	11	1345
1987	1447	62	1385	118	11737	748	637	21	658
1988	2972	20	2952	95	31074	602	2350	30	2380
Avg.	2531	273	2259				1323.8	21.1	1345

* Minimum dollars per soldier = $6,339 used to calculate soldiers costs

Table A.2
Calculations of National Purchases and Total Defense Production: Brazil

Year	Def. Budget	Arms Imports	Nat'l Expend	Soldiers (000)	Dollars / Soldier	Soldiers Cost	Nat'l Purch.	Def. Exports	Total Def. Product
1969	2863	146	2716	360	7546	1414	1302	0	1302
1970	3548	54	3494	375	9317	1473	2021	0	2021
1971	3335	132	3703	375	9875	1473	2230	0	2229
1972	4024	152	3873	410	9446	1611	2262	0	2261
1973	4490	289	4201	420	10002	1650	2551	0	2551
1974	4744	132	4612	435	10602	1709	2903	0	2903
1975	5072	200	4872	455	10707	1788	3084	67	3115
1976	3191	343	2848	450	6329	1768	1080	170	1250
1977	3009	253	2756	450	6125	1768	988	41	1029
1978	2319	336	1983	450	4407	1768	215	168	383
1979	2138	370	1768	450	*3929	1768	0	170	170
1980	2206	184	2022	450	4493	1768	254	198	452
1981	2149	77	2072	450	4604	1768	304	219	523
1982	2888	36	2852	460	6200	1807	1045	819	1864
1983	2533	47	2486	460	5404	1807	679	152	831
1984	2506	169	2337	459	5092	1803	534	732	1266
1985	2626	55	2571	496	5183	1949	622	394	1016
1986	3216	107	3109	527	5899	2070	1038	288	1326
1987	3467	165	3302	541	6104	2125	1176	620	1796
Avg.	3101	175	2926				1278.3	212.5	1490.8

* Minimum dollars per soldier = $3,929 used to calculate soldiers costs.

239

Table A.3
Calculations of National Purchases and Total Defense Production: Chile

Year	Def. Budget	Arms Imports	Nat'l Expend	Soldiers (000)	Dollars / Soldier	Soldiers Cost	Nat'l Purch.	Def. Exports	Total Def. Product
1969	453	29	424	70	6055	113	311	0	311
1970	602	27	575	70	8220	113	463	0	463
1971	609	79	530	70	7576	113	418	0	418
1972	725	25	700	75	9331	121	579	0	579
1973	801	168	633	75	8442	121	512	0	512
1974	1438	153	1284	90	14270	145	1139	0	1139
1975	915	40	875	110	7953	177	698	0	698
1976	426	247	179	111	*1609	179	0	0	0
1977	568	108	460	111	4144	179	282	0	282
1978	647	101	546	111	4919	179	367	0	367
1979	601	278	323	111	2910	179	144	0	144
1980	639	354	285	116	2457	187	98	0	98
1981	699	400	299	116	2578	187	112	0	112
1982	654	340	314	116	2707	187	127	0	127
1983	645	105	540	126	4286	203	337	0	337
1984	670	191	479	123	3894	198	281	23	304
1985	680	55	625	124	5040	199	426	87	513
1986	640	53	587	127	4622	204	383	21	404
1987	852	21	831	127	6543	204	627	176	803
1988	808	30	778	96	8104	154	623	280	904
Avg.	704	140	563	96		167	396	29.7	426.1

* Minimum dollars per soldier = $1,600 used to calculate soldiers costs

Bibliography

Abetti, Pier A. *Linking Technology and Business Strategy.* American Management Association, New York, 1989.

ACDA (Arms Control and Disarmament Agency). *World Military Expenditures and Arms Transfers 1969-1978.* U.S. Government Printing Office, Washington, D.C., 1980.

————. *World Military Expenditures and Arms Transfers 1989.* U.S. Government Printing Office, Washington, D.C.,1990.

Albrecht, Ulrich. "The Federal Republic of Germany and Italy: New Strategies of Mid-Sized Weapons Exporters?" *Journal of International Affairs*, 40 (no. 1), 1986, pp. 129-142.

ASMAR (Astilleros y Maestranzas de la Armada). Annals of the symposium Industria de Defensa Nacional, Valparaíso, Chile, November 1991.

Barke, Richard. *Science, Technology, and Public Policy.* C. Q. Press, Washington, D.C., 1987.

Barros, Alexandre de S. C. "Brazil." In *Arms Production in Developing Countries: An Analysis of Decision Making*, edited by James Everett Katz, pp. 73-88. Lexington Books, Lexington, Mass., 1984.

Bertolucci, Francisco, House Representative. "Contribución de la Industria de Defensa al Desarrollo Socioeconómico del País." Annals of the symposium Industria de Defensa Nacional, ASMAR, Valparaíso, Chile, November 1991, pp. 125-132.

Bilich, F. *Science and Technology Planning and Policy.* Elsevier Science Publishers, Amsterdam, 1989.

Black, Guy. "The Effect of Government Funding on Commercial R and D." In *Factors in the Transfer of Technology*, edited by William H. Gruber and Donald D. Marquis, pp. 202-218. MIT Press, Cambridge, Mass., 1969.

Boisset, Caupolican, Chilean Air Force General. "La Industria Aeronáutica Nacional y su Proyección Futura." Annals of the symposium Industria de Defensa Nacional, ASMAR, Valparaíso, Chile, November 1991, pp. 56-75.

Brigagao, Clovis. "The Brazilian Arms Industry." *Journal of International Affairs*, 40 (no. 1), 1986, pp. 101-114.

Brzoska, Michael. "Other Countries: The Smaller Arms Producers." In *Arms Production in the Third World*, edited by Michael Brzoska and Thomas Ohlson, pp. 251-277. Stockholm International Peace Research Institute, Taylor and Francis, London, 1986.

Brzoska, Michael, and Ohlson, Thomas. *Arms Production in the Third World*. Stockholm International Peace Research Institute, Taylor and Francis, London, 1986.

———. *Arms Transfers to the Third World, 1971-85*. Stockholm International Peace Research Institute, Oxford University Press, Oxford, 1987.

Bureau of International Economic Affairs. "CHILE: Exports, Investments, Economy." Editorial Lord Cochrane Limitada, Santiago, Chile, no.32, March-April 1989.

Cardoen, Carlos. "La Industria de Defensa en la Actualidad y su Proyección Futura: Visión de la Empresa Privada." Annals of the symposium Industria de Defensa Nacional, ASMAR, Valparaíso, Chile, November 1991, pp. 77-86.

CEPAL (Comisión Económica para America Latina y el Caribe). *Anuario Estadístico de América Latina y el Caribe, Edición 1989*. CEPAL, Santiago, Chile, 1989.

Chales de Beaulieu, Juan. "Astilleros Estrecho de Magallanes: Significación Económica y Social." *Revista de Marina* (Valparaíso, Chile), no. 6, 1990.

Chambers, Robert G. *Applied Production Analysis: A Dual Approach*. Cambridge University Press, Cambridge, England, 1988.

CONICIT (Consejo Nacional de Investigaciones Científicas y Tecnológicas). *Ciencia y Tecnología en Cifras No. 3*. CONICIT, Caracas, Venezuela, 1986.

CONICYT (Comisión Nacional de Investigación Científica y Tecnológica). *Indicadores Científicos y Tecnológicos: Informe 1990*. Serie Estudios no. 22. CONICYT, Santiago, Chile, 1990.

Dodaro, Santo. "Comparative Advantage, Trade and Growth: Export-Led Growth Revisited." *World Development*, 19 (no. 9), 1991, pp. 1153–1165.

Dosi, Giovanni; Pavitt, Keith; and Soete, Luc. *The Economics of Technical Change and International Trade*. Harvester-Wheatsheaf, Hemel Hempstead, Great Britain, 1990.

ENAER (Empresa Nacional de Aeronáutica). First author's telephone interview with the public relations officer of the company on April 4, 1992.

Evenson, Robert E. "International Invention: Implications for Technology Market Analysis." In *R & D, Patents, and Productivity*, edited by Zvi Griliches, pp. 89-126. University of Chicago Press, Chicago, 1984.

FACH (Fuerza Aerea de Chile). *Anales del Primer Congreso de Ingeniería de Defensa*. Academia Politécnica de la Fuerza Aerea, Santiago, Chile, 1987.

Fialka, John J. "Fixed-Up Fighters: Old War Planes Get Brand New Electronics, Live to Fight Again." *Wall Street Journal*, September 19, 1991, pp. A1, A8.

Fox, Ronald J., with Field, James L. *The Defense Management Challenge: Weapons Acquisition*. Harvard Business School Press, Boston, 1988.

Frank, Andre Gunther. *Capitalism and Underdevelopment in Latin America*. Penguin Books, Harmondsworth, 1969.

Frankman, Myron J. "Global Income Redistribution: An Alternate Perspective on the Latin American Debt Crisis." In *Latin America to the Year 2000*, edited by Archibald R. M. Ritter, Maxwell A. Cammeron, and David H. Pollock, pp. 41–51. Praeger Publishers, Westport, Conn., 1992.

Frantz, Robert. "X-Efficiency Theory and Its Critics." *Quarterly Review of Economics and Business*, 25 (no. 4), Winter 1985, pp. 38–58.

Freeman, Christopher. *The Economics of Industrial Innovation*. 2d ed. MIT Press, Cambridge, Mass., 1986.

Gansler, Jacques S. *The Defense Industry*. MIT Press, Cambridge, Mass., 1980.

———. *Affording Defense*. MIT Press, Cambridge, Mass., 1989.

Hax, Arnoldo, and Majluf, Nicolás. *The Strategy Concept and Process*. Prentice-Hall, Englewood Cliffs, N.J., 1991.

Heinz, John. *U.S. Strategic Trade: An Export Control System for the 1990s*. Westview Press, Boulder, Colo., 1991.

Herbert-Copley, Brent. "Technical Change in Latin American Manufacturing Firms: Review and Synthesis." *World Development*, 18 (no. 11), 1990, pp. 1457–1469.

Herrick, Bruce, and Kindleberger, Charles P. *Economic Development*. 4th ed. McGraw-Hill, New York, 1983.

Hewish, Mark, and Luria, Rene. "South America's Small But Steady Defense Market." *International Defense Review*, no. 5, 1992, pp. 449–453.

International Labour Office. *Yearbook of Labour Statistics 1991*. ILO, Geneva, Switzerland, 1991.

Jane's All the World Aircraft, 1960. Jane's Information Group, Coulsdon, United Kingdom, 1959.

Jane's All the World Aircraft, 1991. Jane's Information Group, Coulsdon, United Kingdom, 1990.

Jane's Armour and Artillery, 1991–92. Jane's Information Group, Coulsdon, United Kingdom, 1991.

Jane's Encyclopedia of Aviation. Grolier Educational Corporation, Danbury, Conn., 1980.

Jane's Fighting Ships, 1970–71. Jane's Information Group, Coulsdon, United Kingdom, 1970.

Jane's Fighting Ships, 1980–81. Jane's Information Group, Coulsdon, United Kingdom, 1980.

Jane's Fighting Ships, 1990–91. Jane's Information Group, Coulsdon, United Kingdom, 1990.

Jane's Fighting Ships, 1991–92. Jane's Information Group, printed by Butler and Tanner, London, 1991.

Katz, James Everett. "Understanding Arms Production in Developing Countries." In *Arms Production in Developing Countries*, edited by James Everett Katz, pp. 3–13. Lexington Books, Lexington, Mass., 1984.

———. "Factors Affecting Military Scientific Research in the Third World." In *The Implications of Third World Military Industrialization*, edited by James Everett Katz, pp. 293-304. Lexington Books, Lexington, Mass., 1986.

Kellman, M.; Saadawi, T.; Ahmed, S.; Peracha, W.; and Frisch, F. "Foreign Dependency—Theory and Practice." In *Management of Technology III*, edited by Tarek M. Khalil and Bulent A. Bayraktar, pp. 1375-1385. Proceedings of the Third International Conference on Management of Technology, Institute of Industrial Engineers, Norcross, Ga., 1992.

Kindleberger, Charles P., and Herrick, Bruce. *Economic Development*. 3d ed. McGraw-Hill, New York, 1977.

Klare, Michael T. "Who's Arming Who?: The Arms Trade in the 1990s." *Technology Review*, May–June, 1990, pp. 42–50.

Kolodziej, Edward A. "Europe as a Global Power: Implications of Making and Marketing Arms in France." *Journal of International Affairs*, 41, 1987a, pp. 385–420.

——. *Making and Marketing Arms*. Princeton University Press, Princeton, N.J., 1987b.

Landaburu, Federico G. C. "De la Confederación Argentina de las Provincias Unidas del Río de la Plata a la República Argentina." *Tecnología Militar* (Monch Editorial Group, Bonn, Germany), no. 12, 1986, pp. 17–29.

——. "Construcción Naval en la Argentina." *Tecnología Militar* (Monch Editorial Group, Bonn, Germany), no. 11, 1987a, pp. 24–32.

——. "Producción de Armamento Individual en la Argentina." *Tecnología Militar* (Monch Editorial Group, Bonn, Germany), no. 3, 1987b, pp. 28–31.

Letelier, Guillermo, Brigadier General, Chilean Army. "La Industria Bélica Nacional: Visión del Ejército." Annals of the symposium Industria de Defensa Nacional, ASMAR, Valparaíso, Chile, November 1991, pp. 51–64.

Lock, P. "Brazil: Arms for Export." In *Arms Production in the Third World*, edited by Michael Brzoska and Thomas Ohlson, pp. 79–103. Stockholm International Peace Research Institute, Taylor and Francis, London, 1986.

Maldifassi, José. *Introducción a la Energía Nuclear*. Chilean Navy Bureau of Engineering, Valparaíso, Chile, 1988a.

——. "La Industria Privada en el Suministro de Bienes y Servicios para la Defensa." *Revista de Marina*, no. 3, 1988b, (Valparaíso, Chile) pp. 321–329.

——. "Consideraciones para una Política Tecnológica de las Fuerzas Armadas." Centro de Estudios de la Nacionalidad, Essay no. 7, Santiago, Chile, September 1989.

——. "La Tecnología como Elemento de Unión Entre las Fuerzas Armadas y las Universidades." Working paper of the Centro de Estudios Fuerzas Armadas y Sociedad, Instituto de Ciencia Política, Universidad de Chile, Santiago, Chile, 1990.

——. "The Defense Industries of Semi-Industrialized Latin American Countries and Their Impact on the National Economies." Unpublished Ph.D. dissertation, Rensselaer Polytechnic Institute, School of Management, Troy, N.Y., 1992.

Mann, Jorge. "Trasporte de la Fragata Ministro Zenteno." *Revista de Marina* (Valparaíso, Chile), no. 4, 1991, pp. 374–378.

Mansfield, Edwin. *Managerial Economics: Theory, Applications, and Cases*. W. W. Norton, New York, 1990.

Marquis, Donald D. "The Anatomy of Successful Innovations." *Innovation*, November, 1969, pp.28–37.

Martínez, Pedro, and Pérez, Sergio. *La Industria Militar*. Centro de Estudios de la Nacionalidad no. 16, Santiago, Chile, Julio 1990.

El Mercurio (newspaper, Santiago, Chile). Several issues.

Millán, V. "Argentina: Schemes for Glory." In *Arms Production in the Third World*, edited by Michael Brzoska and Thomas Ohlson, pp. 35–53. Stockholm International Peace Research Institute, Taylor and Francis, London, 1986.

Molero, José. "Foreign Technology and Local Innovation: Some Lessons from the Spanish Defense Industry Experience." In *The Relations Between Defense and Civil Technologies*, edited by Philip Gummet and Judith Reppy, pp. 190–212. Kluwer Academic Publishers, Boston, 1988.

Montoya, Gustavo. "Logística Naval y Desarrollo Industrial: La Experiencia Chilena." Third Interamerican Conference in Logistics and Material, Pensacola, Fla., August 1989.

Morita-Lou, Hiroko. "Overview." In *Science and Technology Indicators for Development*, edited by Hiroko Morita-Lou, pp. 3–20. Westview Press, London, 1985.

Mosley, Hugh G. *The Arms Race: Economic and Social Consequences*. Lexington Books, Lexington, Mass., 1985.

National Science Board. *Science and Engineering Indicators—1989*, U.S. Government Printing Office, Washington, D.C., 1989.

National Science Foundation. *Selected Data on Federal R&D Funding by Budget Function*. NSF, Washington, D.C., 1991.

Neuman, Stephanie G. "Third World Arms Production and the Global Arms Transfer System." In *Arms Production in Developing Countries*, edited by James Everett Katz, pp. 15–37. Lexington Books, Lexington, Mass., 1984.

Ominami, Carlos, Chilean Minister of Economic Affairs. "Orientaciónes para una Política de Desarrollo de la Industria de Bienes de Uso Militar en Chile." Annals of the Symposium Industria de Defensa Nacional, ASMAR, Valparaíso, Chile, November 1991, pp. 133–149.

OTA (Office of Technology Assessment). *Adjusting to a New Security Environment: The Defense Technology and Industrial Base*

Challenge. Congress of the United States, U.S. Government Printing Office, Washington, D.C., February 1991a.

————. *Global Arms Trade: Commerce in Advanced Military Technology and Weapons*. Congress of the United States, U.S. Government Printing Office, Washington D.C., June 1991b.

————. *Redesigning Defense: Planning the Transition to the Future U.S. Defense Industrial Base*. Congress of the United States, U.S. Government Printing Office, Washington, D.C., 1991c.

Perry, William, and Weiss, Juan Carlos. "Brazil." In *The Implications of Third World Military Industrialization*, edited by James Everett Katz, pp. 103–117. Lexington Books, Lexington, Mass., 1986.

Piñeiro, Luis. "El Programa TAM." *Tecnología Militar* (Monch Editorial Group, Bonn, Germany), no. 1, 1984, pp. 93–94.

Política Brasileira de Ciencia y Tecnología: 1990 / 95, A. Secretaria da Ciencia e Tecnología, Presidência da Repúblicá, Brasilia, October 1990.

Porter, Michael E. "The Competitive Advantage of Nations." *Harvard Business Review*, March–April 1990, p. 73–93.

Porth, Jacquelyn S. "Argentina." In *Arms Production in Developing Countries: An Analysis of Decision Making*, edited by James Everett Katz, pp. 53–72. Lexington Books, Lexington, Mass., 1984.

Rallo, Joseph. "The United Kingdom." In *The Implications for Third World Military Industrialization*, edited by James Everett Katz, pp. 45–52. Lexington Books, Lexington, Mass., 1986.

Renner, Michael. "Enhancing Global Security." In *State of the World 1989: A Worldwatch Institute Report on Progress Toward a Sustainable Society*, edited by Lester R. Brown, pp. 132–153. W. W. Norton, New York and London, 1989.

Revista de Marina (Chilean Navy, Valparaíso, Chile). Several issues.

Roper, Christopher, and Silva, Jorge. *Science and Technology in Latin America*. Longman, London, 1983.

Ross, Andy Lee. "Security and Self Reliance: Military Dependence and Conventional Arms Production in Developing Countries." Unpublished Ph.D. dissertation, Department of Political Science, Cornell University, August 1984.

Saadawi, T.; Ahmed, S.; Peracha, W.; Kellman, M.; and Frisch, F. "A Methodology for Estimating Industrial Foreign Dependency." In *Management of Technology III*, edited by Tarek M. Khalil and Bulent A. Bayraktar, pp. 1251–1261. Proceedings of the Third International Conference on Management of

Technology. Institute of Industrial Engineers, Norcross, Ga., 1992.

Sadler, George E. "International Productivity Comparisons: Levels and Trends in Output per Hour and Multiple-Input Comparisons, U.S./Japan." American Productivity Center, Houston, Tx., 1986.

Scherer, F. M., and Ross, David. *Industrial Market Structure and Economic Performance*. 3d ed. Houghton Mifflin, Boston, Mass., 1990.

Simon, Denis Fred. "The Technology Issue in Sino-U.S. Relations." In *The Political Economy of International Technology Transfer*, edited by John R. McIntyre and Daniel S. Papp, pp. 243–253. Quorum Books, New York, 1986.

SIPRI (Stockholm International Peace Research Institute). *World Armaments and Disarmament*. SIPRI Yearbook, Oxford University Press, Stockholm, 1990.

Sivard, Ruth Leger. *World Military and Social Expenditures 1987–88*. 12th ed. World Priorities, Washington, D.C., 1987.

Smith, Gordon B. "The Impact of Western Technology Transfer on the Soviet Union." In *The Political Economy of International Technology Transfer*, edited by John R. McIntyre and Daniel S. Papp, pp. 212–242. Quorum Books, New York, 1986.

Sohr, Raul. *La Industria Militar Chilena*. Comisión Sudamericana de Paz, Colección Posiciones y Debates, Santiago, Chile, 1990.

Steinberg, Gerald M. "Technology, Weapons, and Industrial Development: The Case of Israel." *Technology in Society*, 7, 1985, pp. 387–398.

Stoneman, Paul. *The Economic Analysis of Technology Policy*. Clarendon Press, Oxford, England, 1987.

Suri, Rajan; Sanders, Jerry; Rao, Chandrasekhar; and Mody, Ashoka. "Competitive Implications of Modern Manufacturing Technologies and Practices: Insights from an International Study." In *Management of Technology III*, edited by Tarek M. Khalil and Bulent A. Bayraktar, pp. 877–887. Proceedings of the Third International Conference on Management of Technology. Institute of Industrial Engineers, Norcross, Ga., 1992.

Tecnología Militar (Monch Editorial Group, Bonn, Germany). Several issues.

Tromben, Carlos. *Ingeniería Naval: Una Especialidad Centenaria*. Imprenta de la Armada, Valparaíso, Chile, 1989.

Tybout, James; de Melo, Jaime; and Corbo, Vittorio. "The Effects of Trade Reforms on Scale and Technical Efficiency: New Evidence from Chile." *Journal of International Economics*, 31, 1991, pp. 231–250.

UCLA (University of California at Los Angeles), Latin American Center Publications. *Statistical Abstract of Latin America, Volume 28*, edited by James W. Wilkie, with coeditors Enrique C. Ochoa and David E. Lorey. LACP, University of California, Los Angeles, 1990.

UNESCO (United Nations Educational, Scientific, and Cultural Organization). *Statistical Yearbook, 1990*. UNESCO, Geneva, Switzerland, 1990.

UNIDO (United Nations Industrial Development Organization). *Technological Self-Reliance of the Developing Countries: Towards Operational Strategies*. Development and Transfer of Technology Series no. 15. United Nations, Vienna, 1981.

United Nations. *National Accounts Statistics: Main Aggregates and Detailed Tables, 1984*. United Nations, New York, 1986.

———. *National Accounts Statistics: Main Aggregates and Detailed Tables, 1988*. United Nations, New York, 1990.

U.S. Department of Commerce. *Statistical Abstract of the United States, 1990*. 110th ed. Government Printing Office, Washington, D.C., 1990.

Uzumeri, Mustafa Vakur. "The Challenge of Product Variety and Change for Manufacturing." Unpublished Ph.D. dissertation, School of Management, Rensselaer Polytechnic Institute, August 1991.

Varas, Augusto. "Democratization, Peace and Security in Latin America." *Alternatives*, 1985, pp. 607–623.

———. "Economic Impact of Military Spending." *Disarmament*, 9 (no. 3), Autumn 1986, pp. 79–94.

———. "The Transfer of Military Technology to Latin America." *Disarmament*, 12 (no. 3), Autumn 1989, pp. 95–109.

Vayrynen, Raimo. "Economic and Political Consequences of Arms Transfers to the Third World." *Alternatives*, 6, 1980, pp. 131–155.

———. *Military Industrialization and Economic Development: Theory and Historical Case Studies*. United Nations Institute for Disarmament Research, Dartmouth Publishing Company, Hants, England, 1992.

Vessuri, Hebe M. C. "O Inventamos o Erramos: The Power of Science in Latin America." *World Development*, 18 (no. 11), 1990, pp. 1543–1553.

Volker, John. "La Industria Naval." *Revista de Marina* (Valparaíso, Chile), no. 3, 1991, pp. 239–247.

Waisman, Carlos H. "Argentina: Economic and Political Implications." In *The Implications of Third World Military Industrialization: Sowing the Serpent's Teeth*, edited by James Everett Katz, pp. 93–102. Lexington Books, Lexington, Mass., 1986.

World Bank. *The World Bank Annual Report*. World Bank, Washington, D.C., 1989.

Wulf, Herbert. "The West German Arms Industry and Arms Exports." *Alternatives*, 13, 1988, pp. 319–335.

Index

About the Authors

JOSÉ O. MALDIFASSI is a Lieutenant Commander in the Chilean Navy and Project Manager of the Chilean Navy's Research and Development Directorate.

PIER A. ABETTI is Professor of Management and Enterpreneurship in the School of Management of Rensselaer Polytechnic Institute.